Praise from Admissions Officers for
Great Application Essays for Business School

"Totally on target. *Great Application Essays for Business School* is a really terrific, practical, and insightful guide to the kind of writing that can make a difference in winning acceptance at a top MBA program. Many of the things recommended in the book are the kinds of things that I say when I speak with prospective applicants. I also love the level of detail. I really recommend it—a must-read for anyone with business school ambitions."

—ANNE COYLE
DIRECTOR OF ADMISSIONS
YALE SCHOOL OF MANAGEMENT

"Paul Bodine's *Great Application Essays for Business School* is a great 'view from the trenches,' and a careful reading will offer many rewards to applicants. His overall messages—among them 'be yourself, answer the questions, showcase what you feel is important for schools to know'—seem simple but are hard to act on when you are sweating through deadlines. He gives you a practical guide to getting it done. Paul Bodine takes on the essay-writing process and breaks it down into actionable steps. He wants to help you tell your story. Paul knows there is no substitute for hard work and self-reflection, but his book should make an often daunting process much easier. *Great Application Essays for Business School* is a valuable how-to book with a generous spirit."

—JON MCLAUGHLIN
ASSISTANT DIRECTOR OF MBA ADMISSIONS
MASSACHUSETTS INSTITUTE OF TECHNOLOGY
SLOAN SCHOOL OF MANAGEMENT

"Quite effective. If all MBA candidates take to heart Paul Bodine's counsel and advice, we would receive far stronger essays, and applicants would likely see even greater success in the MBA admissions process. *Great Application Essays for Business School* provides an easy-to-follow blueprint for preparing and writing effective essays."

—JAMES HOLMEN
DIRECTOR OF ADMISSIONS
INDIANA UNIVERSITY
KELLY SCHOOL OF BUSINESS

"Paul Bodine does a terrific job in *Great Application Essays for Business School* of capturing the essence of the MBA application process. This guide will be useful to every MBA applicant."

—NATALIE GRINBLATT
DIRECTOR OF THE OFFICE FOR ADMISSIONS AND FINANCIAL AID
CORNELL UNIVERSITY
JOHNSON GRADUATE SCHOOL OF MANAGEMENT

Great Application Essays *for* BUSINESS SCHOOL

Paul Bodine
Accepted.com

McGraw-Hill

New York   Chicago   San Francisco   Lisbon   London   Madrid   Mexico City
Milan   New Delhi   San Juan   Seoul   Singapore   Sydney   Toronto

For Tamami

2 3 4 5 6 7 8 9 0 DOC/DOC 0 9 8 7

ISBN 0-07-145299-0

This publication is designed to provide accurate and authoritative information in regard to the subject matter covered. It is sold with the understanding that neither the author nor the publisher is engaged in rendering legal, accounting, or other professional service. If legal advice or other expert professional assistance is required, the services of a competent professional person should be sought.
—From a Declaration of Principles jointly adopted by a Committee of the American Bar Association and a Committee of Publishers

McGraw-Hill books are available at special quantity discounts to use as premiums and sales promotions, or for use in corporate training programs. For more information, please write to the Director of Special Sales, Professional Publishing, McGraw-Hill, Two Penn Plaza, New York, NY 10121-2298. Or contact your local bookstore.

 This book is printed on recycled, acid-free paper containing a minimum of 50% recycled, de-inked fiber.

Library of Congress Cataloging-in-Publication Data

Bodine, Paul
    Great application essays for business school / Paul Bodine.
        p.   cm.
    Includes bibliographical references.
    ISBN 0-07-145299-0 (alk. paper)
    1. Business schools—United States—Admission. 2. Exposition (Rhetoric)
3. College applications—United States. 4. Business writing. I. Title.
  HF1131.B543 2006
  808'.06665—dc22

                                       2005029015

Contents

Acknowledgments

The author would like to thank Linda Abraham, founder and president of Accepted.com; his Accepted.com clients over the years; the editors of Accepted.com; and Elana Fink. Special thanks are due as well to Anil Phull and Abhey Lamba.

Introduction

The stakes are huge. Once a "feeder" degree for would-be captains of American industry, the MBA has evolved into the essential credential for entrée into management consulting and investment banking and, more recently, a common qualification for entrepreneurs and venture capitalists as well. Today, in fact, a graduate management education is an accepted pedigree even for public-spirited managers seeking to lead international nonprofits, government agencies—not to mention North American superpowers. As the range of organizations hiring business school graduates to lead them has expanded, so too has the pay those MBAs can expect to receive. According to *BusinessWeek,* a newly minted Harvard MBA earned over $117,000 in salary and bonuses in 2004, with 13 percent annual salary increases expected in the years ahead. And that's just the start. By 2002, the average Harvard Business graduate from the class of 1998 was pulling down $195,000, and 10-year veterans in industries like venture capital could envision breaking the seven-figure threshold. Whether measured by pay, power, or career potential, the trend is obvious: if you want to change the world or just your job, a top-tier MBA is increasingly the key qualification for opening the doors of opportunity.

For business school applicants like you, such rosy prospects create incentive, to be sure, but also an acute anxiety to execute the MBA application well. Unfortunately, the days are long past when impressive grades, ninetieth-percentile GMAT scores, and a fast-track career profile could ensure you of a place in a top-drawer management program. With some 62,000 total applications flooding their coffers annually, the top-20 programs know they'll have their pick of applicants with stellar numbers and brilliant résumés. Today, they enjoy the luxury of cherry-picking a class fine-tuned for well-rounded variety not only in terms of industry and professional function but also cultural background, geographic origin, and even personal passions.

The raw data of your application can help schools weigh some of these admissions factors, it's true. But when admissions committees must choose from among equally qualified superachievers, nothing helps them more than your own words. Enter the MBA essay. More than ever, the four to five essays business schools typically require play the critical role in helping admissions officers see you as a unique person deserving of admission rather than a lifeless statistical "profile."

To write such mission-critical documents, you need more than one-size-fits-all "good writing" tips and a stack of sample essays you wish you'd written. As the senior editor since 1997 at Accepted.com, America's premier admissions consulting firm, I've written *Great Application Essays for Business School* to give applicants to the world's best business schools market-tested, MBA-specific methods and strategies for crafting essays that truly communicate the special qualities and insights that make your personal story too compelling for admissions professionals to ignore. Whether you are a confident communicator or a writing novice, whether you're applying from an MBA feeder industry or are a card-carrying "nontraditional" applicant, the focused, practical advice in this book will provide you with the key tricks of the trade that have worked consistently for hundreds of accepted applicants at Harvard, Stanford, Wharton, Kellogg, MIT Sloan, Columbia, Cornell, INSEAD, Yale, Berkeley Haas, UCLA, IMD, Indiana—all the most selective management programs.

Great Application Essays for Business School is the only how-to MBA admissions writing guide to offer the following combination of features:

- Proprietary admissions and writing insights of Accepted.com, one of the oldest and most successful admissions consulting services, whose editors have helped thousands of applicants gain admission to the world's best professional schools since 1994. The advice in this book distills nearly a decade's experience in personally guiding applicants from every demographic and region of the world toward admission offers from the top 50-plus graduate management programs. (A sample of their testimony can be found on Accepted.com's Web site at www.accepted.com/aboutus/EditorTestimonials.aspx?EditorID=2.)

- A flexible, practical system for finding your application's self-marketing handle, brainstorming your essays' raw material using six personal "data-mining" techniques, crafting an outline using theme and evidence sentences, and writing, revising, and editing effective essay drafts.

- Detailed strategies for writing essays for the eight most common MBA admissions essay topics, from goals, accomplishments, and "self-revelation" essays to diversity, leadership and teamwork, failure, ethics, and creative topics. *Great Application Essays for Business School* includes practical guidelines for understanding what schools actually ask (based on analysis of more than 60 MBA programs' essay sets), choosing your appropriate stories for each essay type, and structuring your essays so they provide context, analysis, and "lessons learned."

■ Twenty-five actual, complete essays or admissions documents written by applicants admitted to many of the very best business schools (Harvard, Kellogg, Wharton, Chicago, Columbia, and MIT Sloan, among others). Each sample is explicitly tied to the text's instruction and annotated to highlight the tactics that made the essay "click" with admissions readers.

■ Seventeen interactive end-of-chapter exercises that help you actually begin writing by posing key questions and walking you through the stages of the essay-writing process.

■ Ten practical "What *Not* to Do" tip sections (70 tips in all) that recap the critical learnings in each chapter in light of the most common applicant errors.

■ Specific treatment of special issues like handling social impact, creative, and career-change goals; responding to tricky goals questions; discussing low GMAT scores, grades, and other extenuating circumstances in optional essays; and selecting and approaching recommenders.

■ Candid insights from 23 admissions officers representing 16 top schools.

Chapter 1 of *Great Application Essays for Business School* guides you through the hardest part of the application process—actually writing the essays—by showing you how to create a self-marketing handle that informs your whole application, drill down to the themes and stories on which your essays will be built, use outlines effectively, and approach the first draft and revision/editing stages confidently. In Chapter 2, you learn what schools are really looking for in the goals essay while exploring practical strategies for writing the goals essay's three key sections: career progress, goals statement, and the three "why" questions. In Chapter 3, we consider what admissions officers expect from the seven key non-goals essay topics and provide specific methods for structuring your essays, choosing your content, analyzing your examples, and developing the lessons that the experiences you describe taught you. Chapter 4 shows you how to take advantage of the opportunity that optional essays give to do damage control on potential negatives or provide schools with new stories that strengthen your application. Finally, in Chapter 5, you'll learn the most effective strategies for selecting and approaching recommenders as well as practical, proven tactics for tackling the five most common recommendation questions.

Great Application Essays for Business School is designed to benefit motivated, conscientious applicants to the world's leading business schools who need a no-nonsense, thoroughly authoritative guide to admissions writing. We cannot promise, of course, that following the advice in these pages will ensure admission. "Magic bullets" or rigid systems cannot (thankfully) guarantee you success in a process that is so inherently complex and personal. There are many different ways to approach and write your essays, and you are encouraged to use the advice that helps you and modify or ignore the rest.

This book was written with the assumption that effective admissions writing involves much more than just reading other people's sample essays or trying to figure out exactly what admissions officers "want to hear." Good writing is about uncovering and polishing the special blend of skills, experiences, and values that only you possess. It demands self-understanding, honesty, analysis, and hard work. I have yet to meet a client who didn't have a unique story to tell. You have one too. Helping you find it is why so many of my clients have the MBAs they dreamed of.

A NOTE ON THE ESSAY SAMPLES

All the essays reproduced in this book are real essays—not composites or ideal models—written by actual applicants from a wide range of backgrounds who were admitted to the business school listed before each sample (and in many cases to other top schools as well). To protect these applicants' privacy, personal details like gender and cultural background, proper names, and other nonessential details have been disguised. Otherwise these are the same essays that admissions officers read.

It goes without saying that it is both illegal and unethical to copy or adapt any of these samples for use in your own application.

The author welcomes any input for improving later editions of this book. Contact Paul Bodine at pbodine@accepted.com.

Getting Started

I have admitted applicants based primarily on the strength of their essays. I've actually called up applicants after reading their particularly moving— and honest—essays and asked: How would you like to come to the Illinois MBA program? That can happen based solely on the merits of their essays.

—Paul Magelli, University of Illinois

At first blush, it makes no sense. Why should essays—mere words—determine whether you're among the fortunate few who earn MBAs from the world's very best business schools? After all, CEOs aren't paid millions to turn colorful phrases; their job is to solve intractable problems, motivate organizations, make the tough decisions. Isn't your potential to do that better gauged by hard metrics like career progress, academic performance, and standardized test scores than by a batch of well-spun essays?

However counterintuitive it might seem, the preeminence of the personal statement in the MBA admissions process is no longer open for debate. As the quality of applicants competing for top-tier schools spirals ever higher, the humble essay has become the decisive factor in helping business schools (B-schools) choose the "fat envelope" recipients from the ranks of equally qualified also-rans.

And well it should. When applicants' work experience, recommendations, academic record, intellectual skills, and extracurriculars are all uniformly superlative (at the best schools they often are), business schools could make admissions decisions with a coin flip. How much fairer it is that admissions officials ("adcoms" for short) take the time to let applicants' thoughts about their lives, dreams, and accomplishments guide their decisions. So, as subjective as words can be, business schools are actually doing you a favor by giving your essays so much weight. How so? Because of all the components of your application, the personal statement is the one over which you have the greatest control. Your grades, GMAT scores, and work experience are now all history, your recommenders may (or may not) say what you want them to, and even the success of your admissions interview depends on your interviewer's questions and mood. But your essays are all yours. From the themes you choose to capture your profile and the stories you pick to illustrate them to the lessons you draw and the tone you adopt, business schools give you the reins to shape their perception of your candidacy.

KNOW THY AUDIENCE

Why such generosity? Because, strange to say, admissions officers want to let you in. If you doubt that, consider the background of the typical admissions committee member. If you find any pattern, it will be that of the lifelong admissions careerist—that is, a professional with a human resource (HR)–oriented degree who's worked her way through the admissions food chain, often at several schools. Instead of statisticians, number crunchers, or demographic analysts, you'll find HR and marketing types and eclectic multicareerists, from ex–opera singers, scholars of ancient Greek, and horse breeders to onetime teachers, former business writers, and, of course, MBAs. You'll find, in other words, "people persons" with varied interests who value this same profile in applicants.

Writing is really just a means of striking up a certain kind of personal relationship with a reader, and who you think that reader is will obviously affect what you say to him or her. Too many applicants doom their essays from the start by assuming they're addressing the educational equivalent of a parole board—humorless, ranking-obsessed statisticians sternly sifting their pasts for hints that they've departed in thought or deed from the true MBA way. Though admissions officers must deny eight or nine out of every ten applicants, you must assume that they approach each one with an open mind and the readiness to believe that your application is the one that will draw them a step closer to a full, rounded class. So if the essays of unsuccessful applicants often read as though they were written for an audience of rubber-stamping, degree-issuing automatons or surly Dickensian gatekeepers waiting to pounce on signs of individuality, the essays of successful applicants are usually open, relaxed, confident, and optimistic. That fact alone should tell you what kind of people your audience really is.

Imagine you're at a tony cocktail party where you find yourself competing with the best and brightest of your peers to make a lasting impression on your welcoming but overworked hosts. You're all splendidly accomplished, well-rounded types, but you know your influential hosts are likely to remember only a handful of you when the evening is done. When your moment comes, would you collar them and begin reciting your promotions and academic feats? Let's hope not.

You'd probably turn on the charm, complimenting them on their home, probing for areas of shared interest, telling a few of your choice stories, and generally captivating them with your engaging personality. On one level, your B-school essays represent this same interpersonal challenge: how to put your best foot forward when your personal distinctiveness, not your résumé, is what will separate you from the other superachievers vying for your B-school spot. If there are three applicant categories—the dings (or rejections), the doables, and the dazzling—it's in your essays that you can elevate yourself from the doable to the dazzling.

In the Schools' Words—

Effective business leaders are almost without exception also good communicators, and we make no bones about wanting to recruit good business leaders, rather than narrow analysts.

—Andrew McAlister (aka "Fanatical Fan"),
Wharton graduate and former admissions officer

FINDING YOUR SELF-MARKETING HANDLE

The essay-writing process begins with introspection; there's no shortcut around it. Before you begin writing, even before you know the questions your schools ask, begin developing a short personal marketing message or "handle" that integrates the key themes (strengths, experiences, interests) you want your application to communicate. Picture our admissions cocktail party again. Your hosts' time is limited. They must make the rounds with all their guests before the night's over. Since you can't give them your whole life story, everything you say must communicate a compact, multidimensional message that's distinctive enough for your hosts to remember long after other partygoers have made their pitch. Take your time, cast your net widely, and ask friends and family for their input, so the handle you devise reflects key uniqueness factors from your professional, personal, community, and academic lives.

As a rule of thumb, construct your self-marketing handle out of four or five themes, each one rich enough to build an essay around. If you come up with "a natural leader with strong analytical skills and a social conscience," you're thinking far too broadly. If your handle runs past a sentence or two, unless it's truly scintillating, business schools may lose it in the crowd. The blend of themes should emphasize your multidimensionality. That is, you're not only a Testing Team Lead at IBM, but you're *also* a Norwegian American raised in Ecuador who *also* loves taxidermy and tutoring immigrant kids for the Knowledge Trust Alliance.

Remember that your admissions "hosts" will be bringing a long memory of past conversations to your brief encounter. Simply telling them you're a banker or a marketing manager will trigger all sorts of valid assumptions about your skills and professional exposures. If you're applying from a traditional MBA feeder profession like consulting or investment banking, for example, your handle will come equipped with analytical and quantitative strengths. So round it out distinctively by including themes that B-schools don't automatically associate with your profession, such as creativity (e.g., your lifelong devotion to basket weaving), social-impact causes (e.g., that stint training subsistence farmers in Malawi), or out-of-the-box professional experiences (e.g., your first career as a geography teacher). Or look for unusual childhood or family experiences, distinctive hobbies, or international experiences that offset the predictability of your professional profile—and incorporate these in your handle.

Conversely, if your profession is unusual (e.g., nonprofit or creative), B-schools will already be giving you points for distinctiveness, so balance your handle with themes that show them that you also have the quantitative, analytical, or business skills they automatically associate with consultants and finance types. Instead of "the award-winning African American photographer who grew up in Portugal and organized her church's choir," pitch yourself as "The Lisbon-raised African American photographer who runs her own five-person media studio and handles her church's finances." Like the consultant or finance professional, your goal is to create a handle that communicates multidimensional balance, but you achieve it by reassuring schools that you are MBA caliber—in addition to being unlike anyone they've encountered before.

Your search for your application's self-marketing handle will inevitably involve some comparison with other applicants. Relying only on your own sense of your distinctive strengths may not be enough to separate you from your peers, especially if you're a member of a crowded applicant demographic. For example, an information technology (IT) applicant from India (a large applicant pool) could be forgiven for deciding that the strongest aspects of his profile are his degree from ultra-selective Indian Institute of Technology, his leadership of his school's cricket team and cultural festival, and his fast-track career at Intel.

Unfortunately, at the very top schools this stellar background will only be par for the course among Indian IT candidates. To find a self-marketing handle that really sets him apart, he'll have to dig deeper—perhaps by focusing on unusual aspects of his upbringing (obstacles overcome or cultural or religious uniqueness factors) or hobbies or involvements that few of his peers will share. You can use business schools' class profiles to gain a sense of the educational, geographic, and professional backgrounds of past matriculants. Experienced admissions consultants like Accepted.com can also help you isolate the potential themes that could make your handle stand out.

Although a distinctive multidimensional handle is ideal, it must truly capture who you are. Don't try to force a theme—"internationalism," for example, or "creativity"—onto your profile if you don't have the experiences to back it up. Again, each of your handle's themes must be deep enough that you could write a full essay around it.

DATA-MINING YOUR LIFE

Once you have your self-marketing handle, you will have the multipart message that should inform all your essays for every school (albeit with some tweaking here and there to match particular schools' emphases). Now you need to find the best *specific* stories that illustrate that message.

Unlike medical and law schools, which often give you carte blanche in formulating your subject matter, business schools help you by posing several highly specific "thesis-bearing" essay topics—topics, that is, whose theme is contained in the wording of the question itself. Moreover, within each essay question schools also usually pose several specific subquestions (e.g., What are your goals? Why do you need an MBA? Why now?). This may feel like cruel and unusual punishment when you're writing your essays, but by limiting the scope of the essays for you, schools save you a lot of up-front time. You won't have to do that much brainstorming of topics.

Study the wording of each essay question carefully. You will hear a lot (in this book too) about "positioning" themes and thinking "strategically" about your essays, but none of that will make a whit of difference if you don't reflect in a sincere way on the question the essay poses. After all your savvy positioning, some of that sincerity must shine through, or your essays will be as bland as a committee-written Hollywood script. Schools put a great deal of thought (even ingenuity) into their questions because they're looking for the most effective and varied ways to get you to open up so they can peer inside at the unique you. Since capturing your key uniqueness factors is exactly why I advise you to craft a self-marketing handle, the schools' multiple essay topics should not intimidate you.

Unfortunately, you won't usually be able to simply match each of your themes to individual essay questions. Some schools may force you to discuss several (or all) of your themes in a single essay. Other schools may pose questions that none of your self-marketing themes seem appropriate for. Many essay questions ask you to address several things, so pay special attention both to the question's subject words (for example, *career progress* and *nonprofessional accomplishment*) and the direction words (*describe, discuss, explain*). Yale's "What nonprofessional accomplishment are you most proud of and why?" might seem like a no-brainer, but you can bet that some applicants will discuss a work-related example, assume "are most proud of" means "did others value most," or ignore the crucial "why" question altogether. And many programs pose much more maddeningly complex questions. So read carefully, break out all the subquestions, even send an e-mail to the school if you're unsure, but know what you're being asked.

Review your schools' essay questions to get a sense of the range of topics you'll face. As you'll see in Chapters 2 and 3, there are at least eight basic topic groups: goals (including Why an MBA? and Why our school?), accomplishments, "self-revelation" topics, diversity, leadership and teamwork, failure, ethics, and "creative" questions. Each school poses between two and seven (or more) essay questions. Assuming that you'll be applying to six to eight schools, you may well encounter all eight of these categories in some form. Don't get too strategic here. Stay focused on the range of the themes and stories within each school's essay set. Don't assume that similar-seeming topics from two or more different schools can be answered with the same story. If you try to look for apparent topic "clusters" across a range of schools, you'll risk losing the focus that you need to find the right mix for each particular school.

Review the essay questions once a day for a week or so to get your mind working subconsciously on your essays. Then you'll be ready to identify the individual stories you will build each essay around.

Mind-Plumbing Methods

The data-mining or "life inventory" step is not optional. You should no more exclude it from the essay-writing process than you would omit gathering business requirements before developing a software application, rehearsing a piece of music before performing it publicly, or conducting research before writing a dissertation. It's that essential. Inventorying your own life is by definition a subjective process. Your memory can deceive you: stories you consider unexceptional may actually make outstanding essays, and stories that you're convinced are distinctive and impressive may actually be fairly commonplace. So at this early stage you want to suspend judgment and simply "brain-dump" as much as you can as quickly as you can. The goal here is to find different ways to bypass your inhibitions and trick your mind into disgorging details you overlooked, significant events you've taken for granted, passions you forgot you once had.

Several techniques may help you:

- *Visual mapping or clustering.* Write the four or five themes that constitute your self-marketing handle on separate sheets of paper. Around each of your theme words begin jotting down whatever events, skills, values, or interests these words suggest to you. Each new term you jot down will suggest other words. Follow them where they lead, and connect each new term with a line back to the related term that prompted it. If you go with the flow, you may gain insights into what you value most and the interconnections between your themes. All these may prove useful when you begin writing your essays.

- *Using your résumé as an autobiographical time line.* Your résumé can be a memory aid for generating essay material. Let your mind linger over each section of the résumé, recalling the challenges, breakthroughs, and changes each stage of your career offered you. Recall and write down the full details of the accomplishments listed as well as the achievements you decided to exclude from the résumé that might make good essay fodder. Since many of your essays will involve a chronologically ordered narrative (e.g., your career progress, your greatest accomplishment), this exercise can generate useful material and create a time frame to help you understand your development.

- *Random listing.* Instead of shackling your thought to the rules of sentences and paragraphs, first warm up your writing skills by generating simple lists— favorite music; worst jobs; greatest accomplishments; best vacations; traits that define you; characteristics your friends admire in you; or most unusual things about your childhood, education, homeland, international travels, hobbies, and so on. Then take these lists a step further by looking for any connections between them. Perhaps your list of defining traits is illustrated by your list of achievements.

- *Recording thoughts or conversations.* If you are one of those people who finds any kind of writing exercise inhibiting, a tape recorder may enable you to get your thoughts out. Either record yourself as you extemporize about your life or goals, or record a conversation with a friend as he or she probes you with some of the basic "life" questions listed in the Writing Prompt Exercise at the end of this chapter. Transcribe this recording, minus the "um"s and "like"s, and you'll have a rough but potentially useful data bank of essay content.

■ *Stream-of-consciousness writing.* Perhaps the least structured of writing techniques, stream-of-consciousness or "free" writing simply involves scribbling down whatever comes into your head without stopping, even if it's nonsense. As odd as this may sound, you'll find that, for all the useless verbiage you generate, you'll also unwittingly produce ideas, phrases, and insights that may actually wind up in your essays. Try to organize these ideas, phrases, and insights into related groups. At a minimum, this technique can help you overcome the angst of the empty page.

■ *Journaling.* Nothing will get you into the discipline of writing better than a daily regimen. The operative word here is *daily*—anything less frequent will prevent you from writing naturally and unselfconsciously. Pick a time of day when you can write uninterruptedly for 15 minutes to a half hour. Record your thoughts, dreams, experiences of the past day, whatever you want, but do it without fail and without distractions. Avoid the trap of simply recording your comings and goings, however. Make it a practice to close each paragraph by drawing some conclusion or stating its significance. Writing thoughtfully is a habit you can learn.

What do all these exercises have in common? They get you writing *before* you begin writing your essays, when anxiety and your "internal editor" can cut you off from the creativity and personality that will make your essays live. The mere act of translating your thoughts into words—in whatever form—forces those thoughts to the next level of concreteness and leads you in new directions, while also giving you a paper trail to refer back to as raw material for your essays. Writing, in other words, is a way of thinking, a kind of introspection. The sooner you get into the habit of thinking on paper (or screen), the sooner you'll be ready to shape that thinking into the rigorous, ordered thought that is the essay. Crossing the great divide between your thoughts and their verbal expression in concrete language is what separates would-be writers from nonwriters. It's not easy, but these exercises can help you do it with a minimum of pain.

Everything Has Significance

Your data-mining or "life inventory" process should involve more than merely flushing out the stories that best capture your self-marketing themes. You also want to be continually evaluating their significance. How valuable was that Singapore internship to me? What did it teach me, or how did it change me? To manage your data-mining effort, create a spreadsheet or log divided into sections, say, Career, Academics, Extracurriculars, Community/Volunteering, and Personal/Family. Within each section create three columns: one for describing the event, one for noting its "external" significance or impact, and a third for logging its "internal" significance to you. External significance will include the experience's impact on your career progress (earned promotion, raise, etc.), on your organization (won new client contract), or on others (helped student you tutored raise math grade to B). Internal significance will include how the experience changed you, enhanced your skills, deepened your perspective, strengthened your sense of your potential, and so on.

By getting into the habit of identifying and noting down the underlying significance of your stories as they come to you, you'll sharpen your ability to evaluate your essay material in the same way that admissions officers will, reducing your burden in the essay-writing stage.

Don't perform the critical data-mining stage by yourself. Your perception of your own life is likely to be highly subjective, so ask friends, family, and mentors for any key traits, memories, or accomplishments you may have missed.

From Raw Material to Essay Content

If you've done it right, your data-mining process should leave you with a mass of raw material that could fill dozens of admissions essays. As much as you may want to throw it all into the pot, essay length limits will force you to jettison the bulk of it. So get used to thinking early on in terms of focused stories or experiences that capture in microcosm what's essential about you rather than "overview" essays that superficially skim dozens of key moments. The latter kinds of essays usually come off as glorified lists that lack the detail and context that enable readers to remember your stories and hence you. Look for discrete stories that can "stand in for" or serve as metaphors for your life's themes. By understanding these stories, someone could know nearly as much about who you really are as by hearing your full autobiography. Given the limited length of schools' essays, you will only be able to suggest the breadth of your life experiences by exploring a key handful in depth.

Because you approached the data-mining stage with your self-marketing handle already defined, you were able to group your raw stories or data points into buckets that corresponded to the handle's four of five themes. Your data-mining process may have shown you that your handle was overemphasizing one aspect of your profile or ignoring one that you now think is stronger. Be flexible; make whatever adjustments you need to.

Now begin to evaluate your raw stories critically. Look for the ones that are most distinctive and combine the greatest external impact and personal transformation. If a story scores high in unusualness, objective results or impact, and personal significance, you've probably got a winner. How well does this story illustrate your theme? You may have three stories for your "internationalism" theme: a college internship in Thailand; a customer relationship management implementation in which you worked side by side with Belgians, Russians, and

Brazilians; and last year's two-month engagement in Cairo. Because the internship happened four years ago in college and you were based in the United States throughout the CRM implementation, you tentatively decide to use the Cairo experience as your core story for any essays that focus on globalism or cross-culturalism. (Of course, it may also work for any teamwork or diversity essays, and some schools may give you the space to discuss all *three* of your international stories.) Subject all the raw stories generated by your data-mining process to this same weighing or ranking process until you've arrived at a core set of stories that covers all the topics for the application you plan to tackle first.

Now—at last—you're ready to start the essays themselves.

WRITING YOUR ESSAYS

Because you performed the content-gathering steps in the last section, you should not only know which stories best address each question but you also have done enough raw writing to avoid "blank page syndrome" and other writers' ailments. Still, writing tends to bring out the procrastinator in all of us, so set tight deadlines of a few days or less for completing each stage of your essay. As in the data-mining process, your focus when writing the first draft of your essay is to get something down on paper. Many applicants believe they have to complete a polished, finished draft in one sitting. Don't be so hard on yourself. Good writing is a base-at-a-time game; it's not about home runs. So forget about style, grammar, and word count when writing your first draft.

To keep the pressure off, start with the first applications that business schools make available during the summer or with a school that's not your first choice. After you finish the application, move on to the next school, but *don't* submit the first application. Assuming that there is time before the first-round deadline, finish the second school's application (and perhaps others), and then go back to the first school's and polish it off in light of the tweaks you've made while working on later applications. In this way you can capitalize on the improvements that inevitably occur as you refine your essays without jeopardizing the advantage of a first-round submission.

The Outline Is Your Friend

The outline may summon unpleasant memories of seventh-grade English, but it's one more useful method that can reduce the anxiety and time drain of the writing process. If outlines make you nervous or stifle your creative juices, you *can* develop your essays in unstructured fashion by simply expanding the raw content you generated in the data-mining process into larger chunks or paragraphs. You can then juggle their order until you find one that fits. The (substantial) downside of this approach is its haphazardness and inefficiency.

By failing to map out your essay's organization from the start, you risk chasing tangents down blind alleys and wasting valuable time.

By bringing structure to your essay before you start writing it, outlines maximize your efficiency and enable you to conduct a crucial early test of your essay ideas before you've invested too much in them. Do you have enough material to support your assertions or illustrate your experiences? Does the lesson you're trying to draw from your material have enough substance? Does the lesson really grow organically from the story itself or does it seem imposed and unearned? Outlines can help you answer these questions.

Each outline you create will have the following basic organization:

1. *Introduction.* One paragraph introducing the essay's themes and setting its tone.

2. *Body paragraphs.* Anywhere from two to three or more paragraphs that provide evidence to support the themes asserted in the introduction. Each paragraph in the body should consist of:

   a. *Theme sentence.* The first sentence of the paragraph states the topic or theme that the paragraph will demonstrate: "Though my formal roles are technical, all my growth opportunities have involved leadership."

   b. *Evidence sentences.* These consist of specific examples, anecdotes, or details that support the paragraph's theme sentence: "In my first project, for example, I became the de facto team lead when my implementation proposal was accepted as our project solution."

3. *Conclusion.* This paragraph pulls together the underlying lessons or themes of the preceding paragraphs. It generally includes a summary of lessons learned or insights (from the third column of your data-mining spreadsheet).

Good outlines are the safety rope that keeps you focused on finding that next secure foothold toward your essay's summit rather than staring dizzily into the abyss of the next empty paragraph. Don't cling to your outline cravenly, however. It may need to be revised as your thinking about the topic evolves. In sample outline 1 at the end of this chapter, note how Bill W. (later admitted to Kellogg) focuses himself by using a theme statement at the front of the outline but also keeps his outline informal and provisional by inserting questions to himself.

The First Draft

According to writing coach Elizabeth Danziger, you should devote no more than 15 percent of your total time on writing the first draft of your essay (with the remaining time divided between brainstorming and revisions). Whether that number's accurate or not, the moral is that writing your first draft should not paralyze you with anxiety or perfectionism. You've already done a major portion of your work (finding, selecting, and structuring your material), and the bulk of your remaining work (revision and editing) comes later. So lighten up! Run with your outline, and don't analyze what you're writing too closely—just get it down.

Some writers start with the sections of the outline that look easiest or that they know the most about. And for many writers, the introduction is often the last piece of the puzzle. In the next three sections, however, we look at the three main components of every essay—the introduction, body, and conclusion—in that order.

Introduction

In your introduction, you must tell the reader what you will be accomplishing in the essay. This does not mean that your first sentence should be a monotonous statement of your theme ("In this essay, I will be . . ."). But somewhere in your first paragraph—the last sentence is good—you must directly signal that you will be answering the school's question and what the thrust of your response will be.

More than stating your theme, however, your introduction must catch and hold the reader's interest, which is battered daily by dozens of same-sounding essays. It's critical that the admissions reader finish your introduction thinking "I wonder how this turns out." or "Hmmm, this is interesting." rather than, "Here we go again." (In Chapter 2 we discuss some of the more typical essay openings in the context of goals essays.) Finally, your introduction must also provide some of the essay's key context (answering where, when, who, and what questions) and establish, primarily through word choice, the essay's tone (e.g., dramatic and serious, or wry and subtle).

Body

The body of your essay is also its heart—the human story and the corroborating "evidence" that justifies the claims or promises you make in your introduction. Every paragraph in the body should be built on a basic pattern of *general assertion → supporting example.* That is, whether you're writing a narrative-driven chronological essay, an example-driven "argument" essay, or a vivid detail–driven descriptive essay, every paragraph should begin with a general-focus *theme sentence,* which is followed by several sentences of specific-focus *evidence sentences*—anecdotes, examples, descriptions, or actions—that illustrate the theme sentence.

Each paragraph in the body should advance your case or further unfold your story. Usually, the specific sequence of your paragraphs is dictated by the chronology of the story you're telling (from the past toward the present), but sometimes each paragraph functions as a separate example in a larger argument. In either case, your paragraphs will live or die by the degree of personal, vivid detail and insight you provide. You want to achieve a balance between data—the personal facts and stories that substantiate your themes—and analysis—regularly stepping back from an example or anecdote to tell the reader what it means. Too much data will make for a dull, impersonal essay. Too much analysis will cause your essay to float off into a sea of generalities unsupported by corroborating facts.

Perhaps the greatest disadvantage you face as an applicant is that you cannot read what the vast majority of other applicants write. If you could, you would immediately see how many essays sound identical! The reason for this sameness is almost always a lack of specific detail and personal anecdote. So throughout the body of your essay, always be as personal and specific as you can be.

You know your essay's body is structured well when the opening theme sentences connecting each new paragraph to the preceding (often called *transition sentences*) seem to write themselves. For example, the transition sentence, "The Bristol engagement was not the last time I took on leadership roles outside my job description," smoothly links the preceding paragraph (about the Bristol engagement) to another leadership example the writer is about to narrate in the new paragraph. Try to avoid graceless transitions involving numbers ("Third, success for me means never having to say you're sorry").

Conclusion

Your conclusion needs to do several key things—and briefly. It needs to draw a synthesized (but not vague or banal) lesson or theme out of the body paragraphs that have preceded it. And it must do so without simply repeating the theme statement from the introduction or merely restating the key point of each body paragraph. The conclusion, that is, must create a true sense of "summing up," of loose ends being bow-tied, but in a way that injects deeper or larger insight than was previously provided in the essay. Moreover, to give the reader that peculiar feeling of coherence or unity good writing often has, your conclusion should refer indirectly back to the language or details of the introduction—but as an indirect echo rather than a mirror. Finally, the conclusion's tone must be positive and forward-looking. If you can smoothly refer to your goals or MBA plans, do so. Avoid "In conclusion" or any of its stuffy siblings.

As you work on your first draft, keep your outline in front of you so you don't wander off into tedious digressions. If you start to feel lost or bogged down, pull back and ask yourself, "What am I really trying to say here?" "What do I want the reader to feel, believe, or conclude after reading this?" These kinds of reorienting questions can keep you on track and help you to plow speedily toward your objective: a reasonably coherent document within which lurks a finalized essay.

If it helps, try to think of your essay, not as an argument ("Why I should be admitted") or a proposal ("Consider admitting me for the following reasons"), but as a story about an interesting and sympathetic hero (you) in pursuit of a distant but most holy grail (the MBA). Humans are hardwired to respond to human-interest stories. Tales of sympathetic protagonists overcoming conflict or obstacles by modifying their world to remove those obstacles appeal to our basic hopes in a way that impersonal proposals do not. This is not to suggest that you submit a ripe piece of fiction or melodramatic screenplay. But if viewing your essay more as a creative act than as cold exposition infuses it with personality and reader-friendliness, then give it a try. For example, use some possession or activity that reflects one of your passions as a metaphor for talking about your whole life, connecting specific aspects of that possession or activity to examples from your life that illustrate them. The possibilities for creativity are unlimited.

REVISING AND EDITING

Once your first draft is done, you must schizophrenically repress the uninhibited Mr. Hyde who created it and summon your editorial Dr. Jekyll to make it presentable. You must cease expressing yourself, that is, and begin reading yourself as the admissions officers will. Writing and revising are distinctly different, even opposing, acts. Intermingling them, like trying simultaneously to be a stage actor and theater critic, is to risk misadventure.

Once you've banished your writerly self, your first act as editor is to completely ignore your draft, at least for a day. When you come back to it, you will immediately see things your creative self missed. Before leaping to fix them, step back and consider only macro and organizational changes first, such as contradictory themes or assertions, needlessly repeated points, yawning gaps in context or logic, or weakly developed or poorly placed paragraphs. If you find these, you may need to switch around paragraphs, expunge digressions, or add, delete, or bolster your examples. By attending to these big-ticket problems first, you'll avoid spit-polishing prose that you later decide to cut.

Depending on how thorough your outline is and how effectively you elaborated on it in your first draft, your essay may go through one, two, or even more macro-level revisions before it's ready for editing proper. It's no fun, but you must revise your essays as many times as they require. Continually ask yourself whether your main thesis and secondary points will be clear to the admissions officers, whether your evidence will persuade them, whether you are telling this story as efficiently and clearly as you can. Always choose the simplest, shortest, and most direct expression over the more complex or "sophisticated." Read your essays aloud. Do they flow? Did you notice miscues you missed earlier? Is the tone conversational, and does it sound like you?

Don't try to go through the revision and editing process alone. Whether you ask friends and family; colleagues, MBAs, mentors; or experienced admissions consultants like Accepted.com, seek a reasonable and diverse range of opinions on your essays. But take each opinion with a grain of salt. Too much positioning and "helpful" tweaking will drain all the personality from your work. They're ultimately your essays; keep it that way.

Revising is really the writing you do after your first draft is done. Editing, on the other hand, is not really composition at all. It is cleaning up the essay's mechanics and grammar at the sentence and word level after the writing is completed. Though the changes you make in this stage will affect your essay less fundamentally, they will be much more numerous and, if uncorrected, enough in themselves to torpedo an otherwise tightly organized piece of writing. The potential glitches that editing catches can involve everything from pronoun and subject-verb agreement, dangling modifiers, run-on sentences, and parallelism to punctuation and capitalization errors, incorrect word choice and misspelling, and active- versus passive-voice issues. If you're uncertain about any of these potential problem areas, review *The Random House Handbook* by Frederick Crews or the redoubtable (and brief) *Elements of Style* by E. B. White and William Strunk, Jr. Finally, have a trained editor vet your essays.

LETTING GO

Too many applicants decide that their essays are "finished" only because the school's deadline says they must be, not because they're truly polished. Applicants who give themselves enough time risk the opposite danger: obsessively tweaking their essays until they have the bland plasticity of a corporate press release. The essay is truly finished when you can't imagine how to make it say what you mean more candidly, vividly, or directly. When you've achieved that level of honesty, color, and tautness, let go.

ADMISSIONS ESSAYS: WHAT *NOT* TO DO

We've spent most of this chapter telling you what to do. Now here are some guidelines on what not to do. Don't

1. *Fail to answer the question.* The answer to the question is what the schools want. Remember that schools purposely customize the wording of their essay questions to differentiate themselves from other schools. They don't want cut-and-paste responses. Often their particular spin or twist is subtle and can be addressed by modifying some key words or sentences in your introduction or conclusion. Thus, you rarely need to start from scratch for

each school. Just be sure you're being sensitive to the particular nuance contained in the question.

2. *Write essays that lack a point or underlying thesis.* This mistake is often a result of omitting the data-mining or outlining stages of the prewriting process. Applicants appear to address the individual parts of the essay question, but when you look beneath the surface detail, you can't be sure where the essay is going, why the applicant is relating the experience, or what he or she thinks about it.

3. *Sound negative, whining, or complaining.* Successful leaders are positive, forward-looking types who even describe their failures in terms of the constructive lessons they teach. They inspire respect, not pity. The ideal tone is conversational and confident; energized, fair-minded, and optimistic; self-aware but world-directed.

4. *Use clichés or hackneyed ideas.* These reflect superficial or tired thinking, regardless of whether they're committed on the micro (sentence) level ("I broadened my horizons and learned that hard work and persistence are invaluable.") or on the macro (essay) level.

5. *Write a résumé-in-prose.* This blunder usually stems from the misguided notion that it's better to cram as much material as you can into an essay than to focus on one or two experiences in extensive detail. Believing that admissions officers evaluate accomplishments or experiences on some gross volume basis, the applicant breezes through a long chronicle of mini-achievements, none detailed with enough specificity to distinguish him or her from any other applicant.

6. *Write what you think admissions officers want to hear.* Aside from the fact that this approach is insincere and won't help you stand out (because so many others do it), it assumes that admissions officers know what they want to hear. In reality, admissions officers live to be pleasantly surprised by a story or profile that answers their question and that they couldn't have anticipated because they've never encountered it before.

7. *Fail to catch grammatical and spelling errors.* Don't rely on your own eagle eye or computer's spell-checker alone. Show your essays to other people, ideally professionals with training in the rules and conventions of good writing and the English language. Read Strunk and White's deeply helpful guide to incisive writing, *The Elements of Style.*

8. *Leave out the passion.* Choosing boring material or writing about interesting material in a boring way sends the wrong signal to admissions officers who are looking high and low for engaged, enthusiastic people with multiple interests and a zest for life. All your essays are ultimately about yourself, a subject schools naturally expect you to be somewhat excited about.

9. *Fail to be strategic about your essays.* This means knowing how to strike a balance between standing out from other applicants and having the minimal skills and values to be accepted by future classmates. It also includes the error of forgetting to view each school's essay set in its totality to ensure that you've included all your key stories and that your essays are a multidimensional mix of personal, professional, and community material.

10. *Forget lessons learned.* A B-school admissions essay (regardless of topic) that lacks a closing lessons-learned section should be a contradiction in terms. Whether the school asks for such "takeaways" or not, give the committee reflection, thoughtfulness, and your analysis of the significance of the events you describe.

WRITING PROMPT EXERCISE

The following questions can help you dig deep enough to uncover the kind of thoughtful and searching answers business schools seek in admissions essays.

1. What makes you happiest?

2. What do you fear more than anything else?

3. What one person influenced you more than anyone else in your life? In what ways?

4. What would your friends be most surprised to learn about you?

5. Aside from salary, what motivates you to do your best at work?

6. If you could choose your epitaph, what would it say?

7. What single event changed your life or your values the most, positively or negatively?

8. What was your greatest nonprofessional failure, and what did you learn from it?

9. If you could be any person living or dead besides yourself, who would it be? Why?

10. If you didn't need to work to earn a living, name the one activity you would devote your days to. Why that one?

SAMPLE OUTLINES

The following two outlines show how two ultimately successful business school applicants used outlines as preliminary structuring tools to write their first drafts. Since outlines are for your consumption only, they can take whatever form best helps you organize your thoughts.

Sample Outline 1: Bill W. (Admitted to Kellogg)

Essay Prompt. Each of our applicants is unique. Describe how your background, values, and non-work-related activities will enhance the experience of other Kellogg students. (1 to 2 pages double-spaced)

Theme: Most important values—focus/hard work, leadership, diversity, enjoying life—evolved through changes in my life. Share them with Kellogg classmates in different ways.

I.   The values I will share with my Kellogg classmates—focus, leadership, diversity, and enjoying life—have been driving me in one form or another my entire life.
   A. Major theme in my and my family's life has been change.
      1. In a way these 4 values are my response to change.
         a. Way of optimizing change, making it beneficial, creating opportunity out of it.
   B. Parents'—traditional Serbian family—forced to embrace change by events.
      1. Mom's home burned by Croatians when she was 6.
      2. Uncle slave laborer in WW2.
      3. Most of parents' childhood: bleak years of communism.
         a. No one on dad's side ever owned car.
      4. Change was only option: immigration.
         a. Risky: uncle had come earlier; could only find work picking cotton.
         b. Spoke no English.
         c. Lacked college degrees.
II. Parents minimized shock of change by moving to Serbian-speaking community in Thunder Bay, Ontario.
   A. Second-largest Serbian population in Canada.
   B. Bilingual: spoke Serbian among themselves.
      1. Parochial schools taught Serbian as second language.
      2. Serbian cub scouts.
      3. Grew up speaking Serbian as first language.
   C. Conservative, strict, old-fashioned.
      1. First major "values": hard work/focus/determination.
         a. Dad built home.
         b. I dragged stumps, constructed addition.
         c. Dad: "Earn your keep."
         d. "Work hard, but work smart."
   D. Results of values of hard work/focus/determination:
      1. Began working at 15.
      2. First in family to go to college.

      3. Overcame disappointment of leaving McGill when scholarships were cut back.

      4. Earned certifications of mastery (skydiving, flying).

      5. Paid 100 percent of graduate tuition.

  E. Working hard, staying focused, never giving up: achieve my goals.

      1. Share with Kellogg classmates by [how share with them?]

III. Value: leadership, initiative.

  A. Always naturally taken leadership positions.

      1. Aside from work.

      2. Seeking skydiving, flying certification.

      3. Leading skydiving trips.

      4. Organizing skiing trips at work.

  B. Acronym in skydiving world: "RAPFS"

      1. Relax, Analyze Problem, Focus on Solution.

      2. Make sure you've got a clear head.

      3. Encapsulates my idea of leadership.

      4. Career goal—rescuing distressed companies—also reflects this value.

  C. At Kellogg [how will my leadership manifest itself?].

IV. Growing up speaking English and Serbian, diversity second nature.

  A. Believe as parents believed: be ready to accept change to take advantage of opportunity.

      1. Led me to live in 5 parts of North America.

      2. Travel overseas.

        a. Balkans, Taiwan, France, New Zealand, India.

      3. Most recently, Montreal.

        a. No avoiding multiculturalism.

        b. Bilingual state.

        c. I'm proficient in French.

        d. Office of Michelin engineers speaking entirely in French didn't faze me—like speaking Serbian at home.

        e. In fact, so comfortable with it, have French girlfriend!

  B. Pursuing opportunity means accepting change, accepting diversity.

      1. At Kellogg [how will belief in diversity manifest itself?].

V. Final value will share at Kellogg: have fun, enjoy myself.

  A. Playing hard, pursuing passions enthusiastically.

      1. Flying aficionado since teenager.

      2. Read all flying magazines, travel to largest air shows.

      3. One indulgence: home-built experimental aircraft kit.

  B. Montreal: many ways to relax.

      1. Skiing.

      2. Culture.

     C. Bring these enthusiasms to Kellogg classmates.
       1. Skydiving trips.
       2. International clubs.
VI. First person in family to go to college.
     A. Heard 1,000 times: "if I had had your education . . ."
     B. Still believe in best education.
     C. Kellogg is best.
     D. In return will share values.

Sample Outline 2: Sarita B. (Admitted to MIT Sloan)

Essay Prompt. Describe a situation where you introduced and/or managed change in an organization. Tell us how you influenced others in an organization (business, school, extracurricular activity) and comment on the professional and/or personal attributes you used to do that and how these attributes (and others) might be important to the attainment of your career goals. How do you expect the Sloan School to further the development of these attributes? (800 words)

  I. LEAD: It was unheard of. In March, Resort Financial Solutions (RFS) requested that I, a Stratagem consultant, manage entire $600K upgrade project of resort investment performance system. Because of past perform-ance, RFS insisted and stipulated in contract that I be project manager.
     A. Only full-time person from Stratagem assigned to RFS. Developed plan, wrote contract, got proposal approved in addition to managing RFS employees: 6 technologists, 5 business analysts.
       1. Split time between technical (implementing software upgrade), business side (logistics, staffing, etc.), managing staff, interacting with management.
  II. From beginning, significant challenges from all sides.
     A. Business side at RFS not sold on what value upgrade would bring.
       1. SOLUTION (Attribute used: cross-disciplinary perspective): Knew business and technical side of project so could speak language of client's business side—show them the value.
       2. Worked with quality/testing department, documentation, database, report people, etc., while liaising between RFS management and Stratagem.
     B. Technical side was sold on it but would not provide full-time staff.
       1. Felt 8 people working half time on project could do same work as 4 full-time staff (not true).
       2. SOLUTION (Attribute used: dedication, resourcefulness)

        a. Filled gap by donating more time to training part-time people, giving feedback, explaining fundamentals.

        b. RFS couldn't produce promised human resource, so located him for them.

   C. Abusive RFS technology manager.

      1. Reports of delays enraged him.

      2. SOLUTION (Attribute used: patience, professionalism): Shouting sessions not time-efficient, productive.

        a. Relied more on e-mail to give updates.

        b. Spoke to Stratagem partner—agreed to deliver project, then speak with senior person at RFS after project ended.

   D. Third-party vendor threatened deadline by releasing buggy software.

      1. Every new version reintroduced errors fixed previously.

      2. SOLUTION (Attribute used: build trusting relationships, take initiative to communicate with decision makers).

        a. Established, maintained excellent rapport with vendor's client relationship manager (CRM).

        b. When necessary, told CRM would speak directly to vendor's CTO and president to get their assurance project had highest priority.

        c. Requested time to speak directly with vendor's programmers.

   E. Despite vendor's delays, RFS insisted on sticking to deadline, budget.

      1. RFS did not believe testing each new version of vendor's software was necessary.

      2. My technical experience told me it was.

        a. Could have gone along with client's wishes, installed untested software—thus guaranteeing meeting deadline.

      3. SOLUTION (Attribute used: commitment to quality, always offer solution rather than problem, find creative solutions): But I believed I was obligated to do better job.

        a. Presentation to RFS: will test software to guarantee quality but also meet deadline (instead of estimated 4 rounds of testing, were 9).

        b. Adjust deliverable to allow testing, meet deadline—upgrade finished by deadline, new functionality installed later.

III. Because I brought all these attributes to project, it succeeded.

   A. This project is my most significant business achievement. First time had sole responsibility for entire project's success. Had to combine technical and business acumen to understand and improve RFS's complex system and had to apply political skills to mediate internal disputes. Had to have persuasive skills to manage clients' expectations. Both RFS and Stratagem praised my work, and I was recommended for early promotion. Client wanted me back, praised me; so did Stratagem.

B. Same attributes will be even more essential when I advise future clients on investment strategy.
   1. Must know investments well.
   2. Must be comfortable practicing shuttle diplomacy with different people, interests.
      a. Juggling multiple clients, contacts within clients, my own in-house people.
   3. Will use all skills used at RFS but at more mission-critical level.
IV. More will be on the line in future leadership roles, so need to polish skills at MIT. [Mention MIT resources that will improve my ability to handle leadership situations.]
   A. $50K entrepreneurship competition.
   B. ProSeminar requires me to work within teams to help real company solve a problem.
   C. Specific MIT courses on "soft skills"?
   D. CLOSE.

Scoring the Goals Essay

Goals are really the touchstone of the application . . . In a sense, they are the backbone or framework to which everything else relates.

—LINDA ABRAHAM, ACCEPTED.COM

Make no mistake, of all the essays you'll need to write for your business school application, the goals essay is the most important. It's the one essay in which schools most explicitly ask you to answer the central question that underlies your entire application—why exactly do you need an MBA? Not surprisingly, it's also the essay for which schools give applicants the most space to answer (up to seven or more pages for Stanford). Yet, despite its importance, when admissions officials are asked, "What's the most common mistake applicants make?" failure to describe goals clearly is almost always the answer. In fact, poor execution on the goals essay has been said to account for more than half of all dings.

The goals essay is key because—surprise—adcoms want to know what reasons motivate you to go to all the trouble, expense, and opportunity cost of earning an MBA. No matter how staggering your qualifications, if you don't provide a clear reason for needing an MBA, your application stands an excellent chance of losing out to those that do. Business schools use the goals essay to do a reality check on your maturity and career savvy. Do you really have a career plan that extends beyond your next promotion? If you do, is the MBA really an essential tool for advancing toward that goal? (Maybe you just need more work experience or perhaps a master's in a specialized functional skill.) Schools know all too well that many applicants seek MBAs for the "wrong" reasons—as a desperate measure to escape a lousy job or downsizing or to gain a promotion or bigger salary—not because the MBA really prepares them to do something they could not do without it. A goals essay that implies you need the MBA for purely instrumental reasons or that has the aura of credential-gathering will be viewed skeptically. Well-defined goals are business schools' way of policing the focus and legitimacy of their applicants' aspirations.

But there are other, less obvious reasons for exerting extra effort on your goals essays. First, the goals essay is almost always the first essay question in each school's essay set, and first impressions do matter. Anything less than a compelling initial essay will put you in a hole that will just drain luster from your other essays, no matter how brilliantly executed they are. Start strong.

Second, admissions officers have a weakness for applicants who are, in the well-traveled term, "passionate"—burning with the right Promethean fire to pursue their dreams. It's only human to respond to enthusiasm. And projecting a well-defined reason for pursuing the MBA makes your enthusiasm much more credible and personal. "I need an MBA to advance my career and deepen my skills" won't generate much excitement, but a detailed, elaborated paragraph in place of this sentence could. If you can't define your goals well, you will also be unable to explain why a particular school is the best fit for you. The crucial link between your goals and the school resources that support them will be missing.

Third, schools also use goals essays to make an indirect read on the quality of your mind and thought processes. Do you think seriously about the problems in your company or industry? Are you a realistic person or a vague or flaky dreamer? Can you craft a compelling case in prose that links your past, your goals, and the school you're applying to? Finally, the goals essay gives you the least freedom of any business school essay for "creative" responses. This is because (1) you need to cover so much ground (career progress, short- and long-term goals, why an MBA, why our school) and (2) your goals themselves need to be well grounded and savvy.

For all that, schools' secondary purpose in requiring the goals essay is to learn about you as a person—that is, the distinctive experiences, values, and human traits that make you unique. It's possible to submit a goals essay that is too factual, impersonal, or boring, that succeeds in answering all the school's goals questions but fails to introduce you as a person the reader would want to know better.

In this chapter, we discuss practical strategies for ensuring that your goals essay avoids all the pitfalls and touches all the bases, setting a compelling, concrete tone for your entire application. Let's start by examining the kinds of questions most goals essays ask.

WHAT THE SCHOOLS ASK

Though virtually all business schools pose the goals question in some form, the wording they use, the range of topics they include, and the length they require vary widely. The vast majority of schools assign a broader length limit to the goals essay than to any other essay. Though Stanford's seven-page suggested maximum and Darden's discretionary "you decide" represent the most generous length instructions, the typical limit is roughly two pages (about eight hundred plus words) or one thousand words.

As a general rule, goals essays have three parts: a backward-looking career progress section, a forward-looking career goals section, and a "why our school" section. Wharton's essay 1 is the classic goals essay formulation: "Describe your career progress to date and your future short-term and long-term career goals. How do you expect an MBA from Wharton to help you achieve these goals and why now?" Many variations are played on this theme, however. Some schools ask only generally what your career goals are, a larger number ask you to break them down further into short- and long-term goals, and a handful even ask for a specific time line: "What are your career goals (immediately after graduation, five years out, ten years out)?" (Maryland).

Though most schools let you decide how detailed your goals description will be, others won't let you off the hook: "Please be as specific as possible, including job title/description, industry, and if possible firm" (Fordham). MIT (Sloan) adds another twist by asking for a business-formatted cover letter in which your discussion of goals must be integrated into an "executive summary" or "elevator speech" that encompasses your entire application.

But the greatest variation among schools' goals essays lies in the retrospective "career progress" or career influences section—where you explicitly connect your goals and school selection to your past. Many more programs let *you* decide what "career progress" means. Schools like New York University (Stern) and Illinois help you by asking you about the choices that led to your career path, and MBA programs such as Georgetown's invite you to expand this backward-looking section to include the "prior academic, personal, and professional experiences [that] influenced your career plans." To encourage you to use the goals essay to introduce your total candidacy, other schools welcome a discussion of everything from your "skills, competencies, and experiences" to your "background, experience, interests, and values." All these permutations, however, really come down to the same question: why do you have the goals you do?

In the Schools' Words—

We want students to be their own career counselors before they get to the program. [We want applicants to] make the connection or create the bridge: Here is where I am, this is how the MBA is going to assist me, and this is where I would like to be.

—SABRINA WHITE,
UNIVERSITY OF MARYLAND (SMITH)

A description of your potential contribution to the program is an explicit additional topic posed by a small number of schools. They ask this to get a bead on the diversity you'll bring to your class and to see how much you know about their program. As we'll see in Chapter 3, schools define diversity broadly here to include "uniqueness factors"—the distinctive combination of professional, community, and personal experiences and characteristics that could enhance the variety of your class. Since you should be communicating the uniqueness of your potential contribution throughout your application, even if a school offers a separate diversity or uniqueness essay, you should try to briefly discuss what you'll bring to the program in the goals essay. After all, it's the first essay adcoms will read, and you want to get as many of your themes and uniqueness factors on the table as possible. The most explicit way to do this is to link what you can contribute—for example, "experience leading international teams"—with specific related resources at the school: "I look forward to sharing this through the International Students Club, my classes on global strategy and marketing, and the Chicago Asian Forum."

Because the range of topics you may encounter in the goals essay is so broad, one of your biggest challenges will simply be answering everything the school asks in one coherent, readable essay. The remainder of this chapter focuses on how to do just that.

The Kitchen Sink MBA Goals Question

Goals Statement. Applicants with a plan for their future and with a good grasp of what is expected of them as MBA students are the most successful students in our program. We know plans change, and we know people often pursue an MBA to create new career options. Please tell us about your plans. Ideally, your essay should answer all the following questions: Why are you pursuing an MBA degree? What do you expect to do immediately after completing the MBA program? What is your primary lifetime goal? How do your life and work experiences to date move you closer to these personal objectives? What specific things will the MBA experience contribute to your post-MBA and lifetime career goals? What unique aspects of the University of Washington MBA Program, if any, would contribute the most to achieving your goals? (*University of Washington*)

WRITING THE GOALS ESSAY

The specific focus of your post-MBA goals will and should color almost every aspect of your application—from school selection, to the guidelines you provide recommenders, to interview preparation and the classes you sit in on during school visits. For this reason, you should begin work on a basic goals essay very early in your application process, perhaps after you take the GMAT, but, in any case, before you begin work on your application proper.

Writing effectively about your goals starts with *thinking* about them. Many applicants begin the application process believing that sufficient reasons for seeking the MBA are:

- They have the numbers (GMAT, GPA) and work experience to get into a good business school.

- Their peers are in business school.

- The organization they work for expects them to earn an MBA.

- It's the next impressive credential for the superachieving applicant to acquire.

- Post-MBA starting salaries are high.

- They were just downsized or hit a career plateau and have nowhere else to go.

Though these are certainly common reasons for applying to business school, they all share the same drawback: they aren't goals. Your task is to move beyond these obvious or uninspiring career objectives to goals that fall within business schools' acceptable range.

SO, WHAT EXACTLY ARE YOUR GOALS?

This book is not a resource for a crash course in career counseling. But if you really don't know why you need an MBA, abandon the application process until you do. Alternatively, consult such sources as your university's career services board or CareerLeader, an online career development tool for business school students, and begin doing some serious informational interviewing with alumni or industry elders who might be willing to guide you. If you do have a vague inkling about your career track, flesh it out by performing some due diligence. Read industry magazines, for example, or cruise the Web sites of organizations you'd like to join, noting the career paths of their top managers. Integrate your new knowledge into your post-MBA career story.

We'll assume for now that you do have a rough sense of your post-MBA path but that you just need to refine it so that it passes the high muster of a B-school admissions committee. Stating that you want to be the CEO of a Fortune 500 consumer goods corporation is a start but not nearly enough. For most schools (let alone Stanford, which gives you up to seven pages to describe your goals), you'll need much, much more. Think of your post-MBA career not as a destination but as an evolving narrative, and take a hint from business schools' questions: "Where do you see yourself in 10 years?" At a minimum, use your career research and networking efforts to map out a credible short-, intermediate-, and long-term trajectory.

Concrete goals should be the foundation on which your selection of business schools is based, whether it's because of the specific study tracks and courses they offer or the number and quality of organizations in your industry that recruit there. Once your goals and school selection are defined, you can begin to sketch out your goals essay.

ORGANIZING THE GOALS ESSAY

As we discussed in Chapter 1, using an outline can minimize much of the potential grief of writing admissions essays. This is particularly true of goals essays, where you're asked to discuss multiple topics, while also establishing the themes that unify your application. Fortunately, many schools' goals essays come with a built-in structure that can help you organize your material. For example, Kellogg invites you to "Briefly assess your career progress to date. Elaborate on your future career plans and your motivation for pursuing a graduate degree at the Kellogg School." There are three closely interrelated but distinct topics here:

- Your career "progress": the trajectory, influencing factors, and themes of your career thus far (*not* a blow-by-blow walk-through of your résumé).

- Your career plans (short-, medium-, and long-term goals).

- Your reasons for needing a Kellogg MBA (aka "why our school?").

It makes sense to structure your outline by addressing each of these topics in turn for the simple reason that this is the order in which you would normally discuss your career: from past to present to future. Your career experiences have shaped your goals, which in turn have shaped your reasons for needing an MBA from this particular school. You still must decide what form your introduction should take and interpret what "career progress" means—what it includes and what you should leave out. But you now have a basic organization to guide you.

Don't assume that each of these three sections must be the same length. It's likely that the career progress and influences section will consume half the essay and that your goals may take no more than a paragraph or so. Also, don't assume that schools necessarily expect you to follow this past-present-future order. They only care that you do address each topic somewhere in the essay.

Many schools' goals essays won't give you such a ready-made structure, of course. But no matter how the goals essay is worded, you should structure your essay in the way that makes the most sense for you. If you've been certain of your career goals since high school, you might well discuss your goals first and your career background second, since your goals have presumably been guiding your subsequent career decisions. Similarly, you could legitimately decide to open the essay with the reasons why a particular MBA program is best for you so as to highlight your enthusiasm for that school.

Whichever structure you choose, each section of your essay must be tightly integrated with the others. Your past, present, and future must be shown to logically support one another. Your career progress section must leave readers feeling that the next inevitable step for you is an MBA and a career in your chosen post-MBA field. Your goals section must describe objectives that seem to have evolved naturally from your past experiences, and your "why our school" section must demonstrate that the school is the perfect place for someone with your values, personality, and educational needs. An effectively integrated outline can help you navigate through your past, present, and future without getting lost in minutiae or turning your essay into a glorified résumé.

With your outline in hand you can begin to approach the individual sections of your essay.

In the Schools' Words—

We are not expecting people to have life plans in stone, but we do expect to see clear thinking about how an MBA fits into where someone has been and where they think they are headed. The MBA is an outstanding credential, but it's more than just a relatively quick ticket to higher earnings. It's also an educational experience—and an expensive one, at that—so it's important to know why one is undertaking this. Also, this understanding/focus/passion makes for a much more successful career search.

—Gwyneth Slocum Bailey,
University of Michigan (Ross)

THE LEAD PARAGRAPH

Given the goals essay's importance and serious purpose, many applicants are tempted to play it safe with a plain vanilla lead:

- "My long-term goal is to become CEO of a major multinational corporation."

- "My career goals stem directly from my professional experiences."

- "I need an MBA so I can help benefit society."

While these gambits have the virtue of directness, they will make you sound exactly like the vast majority of other applicants. They're dull; avoid them altogether. Because goals essays focus on nitty-gritty matters like goals, skills, reasons for MBAs, and career choices, your opening paragraph is one of your few opportunities to inject a little pizzazz into this crucial essay. Creative leads can be divided into two broad types: content-focused introductions (where the emphasis is on what you say) and style-focused introductions (where the emphasis is on how you say it).

Content-Focused Leads

- *The direct statement of theme.* "The choices I have made in my career have been shaped by the constant interplay of two sometimes conflicting traits: my desire to gain broad international business experience and my need to have a positive impact on my community."

- *The autobiographical or self-disclosure lead.* "I was raised by a family of inveterate dreamers," or "I'm the inventor of something you sit on every day but probably can't name."

- *Statement of belief.* "I believe nuclear power plants can be designed that exceed the safety records of solar and wind power sources."

- *School-specific leads.* "While sipping a latte in Huntsman Hall, Ward Dilever, Wharton class of '04, described a scene that sounded almost too good to be true."

- *The diverse list.* "An amateur organist, a lapsed millionaire, a postal clerk in Medicine Hat, a shortstop for the Beloit Bison—I've been all these things at one point or another."

- *The imagined future.* "It's March 2015, and the chairman of Iraq Wireless is admiring the scenic view from his fortieth-floor Baghdad boardroom."

- *Vivid description of goals.* "The first truly national online 'campus'—a student-managed student community provided free to every under-graduate—could have a revolutionary billion-dollar impact on industries as diverse retail fashion, media and entertainment, electronics, and distance learning."

- *The big-picture analysis.* "The pet oral hygiene industry is a little-known but potentially billion-dollar market."

Style-Focused Leads

- *The vividly described image.* "In the clearing stood a huge, delicately carved statue of Tawri, the Indonesian fertility god, a quizzical look etched into its red-lacquered face."

■ *The "you-are-there" scene or anecdote.* "As the Lear jet's wheels touched down on idyllic Bekoe Island, Nordlink's CFO whispered two words that forever changed the way I viewed my career: . . ."

■ *The question.* "Is there such a thing as a strategy consulting gene?"

■ *The direct address of the reader.* "Picture yourself standing before an audience that includes Jack Welch, Sam Palmisano, and Bob Nardelli, and you'll understand how I felt when . . ."

■ *The quotation.* "'If you don't know where you're going, you'll end up somewhere else.'—Yogi Berra"

■ *The outlandish assertion.* "I am the president of an invisible company."

Which of these approaches, if any, should you choose? The key question is which one meshes best with your material and themes. The goal is to engage the reader and project your individuality, so choose the lead that best helps you to do that. For example, if you suspect that adcoms will find your work experience or application confusing or aimless, consider a lead paragraph that clearly states your goals and themes. Similarly, if you think your work experience or professional profile suffers from a lack of personality, consider a lead paragraph that accentuates your diversity or highlights a distinctive story or quality. Note that although both Vassily K. (sample essay 1) and John F. (sample essay 4) choose to open their essays with a quotation, they achieve very different effects. Vassily's "You came all the way from Israel?" raises questions that pull the reader in to find answers, while John's "The only way to really win in this world is to run your own show." operates more as a direct statement of theme with an autobiographical twist.

Whichever type of lead you choose, include a reference to your goals and, if possible, the MBA in the opening paragraph. This signals the admissions committee that your essay will, in fact, address the essay question directly, if not necessarily from the first sentence. Don't let adcoms think, "Where is all this going?"

In the Schools' Words—

One of the things we want to do as an educational provider is to help students get from point A to point B, and you can't do that unless you know what point B is.

—HAYDEN ESTRADA,
UNIVERSITY OF NOTRE DAME (MENDOZA)

THE CAREER PROGRESS AND INFLUENCES SECTION

The career progress or career influences section is really two sections in one: a highly selective narrative of your career's key decisions or turning points, highlights, or career-shaping accomplishments and an explanation of how your career goals have evolved to the point where you are now seeking an MBA. These are two complementary but distinct topics. A goals essay that discusses your career path thus far without linking it to your goals will render your essay's goals section incomprehensible and your essay as a whole disjointed. No matter how superb your professional experiences are, if you can't show how they relate to your post-MBA goals, you won't come across as the focused applicant every school seeks.

In the Schools' Words—

[In goals essays], a compelling bridge from past achievement toward clear future goals helps, especially with specific details showing how features of our school can readily help you get there.

—CRAIG HUBBELL, UCLA (ANDERSON)

Conversely, a goals essay that explains how you arrived at your career goals but fails to mention key career choices or pivotal moments will be a wasted opportunity for you to emphasize your strengths, inviting adcoms to give their own, perhaps less favorable explanations for the career choices you've left unexplained. Even if the business school you're applying to doesn't explicitly ask you to address the career progress and influences topic, try to work it in.

The Career Progress and Influences Question: What Schools Ask

- "Briefly assess your career progress to date." (Kellogg)

- "Please describe your career progression to date, highlighting leadership and management positions and reasons for changing employers or career paths." (North Carolina)

- "How will your background, experience, interests, and values enable you to pursue these goals successfully?" (Vanderbilt)

- "Think about the choices you have made in your life. Which choices led you to your current career path and position?" (Illinois)

- "What has helped shape your goals so far?" (Boston University)

- "Indicate how your past experiences have contributed to the definition of these objectives." (George Washington)

- "How does your past education and experience support your career objectives?" (Rochester)

- "What choices have you made that led you to your current position?" (NYU Stern)

The biggest mistake applicants make in the career progress section is to assume that "career progress" means blandly reciting their résumés in sentence form: "Then I . . . and then I . . . and then." In reality, schools want to know only about the inflection points, the key career decisions, the reasons why you moved from point A to point B. In Vassily K.'s essay (sample essay 1), for example, he pivots his entire goals statement around two events: an international marketing course and his discovery of the corporate responsibility philosophy of a prominent firm. Dig for such inflection points by interrogating yourself about your biggest career decisions: Why, after college, did you take a position as an IT consultant when security analysis firms also offered you jobs? Why did you decide to leave your IT consulting firm for another, smaller firm after only two years? Why have you worked for three firms in five years? Why have you worked for the same firm for five years?

Answering these granular-level career questions enables you to answer in turn the larger underlying questions: Why has your career taken the trajectory it has? What did you like and dislike about your key positions? And above all, what have you learned about your abilities and potential as your career has unfolded? The career progress and influences section, in other words, gives you the chance to instruct the admissions committees in how to properly view the raw data of your résumé. Imposing this interpretive, evaluative narrative over your career eliminates schools' specific questions and gives them a context for feeling good about your career.

In the Schools' Words—

You should have a clear focus when applying to business school; things happen pretty fast and you will be turning in your résumé and interviews almost immediately. We want to see that people have really thought through their goals and have done some research on their intended field. We want to be sure that they are realistic and that we can help them get where they want to go. Also, please tell us what in your past has sparked the interest in your intended goal. What do you want to do?

—Isser Gallogly,
New York University (Stern)

The ultimate purpose of the career progress and influences section is to explain as specifically as possible where your post-MBA goals come from and why you enjoy the field you're in and believe you would succeed in it. You want to demonstrate a knowledge based on contact with your post-MBA profession through your current work or community experience. If you're like most people, your post-MBA goals took shape during on-the-job exposure to the field:

During my four years at HollySoft my software development projects
exposed me to the project management and marketing functions. In 2002, I

was my group's main interface with our Marketing Department during the development of XMLBuilder, and in 2003 I was mentored by my project manager in his duties during the XMLEditor project. I was fascinated by market segmentation and target marketing techniques, and also discovered I have a talent for costing project elements and for leading small teams. I deepened my marketing and project management experiences last year when I was named Team Lead on our flagship XMLSuite product. This promotion only confirmed my desire to focus my future career on software marketing management.

In this example, the applicant explains exactly how he gained his initial exposure to his post-MBA career field and how his deepened exposure to the functions mentioned motivated him to seek a career change. But this is only a bare outline. To really make his career progress section come alive, he should insert miniaccomplishments that illustrate the pivotal moments in his path toward discovering marketing as his calling. Thus, in our example, the applicant could flesh out his five-sentence career-influences statement by answering the following questions:

- What was his (1) biggest accomplishment and (2) greatest lesson learned during the XMLBuilder project?

- What was his (1) biggest accomplishment and (2) greatest lesson during the XMLEditor project?

- What fascinated him exactly about the marketing tools and techniques he gained exposure to? What was the appeal?

- What did he enjoy about the financial and team leadership tasks his project manager let him perform?

- What was his (1) biggest accomplishment and (2) greatest lesson during his team-leading experience on the XMLSuite project?

How detailed his answers to these questions are will depend on how much space he has to work with. In a typical 1,000-word goals essay, you may be able to discuss two to four distinct goal-influencing accomplishments. Your evolving career goals can be the "takeaways" or lessons you learned from the mini-accomplishments that you work into your career progress narrative. For maximum effect, you should also quantify the impact of these accomplishments in dollar or percentage terms. Always highlight what was atypical or "fast track" about your path relative to peers. Note how Chun X. (sample essay 2) repeatedly lets the reader know when a major new responsibility was atypical for someone his age.

If your work experience didn't expose you to your post-MBA field, explain what did. Perhaps a purely personal experience opened your eyes. Describe it. Maybe a friend's advice or a news article hinted that this particular career path might best match your personality, so you followed up with personal research and informational interviews with people in the field. Let the admissions committee in on the origins of your goals. Demonstrate that you did your due diligence in identifying the goals that motivate your application to business school.

Be strategic about the content of your career progress section. What you highlight will obviously be influenced by the message you're trying to send throughout your entire application, by the negatives you're trying to compensate for, and by the topics of the school's other essays. If your GMAT quantitative score is lower than the school's average and you want to emphasize your leadership skills to offset the fact that you have no direct reports, you could skew your career progress section to highlight quantitative and leadership accomplishments. Similarly, as we noted in Chapter 1, you need to view each school's essay set holistically. If a school has a separate essay for leadership, for example, you may not need to press the leadership theme quite as hard here in the goals essay.

THE GOALS SECTION

Not all post-MBA goals are created equal. The MBA has traditionally been a feeder degree for careers in investment banking (IB), management consulting (MC), venture capital (VC)/private equity, and executive management for Fortune 500 manufacturing and consumer goods firms. That business schools are increasingly welcoming nontraditional post-MBA career paths is obvious from the growing prominence of entrepreneurial and social impact goals among B-school graduates. Nevertheless, applicants considering nontraditional goals still need to make the extra effort to prove to schools that their future career actually exists in the real world and that an MBA is an accepted and helpful credential for achieving it. You can test the credibility of your goals by evaluating your answers to the following questions:

- Do people succeed in this goal who have my work experience and the MBA I hope to earn?

- Is this goal related in some direct and explainable way to my past professional or nonprofessional experiences?

- Is an MBA a preferred or accepted credential for professionals in the position(s) I'm targeting?

- Is my goal one that clearly leverages the strengths of the business school I'm applying to?

If you can answer an emphatic yes to these questions (and provide evidence for your affirmation), then your goals will pass the adcom's credibility test. Never forget that business schools view themselves as temples of personal metamorphosis, not diploma mills.

Structure

How you go about describing your goals in the goals essay will be dictated by the specific wording of the school's question. Many schools merely request that you describe your goals, period. A larger number insist that you at least divide your post-MBA plan into short- and long-term goals. A handful of schools are scrupulously exact:

- "What are your career goals (immediately after graduation, five years out, ten years out)?" (Maryland)

- "Describe your post-MBA short (+2 years out), medium (+5 years out), and long-term (+10 years out) professional goals." (Pennsylvania State)

Finally, some schools help you structure your goals section by indicating the depth of detail they want:

- "Be as specific as you can concerning the types of positions and responsibility levels to which you aspire." (Buffalo)

- "Please describe the professional environment in which you envision yourself one year after obtaining your MBA. Please be as specific as possible, including job title/description, industry, and if possible firm." (Fordham)

No matter how vague the question's wording is, you should strive to be as specific in your response as you can be. Identify which industry you're targeting, of course, but also the type of company (multinational? start-up?), geographic region, your rough job responsibilities ("CEO" is not enough), and perhaps some of the challenges you may encounter. You won't be dinged if your description isn't a note-perfect rendition of the occupational realities of that industry. You will be, if you sound like you really haven't given your goals much thought. Again, show the school that you've done your homework.

The most logical way to structure the goals section is chronologically, from short-term goals to long-term goals. Devote several sentences to describing what you plan to do professionally for the first three or four years after you graduate from business school. (Note that some schools consider your time in business school as part of your short-term career plan, so be prepared to sketch your learning goals.) If your post-MBA plan includes an intermediate goal between your short-term career and your ultimate objective, then devote several sentences to detailing this middle period—from, say, five to ten years after you get your MBA. Finally, close the goals section by describing your career's "end game." Since most schools don't expect you to know where you'll be more than 10 to 15 years after you receive your MBA, you don't have to map out what you'll be doing when you're 64.

If your short-term goal makes sense only as a stepping-stone toward your long-term goals it's perfectly valid to describe your long-term goals *first.* You can then present your short-term goals as the bridge to your long-term goals. This is exactly what Vassily K. does in the fifth paragraph of his essay (sample essay 1). If the connection between your short- and long-term goals isn't immediately obvious (such as, short term = consultant, long term = partner), then make it so. It doesn't help you to have superbly detailed short- and long-term goals if the adcoms can't see how one leads to the other.

In the Schools' Words—

I joke that I don't follow around students with their goals essay saying you said finance and now you are doing marketing! . . . [Students] can change their mind once they are here, but I want to know they have a good sense for where they are headed. You can get overwhelmed otherwise. Too many choices.

—KRIS NEBEL,
UNIVERSITY OF MICHIGAN (ROSS)

Goals: How Specific?

"Please be specific" is an insistent refrain in many schools' goals essay instructions. How specific is specific? From a purely practical perspective, understand that by presenting focused goals, you are telling adcoms that you have a better chance of succeeding in their program than applicants without them. Instead of the leisurely four years you were given in college, business school gives you two years, and sometimes sixteen months or less, to master a comprehensive set of intellectual disciplines. The more focused your educational goals are, the more likely you'll be to make the right choices, minimize wheel-spinning, and rejoin the workforce as a productive graduate capable of doing your alma mater proud.

So specific is good. But you can actually clear the "be specific" hurdle merely by sketching out what industry, general type of employer, and functional roles you plan to join over your career's near and distant future. Most applicants don't even go this far. They say, "I want to be an executive in finance" and leave the adcoms to fill in the rest. You must dig deeper. What niche in finance will you pursue? Investment banking? Venture capital? Private equity? What kind of executive will you be? CEO? CFO? VP? And what will your responsibility path be before you earn that title? What functional area will you focus on while you're waiting for the top spot? Accounting? Marketing? Finance? Operations? Further, in what part of the world will your employer be located? What size firm will you likely target? Even general answers to each of these questions can put you well ahead of the typical applicant.

Here's a compact example of a specific goal statement: "My long-term goal is to become CEO or CFO of a midsized e-marketplace or B2B e-commerce company in Europe, such as EuroPlace PLC or e-Markt GMBH, where my experiences wringing cost efficiencies and creating strategic partnerships at RoyaleNet can help scale my organization into a global player." Note that this applicant (we'll call her Roberta) names two specific functional roles (CEO, CFO), a focused but still encompassing niche (e-marketplace or B2B e-commerce), a specific but still broad region (Europe—not "in Liechtenstein"), two actual potential employers for credibility, and a specific tie in to her previous relevant experiences. Fleshed out—and with a similar level of specificity applied to her short-term goals—Roberta's statement will meet business schools' "be specific" requirement. You should present your short- and long-term goals with this kind of specificity, even for schools that do not explicitly ask you to.

If space allows, Roberta could also have enhanced the credibility of her goals by displaying deeper savvy about her future industry's fundamentals. For example, discussing trends or emerging challenges (e.g., labor costs, competing technologies) would further drive home the message that this applicant knows why she needs an MBA. (Don't get carried away with this, of course; keep the focus on you.) Briefly discussing why specific executives (by name) at the organizations she might join have been role models for her would be another creative way to deepen her goal's believability. These discretionary elements can add value and resonance to your goals essay.

For the sake of your goals essay you should specify one future career track rather than two or more. It's fine to say, "I want to be a serial entrepreneur" but not, "I want to be an entrepreneur or an investment banker or a management consultant." There's a limit to how far you should take "be specific." Avoid stating that you want to be a consultant at McKinsey or CEO of IBM, for example. Implying that you've got your heart set on a single employer sounds not only unrealistic but immature. Likewise, "be specific" does not mean "submit a business plan." If your goals are too tightly defined, business schools will think you're just looking to get your vocational or entrepreneurial ticket punched rather than learn a transformational way of thinking and leading that could benefit many organizations over your career.

Schools want to unleash multiple achievers and serial entrepreneurs, not one-trick, get-rich-quick managers. You can signal that you are one of these high-impact types by using your goals section to hint at *why* you have the specific professional goals you do; for example, because you like to manage creative technology teams in creating value, enjoy growing companies or new product ideas, or want to help spur business development in underdeveloped economies.

Finally, keep in mind that your goals statement doesn't necessarily have to be limited to your professional goals. Some schools deliberately welcome a wider-ranging discussion of how your professional goals meld with your values and life goals (e.g., the University of Washington asks, "What is your primary lifetime goal?"). If space permits, you may therefore want to include a brief discussion of your community/volunteer goals in your goals essay, especially if an MBA will help you achieve them.

Career Switching

At least half to three-quarters of all MBA students typically use the degree to transition into an entirely different field, for example, from IT to management consulting or from consulting to general management. Schools know that the MBA is the perfect vehicle for making a sharp, clean, and successful career change. So you need not feel bashful about declaring your career-switching intentions in your goals essay. Demonstrate a grounded understanding of the field you want to break into by detailing the extent and depth of your current pre-MBA exposure to it. Stating that you want to make a career switch does not mean dwelling on your loathing of your current career, however. You can describe the limitations of your current career track without sounding desperate or trashing your current employer.

Creative or Unusual Goals

Banish the notion that you should state nontraditional post-MBA goals just to stand out from the pack. Business schools do love unusual (qualified) candidates, but when it comes to your post-MBA goals, they tend to be more conservative. Here, they look for reassurance, not grandstanding. Can they place you in the field you've claimed as your post-MBA objective? Is an MBA an established career requirement in that industry? Is your goal to start a firm that uses third-world microlending techniques to promote commercial space flight even plausible?

The point is not to discourage you from describing goals that lie outside the traditional "MC, IB, VC, CEO" MBA circuit, but to dissuade you from cobbling together creative goals just for the sake of distinctiveness. "Will an admissions officer remember my goals after reading hundreds of other goals essays?" This is *not* the question you should be asking. When describing your goals, play it safe. An essay in which you project the unique personality, perspective, and passion you'll bring to a post-MBA strategy consulting career can be every bit as memorable—and a great deal more credible—than an off-the-wall manifesto about starting a hedge fund in the Galapagos.

Your goals may be legitimately unusual—the niche you want to fill is a real one but so specialized or new that the adcoms aren't familiar with it. If this is the case, you will have to bend over backward to document how your past work experience connects with this goal and how an MBA is essential to achieving it. Calibrate your goal against the short-term career tracks of the school's recent graduates who have backgrounds like yours. Which industries and companies

> Goals . . . can be a real differentiator—not so much by having an unusual goal, but in your depth of discussion, preparation, vision. Even if you describe a planned career path that is fairly typical, if you show a clear, personal, distinctive vision for what you will do, achieve, and contribute in that role, it will differentiate you.
>
> —Linda Abraham, Accepted.com

typically recruit there? Alumni placement information is often available officially from the school or anecdotally from alumni. Use this to gauge the credibility of your goals. Keep in mind also that some schools that are concerned about the marketability of an applicant's goals may ask a member of their career services office to review your application and evaluate your "placeability." Provide details of your own plan for using your established network to help place yourself.

Social Impact Goals

More and more business school applicants have begun declaring social impact career goals. This is partly a result of the mainstreaming of the corporate social responsibility movement in America's boardrooms and thus in the curricula of top MBA programs. But social impact goals have also offered an easy solution for applicants trying to avoid cookie-cutter profiles as future consultants or investment bankers. They think that stating selfless social objectives can separate them from the mass of applicants merely looking to gild their nests. Stating such goals only to improve one's admission chances, however, poisons the well for applicants who actually do intend to pursue social impact (often nonprofit sector) goals. In fact, Wharton has admitted that fewer than 1 percent of its MBAs actually wind up in nonprofit careers—a figure that's probably typical at most schools.

To ensure that your altruistic goals are taken seriously, you must be able to show through your work or extracurricular experience that public service has been a long-standing motivation for you. Make these past experiences the focus of the career progress and influences portion of your goals essay. No one reading Vassily K.'s essay (sample essay 1), for example, would have any doubt that he has "walked the walk" and not just "talked the talk" of his social impact goals.

Ambitious Goals

One danger that faces the applicant who has not done his post-MBA due diligence is stating overly ambitious goals. No matter how talented you are, you should never declare your intention to become the next Bill Gates or even the CEO of a major existing corporation. First, not even Bill Gates knew he would grow up to become Bill Gates. Why should you presume to be more prescient? Second, even declaring your intention to become CEO of a Fortune 500 company smacks of egotism at best and immaturity at worst. Of course, it's legitimate to state senior management or other lofty goals if your experiences already demonstrate an executive boardroom career profile. But that's a big if; most applicants will not fit this category. Sample essays 2, 3, and 4 all state ambitious goals—starting or growing global businesses—but all the writers legitimize their big dreams through career progress sections that show them to be fast-track achievers, already used to big responsibilities.

Tricky Goals Questions

- Some schools include questions like this in the goals essay: "How do you plan to use what you learn?" (Boston University) This is really just a devilish variation on the standard goals question. They want to know how, specifically, you plan to apply what you learn in business school in your post-MBA career. Rather than a paragraph of smoke and mirrors, it's better to actually provide hypothetical applications of, say, three of the specific knowledge areas you'll gain at business school. That is, if marketing will be one of your specializations, give them a rough sketch of how someone in your post-MBA role would typically apply key marketing methods or concepts. This answer will not only show that you know what you'll be studying at business school but will demonstrate that you also have done your homework on your future career.

- Another trick goals question is "What type of alternate preparation might you seek if MBA programs did not exist?" Here, schools want to know whether you are a forward-thinking person who plans for contingencies and has the problem-solver's ability to resourcefully create multiple opportunities when obstacles arise. So give them three or four different ways in which you would try to achieve your same career goal if an MBA were not an option. (Don't say "I'll just get my MBA at another school.") These ways could include part-time classes, self-teaching, a job or career change move that gives you a sharper learning curve, or striking out on your own as an entrepreneur or even a world traveler. Be creative, mention multiple paths, and show determination.

- Presenting revised goals in a reapplication essay can be tricky if those goals are so radically different from your last application that you seem flaky or capricious. At worse, you want your "new" goal to simply be a refinement of your last application's goal, and you should describe the specific recent experiences that caused this refinement. If your goal was vague last time and the recent experiences that refined it are impressive, then changing your goals in a reapplication essay is a positive move.

THE WHYS

After polishing off the career progress and goals sections, you may think the rest of the goals essay is just a matter of dotting the i's and crossing the t's. Think again. Though not all schools ask applicants to detail why they need an MBA and why now, virtually every single school insists that you explain why you are applying to its program. This process of customizing your application to the specific offerings and culture of each school is an essential part of the goals essay. If you expect your application to be taken seriously by a top-20 business school, don't write a generic goals essay that you submit unchanged to every school. Customization is all.

Why an MBA?

Many schools' goals essays ask you to explain why you need an MBA and also why you need to earn it in their program. This might seem redundant, but schools do this to get you to dig in and truly address the underlying needs or motivations that drive you to business school—any business school. They know that it's entirely possible to provide 20 wonderfully specific reasons why Duke would be a great place to earn an MBA without ever really saying why you need one in the first place. Though "why an MBA?" is an important question, too many applicants answer it with boilerplate, if at all.

The best way to approach this question is to write terrifically compelling career progress and goals sections. If you do those sections right, you will have created so inexorable and compelling a case for needing an MBA that the adcoms may feel they can answer "why an MBA?" for you. "Of course she needs an MBA. She's proven she can lead teams that are culturally and functionally diverse, and since that WessCo project, she's obviously known that operations management is the best way to use her leadership and problem-solving skills." If you've managed to get adcoms rooting subconsciously for you like this, you needn't belabor the "why an MBA?" section with vague references to "enhancing my skill set" and "honing my soft skills." Quick test: if your "why an MBA?" section reads like it could describe every person who's ever graced the campus of an accredited business school, then you need to dig deeper.

There are, of course, a common set of good reasons for wanting an MBA: it is an accepted, even required, credential for advancement in many industries; it's a universally recognized degree that will enable you to jump from one industry to another or from one region or country to another; it gives you the broad management skills you need to launch and then lead a start-up business; and so on. These are compelling reasons, but they are so general and commonly held that they almost go without saying. Worse, these reasons aren't too far from the "I need a shiny credential" type reasons that schools are loath to dignify. As noted, management schools pride themselves on being in the transformative education business, not the credentials game.

So if you do state a general reason for needing an MBA, fortify it with some concrete reasons specific to you, like the functional skills—for example, accounting, marketing, operations—that you lack. Starting with your goals section, (1) list the functional skills usually required in the career track you've specified, and (2) inventory your own skills. Subtract (2) from (1). Now, in your goals essay simply state which of the post-MBA career skills your education and work experience have given you and which skills you still need. This is the heart of your "why an MBA?" section—what skills will the MBA give you that you don't already have? A short, plain-spoken paragraph will usually suffice.

Since it is unlikely that business school is the only route to your gaining these skills, you should also note that the MBA is the most accelerated, rigorous, and integrative path to these skills, one that also provides benefits (network, soft skills) work experience alone can't give you. It's perfectly fine to tell schools that you seek the pure intellectual challenge of learning more about market segmentation or derivatives. Just don't let them think that such scholastic motivations are your main purpose—there are other research- or academic-oriented degree programs for that.

If length limits are an issue (and they usually will be), consider combining your "why an MBA?" and "why our school?" sections. That is, state the functional deficiencies you have that an MBA can fill and then follow this directly by describing the two to three specific resources at your target school that address this need. As long as you show schools that you know that needing an MBA and choosing a school to earn it are two separate things, you will be fine. Notice how Vassily K. (sample essay 1) is able to do away with a separate "why an MBA?" section by drawing a direct bridge between his goals and Kellogg's program: "The Kellogg School of Management—renowned for the excellence of its marketing program and its commitment to community—represents the same fusion of marketing and community I seek in my career."

Why Now?

Many schools explicitly ask you to explain why you are applying now:

- ■ "Why do you want an MBA from Berkeley at this point in your career?" (Berkeley Haas)

- ■ "Why are you pursuing an MBA degree at this time in your life?" (Pepperdine)

- ■ "Why is a Stern MBA necessary at this point in your life?" (NYU Stern)

Why do they ask this? In one sense, it's another way of getting a fix on how certain you are that an MBA is right for you. That is, the "why now?" question is a disguised maturity and focus question and, as such, a complementary variation on the goals and "why an MBA?" questions. You may have detailed, rock-solid career goals and an airtight case for how the MBA gets you to them, but if you can't say why you need to begin the MBA process *now*—rather than two years from now—adcoms may conclude that you're applying now for the wrong reasons. A good "why now?" message gives your application that extra sense of urgency or momentum that can move you from the ding or wait-list piles to the admit basket.

So, whether your school asks the "why now?" question overtly or not, you need to provide an explicit or implicit answer. The implicit answer will be the subliminal message that should be flashing throughout your career progress section: that the trajectory of your skills, leadership roles, and functional breadth has been rising inexorably, so only the lack of an MBA keeps you from bursting in glory into the management ranks. Your explicit answer will support this subliminal answer along the following lines:

- *Career plateau.* Your learning curve has flattened, and no new challenges are foreseeable in the next two years. If you stay any longer in your current career path, you will risk being pigeonholed as a "[insert your job here]," and breaking out will only become harder.

- *Goals epiphany.* You have only just recently realized what your career's purpose (post-MBA goal) is, and now that you know it, there's simply no reason to delay.

- *Post-MBA goals have time element.* Your post-MBA plans are linked to trends that will begin to gel about the time you earn your MBA. You can't afford to wait to gain the skills to capitalize on these trends. (This is Ingrid T.'s tack in the sixth and seventh paragraphs of sample essay 3.)

- *Maturity.* You finally have the professional and personal savvy, balance, and perspective to make the wise decision to invest in your long-term future. (This is the acceptable way of saying "My age matches the median age of the people you admit.")

- *Natural break in career.* You're approaching the end of a clearly demarcated career phase, such as a corporation's two-year management training program or a one-year overseas posting.

The "why now?" issue is even more important for applicants who are younger (two years or less of work experience) or older (32 years old or older) than the norm. Younger applicants will have to go out of their way to convince schools that they can't wait another year or two more. The best way to do this is to show that you are exceptional for your age. You have the skills, career track, or leadership responsibilities of an older applicant. If you aren't exceptional professionally, you can compensate by outlining well-defined goals. Schools may admire your career focus and overlook your relative lack of experience. Alternatively, you may argue that while your work experience isn't the equivalent of that of older applicants, you can compensate by bringing other positives to your class—perhaps unusually deep international experience, a personal story that shows maturity and fortitude, or distinctive extracurriculars. Showing in your essays or letters of recommendation that you have a track record of interacting effectively with more senior teammates will help.

Older applicants will be expected to have more sharply defined career goals than younger applicants. This is partly because they are expected to be more mature professionally and partly because the school's career services office may have more trouble placing them than younger applicants and will expect them to play a bigger role. For this latter reason, older applicants have to be careful about stating goals that represent radical career switches, particularly into fields like management consulting and investment banking. Entry-level positions in these time-intensive professions are typically filled by younger types with the energy and unencumbered personal lives to work the appalling hours.

In their goals essays, older applicants will have to convince the adcoms that they already have the professional network and job opportunities to "place themselves" after they get their MBA. Since the depth of older applicants' experience only underscores their age, they should downplay the "seen-it-all" rhetoric in favor of energized descriptions of recent experiences that reinvigorated their outlook by pointing them toward a new professional goal.

In the Schools' Words—

It is never about age. It is always about realistic goals and how they plan to achieve them.

—LINDA MEEHAN, COLUMBIA BUSINESS SCHOOL

Why Our School?

Today, otherwise superb applicants with superhuman numbers and glowing résumés are regularly dinged simply because they give no compelling sense that they've given any thought to their potential match with the schools they apply to. Admissions officials do not believe it is their obligation to figure out whether you would fit in well in their program; they expect you to make that case.

Perhaps the best way to view the "why our school?" section is to treat it as an elaborate courting ritual involving a somewhat conceited future spouse. She (or he) will not surrender to your overtures merely because you are handsome, rich, and charming. You must also flatter her that it's *personal*, that despite all those *other* schools you've known, you are sincerely, passionately, and uniquely interested in her tastes and self-image and will defend her reputation and honor as a generous future alumnus. This wooing metaphor is not entirely facetious. The application process is undeniably a human, subjective process, not a scoring system of numbers and indexes. A convincing—that is, a highly specific—answer to the "why our school?" question persuades adcoms that, despite the marriage proposals you've casually tossed out to six other rivals, you will actually pick them if they say yes. For adcoms, as for potential marriage prospects, the yield factor is critical.

For this reason, you should avoid giving any reason for attending a school that can also be said to any other school. "I'm attracted to School X because its flexible curriculum, collaborative learning environment, strong alumni network, and outstanding faculty are unique." Unique? Virtually every school accredited by the Association to Advance Collegiate Schools of Business could claim that this sentence described it. You must refer by name to aspects of the school's program that will individualize your areas of interest. For example, almost all business schools have some program for getting students involved in the community, but only the University of Michigan's Global Citizenship organization raises funds for "Focus: Hope in Detroit." Simply by citing this initiative by name you lift your "why our school?" section one level above the typical applicant's.

Any effective "why our school?" section *must* be preceded by serious personal research on the school, not just a quick skim of the school's Web site and *BusinessWeek's Guide to the Best Business Schools.* A visit to the school is strongly advised unless it's financially impossible. Even attending information sessions in your city can give you a better sense of the school than impersonal research. One helpful source of information is business schools' student newspapers, such as Harvard Business School's *Harbus Online* (www.harbus.org) and the University of Chicago's *Chicago Business Online* (www.chibus.com). They give you an honest, student-level version of campus reality without the marketing embellishments of official school publications. Besides, mentioning such "insider" resources in your essay will impress the adcoms with your interest and thoroughness.

There is no formula for how long your "why our school?" section should be or in what order you should present your reasons. If you deeply believe the school is a strong match with your needs and you have many examples that demonstrate it, your school section may be comparatively long, say, three paragraphs in a two-page goals essay. If the school's curricular resources perfectly complement your intended specialization, then you could devote more space to these academic factors and perhaps launch your school section with this information. Similarly, if your campus visit is what really sold you on the school, consider talking about it first and giving it the most space.

The only guideline is to take the space you need to show that your interest is genuine and specific to that school. A "why our school?" section should be at least one paragraph in length but should generally not consume an entire page (except for Stanford, of course, which gives you up to seven or more pages to work with). You do, of course, want to show that your interest in a program is multidimensional—you're not only interested in academic resources but in extracurricular and cultural factors too. Note, for example, how Chun X. (sample essay 2) manages to work in 11 diverse references to Wharton-specific resources in the span of an eight-sentence paragraph.

Content

As a rough guide, your "why our school?" section may touch on four categories of school-specific information:

1. *Academics.* This includes everything from academic tracks or specialties, specific courses, and nontraditional learning environments to faculty members (including research interest), teacher-to-student ratio, teaching methods, and joint-degree opportunities. *Hint:* research books, articles, or case studies by professors whose interests match yours. Consider mentioning one or two of these publications in your essay to show the school you've done your homework.

2. *Extracurricular features.* This is where you show the schools that you are a joiner who enjoys people and means to contribute. You can refer to everything from student clubs, athletics, and social groups to alumni network, overseas or exchange opportunities, internships, business plan contests, and community involvement initiatives. *Hint:* if the school has no organization in one of your interest areas, consider stating that you will start one (if you would). Adcoms may be impressed by your initiative.

3. *General and "cultural" features.* This is where you show that you understand the school's specific culture, its self-image, the message it sends about what it believes makes it unique. This is where you might discuss Kellogg's team orientation, Yale's social impact emphasis, MIT's finance strengths or culture of innovation, etc. *Hint:* refer back to the notes you took during your school selection process. Many of the reasons you originally used to winnow your list can actually be mentioned in this section, so long as you also link them to specific school resources by name: urban versus rural campus, large or small school, proximity to cultural or business opportunities, and so on.

4. *Campus visit and personal interaction.* Making a campus visit is an excellent way to show interest. Capitalize on your visit by noting which classes you sat in on, which adcoms and students you spoke with (by name!), and what you learned about the school that you didn't know before. You can use all this information in your goals essay to personalize your "why our school?" message. But such personalization can also extend beyond a campus visit. If you know alumni, mention them by name, how you know them, and what you have learned from them about the school. *Hint:* Consider contacting one or two faculty members whose research interests match yours and arrange to discuss your interests with them. You could then refer to these conversations in your essay.

Be School-Specific

Business schools don't have "preferred" career goals, but they are aware of how well your goals match their resources, whether they stem logically and reasonably from your work experience, and whether they seem typical or distinctive. Schools also have distinct strengths. You may have mixed goals that allow you to modulate your goals description to emphasize your fit with particular schools. For example, if your post-MBA goal is health care and consulting and you are applying to Duke and Tuck, for Duke you could emphasize the health-care goal and Duke's health-care management program, and for Tuck you could emphasize the consulting goal and Tuck's general management focus.

The "why our school?" section is not the only place in the goals essay where you should be sending your customized school-specific message. The whole essay should be communicating school fit on some level. Revisit your entire goals essay to see if its themes and key words need tweaking to match the school's particular culture.

THE CONCLUSION

Because the goals essay is your application's first and most formal essay, you need to be extra careful not to commit any of the blunders applicants typically make in conclusions. One is to simply let the essay end abruptly: "Fourth, Stern's International Passport Day will enable me to share my Estonian heritage (from red beet potato salad to *runo*-songs) with my diverse classmates." Even if you have room to insert only one sentence, add a summarizing closing thought, lest the adcoms think you hastily submitted a rough draft.

The most common error made in closing a goals essay is to rely on stale boilerplate prose: "I am confident I can succeed at GSB and look forward to making an invaluable contribution to my talented and diverse class." This kind of language adds no value because (1) it could have been written by anybody, (2) it could apply to any school, (3) it doesn't reinforce any of your specific themes, (4) it doesn't (one hopes) echo your opening paragraph, and (5) schools see millions of conclusions like this, so it doesn't help you stand out.

As we discussed in Chapter 1, the safest way to avoid these deficiencies while also creating a nice sense of closure is to indirectly echo or refer back to your opening sentence or opening paragraph. Think of this as repeating your lead but with a twist, restating what you began with but with some forward-looking variation on it. Locate the key word, phrase, or idea in your opening sentence and find some way to connect it to a positive, flattering, declarative statement about this specific school:

Lead. "When I asked my friends what they thought of my decision to leave Lance & Boyle, they replied in unison: 'You're out of your mind.'"

Close. "Earning my MBA at Kenan-Flagler makes the best personal, professional, and educational sense. You might say I'd be out of my mind not to."

Lead. "In 2003 I was the key client contact for the largest strategy consulting engagement in Chinese business history."

Close. "With a Tuck MBA the next historic engagement I witness will be the one I lead."

Lead. "My father once told me, 'Put your trust in friends, your faith in hard work.'"

Close. "Put my trust in friends, my faith in hard work? Of course, but I'll also put them in the transforming power of a Yale MBA."

Echoing your introduction in this way is a convenient way to avoid a generic ending. If your introduction is, as it should be, personal and engaging, then your conclusion, in echoing it, will borrow some of that flair. Finally, the short-is-sweet rule of thumb applies to goals essays too. A brief, punchy final sentence can give your essay a nice closing jolt, like an exclamation point:

"More than ever, I'm ready to seize that chance."

"I can't wait to begin."

"My next step is clear: a Columbia MBA."

Now that you've finished your goals essay, go out and treat yourself—you deserve it. You've cleared a major hurdle on the way to creating a successful application.

GOALS ESSAYS: WHAT *NOT* TO DO

When you're writing your goals essay, keep in mind the following common blunders. Don't

1. Start your essay with a bland lead paragraph: "My career goal is to . . ." The range of topics business schools ask you to address in the goals essay prevents you from getting too creative, but this doesn't mean you should start the essay like an auditor's opinion letter. An anecdote, a vivid moment, a pivotal scene from your career—each of these can give your goals essay a bit of color while projecting your themes.

2. State the obvious or the impolitic. Increased salary, promotions, or the prestige a degree from a top-10 school adds to your résumé are not reasons for earning an MBA that schools want to hear.

3. Be vague—about your career progress thus far, your goals, or your reasons for applying to this business school. If you're avoiding concrete details (1) because you think the schools aren't interested, think again; (2) because you don't think you have enough space, then find an editor to help you make it all fit; (3) because you don't want to think that hard, then you're not taking the application process seriously enough. Be specific!

4. State goals that are too creative or off the wall. Yes, you want your application to be distinctive and stand out from the pack. But the goals section of the goals essay is not the place to do it. Anchor your goals in reality by doing thorough research into actual career paths for MBAs in your desired field.

5. Write your essay without an outline. An outline can help you ensure that your goals essay's three sections—your relevant career experiences, your goals, your reasons for wanting an MBA—all interconnect and comment on one another.

6. Fail to connect your goals to the past experiences that shaped them. It is imperative that you explain what experiences or influences prompted your decision to earn an MBA and select the post-MBA path you hope to pursue. If your goal is strategy consulting, perhaps you worked with strategy consultants on a key company project, learned about it through a friend in the field, or saw a *BusinessWeek* article that prompted you to read *The McKinsey Way*. Whatever the reason, explain it.

7. Neglect to create a "why our school?" section that discusses resources unique to that school. The garden-variety goals essay will chatter on unctuously about the school's "student-driven learning environment and sense of community," "powerful alumni network," and "balanced teaching methods and flexible curriculum." But since these things can be said about 90 percent of all business schools, you must go several steps further and connect these "selling points" to specific resources (by name) of the target school.

8. Write a résumé in prose. *Career progress* does not mean a blow-by-blow account of your work experience since college. It means explaining why

you've made the career choices you did (think inflection points) and using brief descriptions of a few of your key accomplishments to account for where your post-MBA goals have come from.

9. Forget to explicitly address the "why now?" question. You don't need to devote an entire paragraph to explaining why this is the right time to earn an MBA, but adding at least one declarative sentence about the timing of your business school decision will show the adcoms you're answering the question.

10. Fail to inject some of your values, personality, or nonwork uniqueness factors into your essay. Even if the school does not explicitly ask you to, try to communicate the scope of your contribution: "In turn, I will offer my classmates my intensive experience in the bioinformatics industry, multicultural depth as a Japanese-Canadian who has lived and worked in Europe, and creativity as reflected in my award-winning poetry and saxophone compositions." You should also communicate your personality and values through the passionate way you describe your career progress.

WRITING PROMPT EXERCISES

The following four exercises show you one hypothetical path toward translating the advice of this chapter into words on the page. Your own path will probably differ because your goals are distinctive to you. Don't be afraid to improvise.

Exercise 1: Goals

The heart of your goals essay is your goals, so it makes sense to start your essay there. Assuming that you're limited to two pages, aim to devote a third of a page to a half a page to your goals. Assuming you plan to use the MBA to make a career switch, you'll need to show that you understand your target industry. Online industry information sources like Hoovers.com (www.hoovers.com), Vault.com (www.vault.com), or WetFeet.com (www.wetfeet.com) will enable you to focus your effort.

Suppose you want to rise to senior management in the snack foods industry. Using Hoover's "Browse Industries" feature, you could browse the food industry for snack food companies such as Altria Group. Linking to its home page, you would find that, like many major companies, Altria offers a careers section with descriptions of positions available and even career profiles, including descriptions of duties, training opportunities, and cross-functional transfer opportunities. By researching the Web sites of half a dozen of the leading companies in your target industry, you can quickly gain a sense of the career paths and responsibilities for managers in your post-MBA industry. Select the details that most appeal to you, and integrate them selectively into your goals statement. Don't overdo it, however. Keep the focus on you.

Now do this same type of due diligence for your short-term goals. Do they match the path of the career profiles that your research uncovered? Twenty minutes of your time can give you details that will separate your essays from 80 percent of the competition. Better yet, a little extra time spent on informational interviews with two or three people in your target industry can give you names and hard knowledge that will give your goals essay the ring of truth.

Exercise 2: Career Progress

Now that you've mapped out your goals and translated them into two or three paragraphs of meaty prose, use your résumé as a guide for reexamining your work experience in light of the typical career paths you discovered in the industry you've chosen for your post-MBA career. First, beginning with your college major, write down a one-sentence explanation for each inflection point in your career: Why did you major in finance? Why did you choose to work for your first postuniversity employer? Why did you move to the second? And so on. Second, in light of the skills that you now know your post-MBA industry requires, identify experiences you had with each of your postuniversity employers in which you gained or applied these skills.

Identify the two experiences in which you had the greatest impact, and turn these into one-paragraph achievement anecdotes: What was the problem you or your organization faced? What was your role in solving the problem? What post-MBA-relevant skills did you apply to solve the problem? What was the outcome in quantitative terms of the solution you and your teammates developed? Third, briefly trace the history of your interest in your post-MBA industry. How did you learn about it? What interests you about it? How did you go about learning more about it? Why do you think you would be good at it?

Using your résumé as a guide for structuring your career progress and influences section, arrange your responses to each of these three sets of questions into a chronological narrative built around your one-paragraph achievement anecdotes. It should tell the story of why you decided to pursue your post-MBA career. Now, your goals essay is really taking shape.

Exercise 3: Why Our School?

After mentioning a few specific, personalized reasons why you need an MBA and why you need it now, prepare a roughly three-part outline for the "why our school?" section. First, relying on the school's Web site and other information sources, identify at least five academic-related resources that directly address your post-MBA goals and your learning needs—from specific course names and professors to on-campus research institutes, student clubs, and lecture series.

Make the strongest, most detailed case you can that someone with your career goals would benefit from this school's program. Second, broaden your focus from academics to include the school's extracurricular resources, its relationship with other university resources, the resources of its surrounding community, and above all the general tenor or spirit of the place as communicated by the school's self-description. List specific examples of each of these elements, and work them into your essay.

Finally, pull out your notes from your campus visit (you did visit, didn't you?). Build a paragraph around the classes you sat in on, the students or alumni (by name) whom you spoke to, and the specific insights you gained from that visit that deepened your desire to go there. After running a word search to eliminate words like *ranking*, *prestigious*, or *reputation*, review your "why our school?" section. Make sure every single sentence names at least one specific resource unique to that school.

Exercise 4: Introduction

Review the three-section essay you've developed so far, covering your goals, your career progress, and your reasons for applying to this school. What kind of tone and image is this rough draft projecting? Does it come across as dynamic? Matter of fact? Mature? Adventurous? Dry?

The type of introduction you choose can modulate or reinforce the flavor of the essay as a whole. Next, estimate how close you are to the school's length limit. The amount of space you have left will also influence which type of introduction you choose. Referring to the examples of creative openings shown earlier in this chapter, look for the one that will best "cap off" your essay as it stands now. If your draft seems a little dry, the imagined-future, "you-are-there" scene or out-landish-assertion leads might compensate. If you're running short on space, the direct statement of theme or vivid description of career goals might help you cut to the chase. If you're concerned that your work experience will make you seem unfocused or opportunistic, perhaps statement-of-belief or big-picture analysis leads will give the essay the sense of integrity or weightiness it needs.

Finally, ask yourself whether you'll be able to use all your key accomplishments and stories in this and the remaining essays. If there's a powerful anecdote left over, it might be an excellent candidate for your lead paragraph.

SAMPLE ESSAYS

The authors of the following four goals essays were admitted to Kellogg, Wharton, and MIT Sloan. These samples are not meant as models to be slavishly imitated but as prompts to encourage you to write the concrete, honest, and tightly structured essay that will best express your own career path and reason for needing an MBA.

Sample Essay 1: Vassily K. (Admitted to Kellogg)

Essay Prompt. Briefly assess your career progress to date. Elaborate on your future career plans and your motivation for pursuing a graduate degree at Kellogg. (1–2 pages double-spaced)

"You came all the way from Israel?" Though my initial reason for visiting Honolulu was in fact a study abroad program at the University of Hawaii, my tour guide at Olakino Life's international headquarters could have been forgiven for getting it wrong. My personal pilgrimage to Oahu to see the birthplace of the firm that epitomizes socially and environmentally responsible business on the Pacific Rim was one of the true highlights and lasting influences of my semester. My conversion was total: I studied Vance Nakamatsu's book "Pacific Healthy," visited Olakino Lifes all across the Pacific Rim, and even sent a letter to Mr. Nakamatsu himself. *[Effective word choice ("pilgrimage," "conversion") convinces reader that Vassily is a true believer in corporate social responsibility.]*

Though I had learned about Olakino Life during my international marketing course at University of Hawaii, it only crystallized a realization that had been forming since my first marketing class at the Jerusalem College of Technology: marketing, not software engineering, was my real calling. *[Deftly introduces essay's second theme—marketing—by tying it into story he opened essay with.]* I was gripped by the world of consumer behavior, brand management, and marketing strategy I glimpsed through that class, and after returning to Israel added a second major in marketing. Since that semester abroad, my career path has become an unconsciously choreographed dance between two themes: corporate marketing and social responsibility. My experiences with Olakino Life and Wolfgang Puck Worldwide have shown me that, with an MBA, it will be possible to fuse these two themes into one. *[←Wisely ties story into need for MBA at earliest opportunity.]*

I joined Tel Aviv Consulting after graduation because I knew that as a mid-sized management consulting firm specializing in marketing and sales it would offer me an ideal blend of functional focus and project variety. Over the next two years, I helped grow its first global product marketing strategy project to more than 35 people; rose to Manager of the firm's flagship market analysis tool, MarketTouch; and, in my last assignment, helped plan the launch of a new $17 million data security product for one of the firm's largest clients. I moved to Wolfgang Puck Worldwide in 2002 to gain exposure to qualitative, more traditional consumer-focused brand marketing and to work with a corporation with a fully developed corporate responsibility program. Starting with the Market Research department enabled me to lead both quantitative and qualitative consumer research market studies while I learned about the industry. I transferred to the brand marketing team for Wolfgang Puck's Catering & Events Group in November 2002 because I knew working in the company's smallest operational unit would expose me to many different functions and enable me to assume greater responsibility than marketers working on larger brands have. I did everything from manage the marketing campaigns, develop long-term event schedules, and create custom marketing programs to ensure integration between reputation and execution and train the marketing department. [←*Paragraph deftly interweaves accomplishments with his explanations for his career shifts.*]

The responsibilities of jump-starting the Catering & Events Group were demanding. Almost immediately after joining Wolfgang Puck Worldwide, I had joined its Community Participation Team for the environment, where I had the pleasure of participating in such events as a local park clean-up and an Earth Day clean-up/celebration. Because the Catering & Events Group was undergoing a transitional period, however, I frequently had to work 12-hour days, which left me virtually no time for the community involvement that gave my career balance.

To find that balance I seek a career that will marry my parallel interests in marketing and corporate social responsibility. My long-term career goal is to start or join a consultancy that specializes in corporate social responsibility issues or cause-related marketing/branding like The Wishnow Group or Sutton Social Marketing. By showing for-profit companies how to integrate values and social issues into their brand equity, organizational identity, and daily business practices, I will help firms build sustainable competitive advantages in a socially and environmentally responsible way. Toward that end, my short-term goal is to work for one of the elite socially and/or environmentally responsible companies or brands such as a Brand Manager for Avon or Marketing Manager for Olakino Life or Chiquita Brands. [←*Compact but meaty description of two-stage career plan.*]

To establish a foundation to make my career goals plausible, I chose to leave Wolfgang Puck Worldwide in August 2003 and pursue an experience that would bring my dual community and marketing interests back into balance before beginning an MBA program in 2004. In August 2003, I became a member of Points of Light Foundation, a Washington-based volunteer center and national network that recruits and mobilizes millions of volunteers nationwide to solve serious social problems in thousands of U.S. communities. Today, through Points of Light Foundation's Youth & Family Outreach program I analyze data from the national evaluation of the Points of Light Youth Leadership Institute; help create reports to communicate results of the PLYLI evaluation to stakeholders and funders; and help design and format the Service-Learning Impacting Citizenship curriculum.

The Kellogg School of Management—renowned for the excellence of its marketing program and its commitment to community—represents the same fusion of marketing and community I seek in my career. *[←Nicely establishes paragraph's theme: the tight link between his career goals and Kellogg's program.]* As a dual marketing and public/nonprofit management major, I can build an in-depth understanding of such advanced topics as product development and design, marketing channel strategies, and sales promotion to prepare myself for a position in brand/marketing management after graduation. To develop a framework for socially responsible business, I will study nonprofit management, social entrepreneurship, philanthropy, and change management among other topics. Supplemental courses in subjects like finance, management and strategy, and organizational behavior will help prepare me for my longer-term interests in consulting and entrepreneurship.

More generally, the accelerated, flexible nature of Kellogg's four-quarter MBA program will enable me to return to the workforce as quickly as possible. *[←Note shift in this paragraph from curricular to extracurricular reasons for choosing Kellogg.]* I plan to participate actively in such student organizations as the Social Impact Club, Marketing Club, and Business With a Heart. I am also interested in participating in a Kellogg Service Initiative before the fall quarter and in one of the Global Initiatives in Management (GIM) in the winter. Finally, Kellogg's noncompetitive, team-oriented culture is an excellent fit for me. Three campus visits and conversations with Kellogg friends Norm DeVry (Class of '02) and Sharon Weisberg (Class of '00) have already made me feel a part of the Kellogg community. *[←References to multiple campus visits and specific Kellogg people show true interest.]* Time and again I have witnessed students' cooperative, supportive team spirit in my visits to the Jacobs Center to attend classes, Social Impact Club meetings, and TGF social events. I am continually impressed by the caliber of Kellogg students and their willingness to help others even during this year's ultra-competitive recruiting season. *[←Ends somewhat abruptly but only after making very strong case.]*

Sample Essay 2: Chun X. (Admitted to Wharton)

Essay Prompt. Please discuss the factors, both professional and personal, influencing the career decisions you have made that, in turn, have led to your current position. What are your career goals for the future, and why is now the appropriate time to pursue an MBA at the Wharton School? How will you avail yourself of the resources at the Wharton School to achieve these goals? (3 pages or 1,000 words)

When I was growing up in Doalong, China, I used to fantasize about conducting international business on a global scale. I had never been overseas, and I had little concrete idea what global business was all about, let alone how I could set my life on a path that would make my fantasy real. But I never forgot my childhood vision and doors kept opening for me. My academic achievements—such as ranking first out of 22,439 students in tenth-grade exams and placing in the top five hundred out of 50,000 applicants in a college admission exam—ensured that I could stay in China and get government-paid undergraduate education at the school of my choice. As an operations management student at Beijing University I was deeply involved in research activities in robotics and just-in-time logistics, presenting three papers at conferences and submitting four more for an international conference. I viewed graduate study in North America as an exciting opportunity to learn new skills, explore the world, and alleviate my family's financial circumstances. When two Canadian and three U.S. universities offered me financial aid to pursue my graduate study I knew I could make that dream come true. [←*Manages to cover a lot of ground in first paragraph, including several accomplishments.*]

During my first semester at Western Ontario University, I realized that Canada, like the United States, was undergoing a massive shift from a manufacturing to a services-based economy. Moreover, the experiences of the international Western Ontario graduates who preceded me suggested that as an operations engineer my prospects for obtaining a job after graduation were slim. I therefore decided to broaden my educational background, transferring to the interdisciplinary industrial engineering program at the University of London. My decision bore fruit almost immediately. While still in graduate school, I led innovative productivity-improvement projects as a consultant at Tipperary Steel Products, a manufacturer of steel piping products that was facing bankruptcy due to cheap imports. As the team leader, I directed our efforts to improve assembly-line efficiency by performing time-slice analyses, identifying critical paths, and simulating the assembly lines. I then presented a new assembly plan to Tipperary, explained our proposed improvements, and took a huge risk by deciding to persuade management to let me direct a test run. The test showed our new system reduced assembly throughput time by 60 percent. Our success led to other projects designing cheaper and better pipe systems, reducing redundant parts, and eliminating setup times for machines. At Tipperary, I came to understand not only the role IT can play in creating value in manufacturing industries but also the enormous opportunities it offered for my career. As a result, I decided to broaden my skills again, this time into software engineering by taking seven more courses in this field than I needed to graduate. [←*This early career success already shows Chun to be a high-impact leader.*]

A brief stint at Wessex Royal Industries in Manchester gave me my first real-world lessons in quality and software engineering, but my decision to move squarely into software development began to pay real dividends when I joined Sassoon Media PLC in 1996. They offered me an opportunity to play a key role in an exciting, strategic project to reposition the company from a print-based media publisher to a multimedia model using IT as the vehicle of transformation. Being a part of this 300-person reengineering effort taught me the importance of "soft skills" as well as the implementation risks of IT. Later, as a systems analyst at Sassoon Electronic Media (SEM), a Sassoon business division, I used both these skill sets to successfully lead their turnaround efforts.

At SEM, I was fortunate to be challenged by more than just engineering and IT issues; I worked with key people in every division and saw how IT could serve as a catalyst for teamwork and communication. My work at SEM led to greater challenges at Sassoon corporate, where as the Publishing Technologies Team Lead (senior systems analyst) on a technology-enabled business transformation project, I led a team of ten software engineers in developing a new e-publishing system (called "SEMPub") that replaced legacy systems in six counties in southern England. Senior team members were initially reluctant to accept me as their lead because we were short on resources, always worked on older technologies, and had to work with individuals who resisted change. With the youngest team member as the lead, they felt things could only get worse. I decided to prove them wrong. I began by negotiating with management for a larger share of the limited resources. By showing cost benefits, I also persuaded our project director to approve an Internet interface to SEMPub that enabled the product to exploit the latest technologies. I then ensured that my team would be asked to develop it. I motivated my team with tangible benefits, such as flash bonuses, and I vigorously pursued process improvements. When my performance reviews rocketed, I knew I had won the senior members over. [←*Increasing impact of Chun's accomplishments creates snowball effect.*]

With increasing confidence in my leadership abilities and my understanding of the software industry, in 2003 I helped two college friends start a printing technologies business (through China Publishing Agency) in Shenzhen province, China. I arranged the financing and the registration and worked around the bureaucratic obstacles and corrupt officials. To ensure the firm's success, I negotiated a partnership with a larger firm to supply needed training and course material. To work our print runs around intermittent paper shortages, we used contacts on the government media committees to convert unpredictable paper deliveries into regularly scheduled shipments. We worked through local community leaders to deal with the Chinese bureaucracy, for whom patience is the only virtue. While buying printing presses I learned that, at least in China, even business deals that are signed and sealed are sometimes still "negotiable." Today, the printing business is financially successful. Although I was partly motivated by my desire to help my friends' economic situation, it gives me great satisfaction to know that ten of our new-hires have already been promoted to middle management.

The decision I made to go to Canada and then the United Kingdom, and the decisions I have made since, have provided me with exciting challenges and, most important, personal fulfillment. They have also fueled my desire to establish my own new media company in the Internet or e-books space, preferably in China. To make that entrepreneurial dream possible I need an MBA. After my MBA I will work as a business development manager in a small media company in the Internet or e-publishing niches where I can utilize my competencies in IT to identify and develop new business opportunities. For example, I could help a traditional publishing company like China News create the products that facilitate Web-based news delivery across China's growing Internet market. My medium-term goal is to gain multifunctional experience in international management by working as a senior manager for a multinational media firm like Bertelsmann or TimeWarner that is expanding its global markets.

My long-term goal is to establish my own global business that takes advantages of the lower labor and production costs of countries like China to create innovative media products. For example, advances in print-on-demand and web-delivered data will someday make it possible to deliver information and entertainment so even consumers in remote provinces of China can gain access to the media of Western markets. *[←Discussing future trends in his industry lends credibility to his goals statement.]* My company will pursue such opportunities. Although I understand the risks and rewards of technology and IT's tremendous potential for creating value for emerging economies, I lack depth of understanding in such key functional areas of management as marketing and finance. *[←Uses his two-paragraph goals section not only to describe his goals but the skills he will need to achieve them, thus answering the "why an MBA?" question.]*

The Wharton MBA program will give me this knowledge in a more focused and rigorous way than any other program. Wharton's unique major "Technological Innovation" will be the glue that binds together my competencies and work experiences. Through Wharton's strong Entrepreneurial Management program, I will learn the pitfalls of business start-ups, and I will gain indispensable experience through the Small Business Development Center and the Global Immersion Program. Wharton's team-based learning approach will teach me important people skills for the long run. Finally, courses such as "Technology in Global Markets: Corporate Strategy and National Policy" and "High-Tech Entrepreneurship" will complement my operations and technical expertise. In addition, I will take a lead role in organizing the Entrepreneurship Conference and Wharton Asia Club. I also hope to start the Cinema Club, which, surprisingly, WGA lacks, and help the Admission Committee evaluate and interview applicants. With an MBA from the Wharton School I will have the key to making my ambitious childhood dream a reality. *[←Chun's longish career progress section gave him less space for his goals and "why our school?" sections, but he uses specific detail to make the most of them.]*

Sample Essay 3: Ingrid T. (Admitted to MIT Sloan)

Essay Prompt. The cover letter serves as a sort of executive summary for your application. It is also the written equivalent of the first impression which you make when meeting someone for the first time. As such, it should reflect a great deal of time, thought, and energy. Ideally, we will finish reading your cover letter eagerly anticipating reading the rest of the application. (500–800 words)

Dear Admissions Committee Members:

It is with the single-minded determination to become a new product development manager in the supercomputing industry that I am applying for a seat in the MIT Sloan MBA Class of 2003. [*←This lead would be too stolid for an essay, but because of MIT's business-letter format it works here.*] Pursuing an MBA at this time fits perfectly with my career goals and eventual desire to start my own venture.

Ambition, achievement, and acceleration are common themes in my academic and professional experiences. I chose the Hamburg Technische Institute (HTI) for undergraduate studies not for its top-ranked Advanced Computing program, but for its unparalleled emphasis on developing well-rounded leaders and managers who can take charge in tough situations, readily address any audience on any topic, and provide effective and efficient solutions for challenging problems. No other college in the world offers its students such extensive practical summer training; by the time I graduated, I had been a contributing member of a hot-air balloon team, a Baltic resort design group, a Berlin art museum renovation technology team, and a DM400 million government supercomputer project. [*←Responds to MIT's instructions for a "summary" by telegraphing several key projects that pique the reader's interest in her other essays.*]

I was one of only a select few engineering students to pursue a minor in Arabic, and was among only 4% of my classmates admitted to an early-entrance fast-track graduate program in my third year at HTI. Now, in considering graduate business programs, I am seeking a rigorous academic curriculum with parallel opportunities to put theory into practice. In this regard Sloan stands out among the top MBA programs, setting the standard with programs like the MIT $50K Entrepreneurship Competition and by providing MBA students with special access to the world-renowned Media Lab.

The leadership and service experiences I had as an HTI honors student and government consultant have had a tremendous impact on my interests outside of work. Whenever possible, I have committed my time and energy to my local community whether co-directing an orphanage in Ethiopia, helping the children of Turkish Gastarbeiter seek job opportunities, or raising funds for the reconstruction of the Marienkirche in Dresden by participating in cross-country skiing events.

I feel very fortunate to be able to share my most substantial accomplishments with you: *[Use of bullets provides visual relief and allows Ingrid to cover wide-ranging material without seeming to ramble.→]*

- Graduating 1st in the HTI Supercomputing Department's Scientists Training Program, and later ranking 1st among 35 peer HTI undergraduate researchers assigned to the Bundes Wirtschaftliche Agentur (BWA); being personally selected to serve on the BWA Director's East German Integration Team

- Leading, managing, and motivating 106 scientific and business personnel in four different organizations responsible for computer design, marketing, commercialization, and supercomputing project evaluations

- Earning the designation Zeugnis für Supercomputing Systeme Bauweise Fachmann (ZSSBF), earned by fewer than 4,900 high-speed computing professionals and equivalent in the industry to the CPA and CFA certifications

- Achieving success as a commercial project and account manager for China's largest chemical products distributor and the world's largest robotics manufacturing company, delivering over DM$15M in scientific consulting services

[←Ingrid offsets her letter's somewhat formal tone with several truly impressive miniaccomplishments.]

My past scientific and commercial experiences involved immersing myself in the management issues of high-tech organizations, honing my leadership and organizational skills, and allowing me to develop extensive expertise in supercomputing. I now wish to apply these experiences and knowledge towards improving existing private-sector computing applications by employing advanced computing designs, as I am certain that the next few years will witness a surge in the efforts of businesses to exploit the data-mining and modeling benefits supercomputers permit.

Considering my rapidly building career momentum and interests, now is the most appropriate time for me to pursue an MBA and grow my new technology product development skills. Sloan's MBA curriculum will supplement my engineering background with a solid understanding of marketing, finance, and technology management. A new product development manager must interface effectively with different business functions, identify and manage the best design strategies, and quickly make sound decisions on the basis of often limited information. The New Product and Venture Development track's focus on innovation will help me to become an adaptive and strategic-minded new product development manager. The chance for hands-on experience through MIT's Entrepreneurship Lab will enhance my grasp of the management tools and techniques successfully applied by rapidly growing ventures. Immediately following my MBA, I intend to assume a position as a technology design manager at a high-intensity startup where I can lead teams in building innovative, useful, high-quality, and profitable supercomputers, such as those now offered by Siemens, Cray, and IBM.

Reflecting on the strong relationships I have maintained with my Hamburg Technische Institute classmates, I welcome the chance to build equally strong bonds with my Sloan classmates, enriching my classroom experiences by interacting with them on both social and professional levels. Looking five to ten years into the future, I would like to start my own venture involving supercomputing technologies. Being able to tap into the extensive experience of Sloan School alumni and the greater MIT alumni communities will be a powerful catalyst for my efforts to create a viable business plan, secure funding, and successfully build a profitable company.

My direct and very recent experience as an early employee of a startup reveals that the road of an entrepreneur is freshly paved with calculated risks and varying uncertainty. Since experiencing the German government's rejection of my application for research funding earlier this month, I am undeterred in my resolve to improve myself as a leader, manager, and supercomputing professional, and am eagerly awaiting my next opportunity for growth and success. [*←Takes risk by mentioning a setback so near the end of the essay, but preceding paragraphs have shown Ingrid's successes, goals, and knowledge of MIT's resources to be so strong that this admission only enhances her credibility.*]

I look forward to the opportunity for a personal interview and would be pleased to answer any questions you may have regarding my candidacy.

With warm regards,

Sample Essay 4: John F. (Admitted to Kellogg)

Essay Prompt. Briefly assess your career progress to date. Elaborate on your future career plans and your motivation for pursuing a graduate degree at Kellogg. (1 to 2 pages double-spaced)

"The only way to really win in this world is to run your own show." That was the advice my uncle, a successful entrepreneur, gave me when I was a young kid growing up in Peoria. I tried to follow his advice by trading baseball cards on the street behind Peoria's main post office, and I still remember the pride I felt when I brought home the first Apple PC I had purchased with my card-trading income. *[←John's lead establishes a personal, even folksy tone that immediately humanizes his application.]*

Building a successful company of my own has always been my goal. I joined America Online in September 1999 to become the best software design engineer I could be because I knew superior technical skills would enable me to become a truly hands-on entrepreneur some day. During my first year at AOL, I was chiefly responsible for the design of AOL's gaming site (now AOL Arcade), giving me exposure to state-of-the-art eCommerce development. After only eleven months at AOL, I joined the prestigious Netscape Navigator group where I gained a perfect opportunity to participate in the making and marketing and observe the branding of a major product in the ultracompetitive high-tech industry. I matured technically on this project and become a respected member of AOL's engineering team. *[←Focuses on two key accomplishments here and in the next paragraph, but takes care to explain their significance and tie them into his maturing career goals.]*

Even while living the fantasy of many programmers—developing software for AOL—I was looking for opportunities to put my uncle's advice to work. *[Referring back to uncle's opening words reinforces essay's unity.]* Luckily, AOL's culture fosters entrepreneurial thinking, and in 2001 I faced a challenge that mirrored the obstacles every new start-up faces. I believed firmly that AOL should build support for wireless into AOL version 5.0, but since Windows 2000 was already in Beta 2, the "war team" of developers and testers was not willing to take on a new feature. Nevertheless, I presented the advantages of supporting wireless in detail, convinced them it was an important emerging technology, and then persuaded them to assign me one developer. Coordinating the cross-team effort, I brought the feature to completion within a week, just in time for AOL 5.0's update release 1. Taking ownership of this innovation raised my visibility, and the entire experience showed me that I could identify a business opportunity, develop the plan to implement it, sell it from inside the company, and successfully execute my plan. I enjoyed entrepreneuring from beginning to end and began looking for the next opportunity—my own venture.

This March I co-founded MangaWorks, a small graphic-novel publishing house. Managing it in my spare time, I have built a team of five writers/illustrators in only seventeen months and managed our first project—the Aleph Man series—to publication. Because of my drive for results and hands-on leadership, our investors have recently agreed to let MangaWorks begin marketing our titles in Europe to take advantage of the growing taste for graphic novels there. Only one thing could compel me to give up the exciting opportunities AOL continues to offer me, and that is the opportunity to take MangaWorks to the next level. As I write this, my plan is to "parachute" into London this November to set up shop and deliver our first European editions by next September. [←*Revelation that John is willing to walk away from prestige job underscores seriousness of his goals and need for Kellogg MBA.*]

My long-term goal is to grow MangaWorks into an international publishing firm with a presence in the United States, Europe, and the Pacific Rim. This will position us to capitalize on the abundance of demand for graphic novels in the United States and Europe and the traditional interest in manga in Asia. To execute this vision, our biggest challenge will be to convince potential customers that we have the creative resources and plan to publish profitable titles without jeopardizing quality. Because none of MangaWork's partners has marketing experience, we have been marketing our firm by the "trial-and-error" method. We have also had limited success taking our projects overseas. It has become obvious to me that I need core management skills, from economics, accounting, finance, and statistics to marketing, human resource management, and international business strategy. An MBA from a rigorous program will give me those skills as well as the credibility to attract partners and potential investors. With credibility and a better network of contacts, I will have greater access to decision-makers in all my future business endeavors. [←*Strong argument for needing MBA.*]

Kellogg's MBA program, with its outstanding marketing and finance curricula, directly addresses my career goals. For example, its curriculum is unusually integrated across disciplines, and such courses as "Accounting for Decision Making," "Finance I," and "Microeconomic Analysis" will give me the solid foundation for more advanced management study. Similarly, "Entertainment Culture and Marketing," "Media Strategy and Implementation," and "Marketing Management" will help me better formulate and articulate marketing and business development strategy. With its "school for people who like people" philosophy, Kellogg will also give me a perfect opportunity to network with the future business leaders I'll meet in the International Business Club, the Entrepreneurship/Venture Capital Club, and Catholics@Kellogg. My uncle had it partly right: the only way to really make it in this world is to be my own boss—and earn a Kellogg MBA. [←*Economical one-sentence conclusion rounds essay out with echo of lead paragraph.*]

Getting to Know You:
The Non-Goals Essays

You must remember that you are unique. Your choices throughout life are unique. Just be yourself and tell your story.

—KRIS NEBEL, UNIVERSITY OF MICHIGAN (ROSS)

There, it's done. You've hammered out your goals, short and long term, crafted a gripping account of your career thus far, and persuasively detailed the reasons why a top-10 business school is your life's destiny. Surely, it's all smooth sailing from here.

Alas, your goals essay, though critical, is just one of several legs on which your candidacy must stand, or fall. In addition to it, almost all schools pose two to four other essay questions (some as many as six or more) whose intent is basically the same: to get to know the person behind the goals, career progress, and earnest yearning for admission. What specifically and uniquely do you bring to their program? Based on the essay questions of the top 75 MBA programs, the seven essay topics discussed in this chapter all play variations on that single insistent theme.

These seven categories are not mutually exclusive. Accomplishments, leadership moments, and teamwork stories, for example, are often the same experience seen from different angles. A diversity essay asking about your potential contribution or unique characteristics will obviously cover some of the same territory as an essay about your life experiences or passions. Though you can use your basic stories in some form with a wide variety of essay topics, each of the topics covered here is distinct enough to prevent you from simply "cutting and pasting": you will have to revisit, rethink, and often fundamentally modify your stories to get at the particular insight each topic seeks.

ONE GOOD DEED: THE ACCOMPLISHMENT ESSAY

After anxiously scanning all the "touchy-feely" essay topics common in B-school applications these days, you can be forgiven for seizing on the accomplishment essay with a sigh of relief. "At last, an essay that asks me what I've actually *done* instead of 'who I am,' 'want to be,' or 'care most about.'" What could be simpler? Don't delude yourself. The purpose of the accomplishment essays is not merely to "get more facts" about the career highlights hinted at on your résumé and telegraphed in your goals essay. Because these essays often let you choose experiences from *any* part of your life and give you the space and freedom to emphasize and evaluate them in *any* way you like, schools can gain as much insight into who you are from them as into what you've done.

Qualities That Accomplishments Can Reveal

Dedication or focus

Persistence

Expertise or special talent

Concern for something larger than oneself

Initiative

Modesty (or lack of it)

High personal standards

Leadership

Team skills

Self-discipline

Organizational ability

On one level, accomplishment essays enable admissions committees to gauge whether you have the "right stuff" for business school. Are your accomplishments substantial enough to justify the ambitious vision you paint in your goals essay? Can you show that you actually have managerial potential? Have you translated your skills into concrete results that demonstrably improved your organization's effectiveness?

The magnitude of the achievement(s) you describe helps to answer these key questions. The details you convey about your accomplishment(s) will prove your ability to facilitate teams, direct projects or resources, analyze complex problems, make tough decisions, and improve your organization. Naturally, the applicant who can show that his or her achievement led directly to a multimillion-dollar revenue gain has an advantage over the applicant whose "greatest achievement" was assisting 13 others in an aborted project whose bottom-line impact was indeterminate.

Fortunately for the latter applicant, however, the schools are interested in you much more than in your bottom-line impact. Which accomplishment you choose to write about, for example, tells them what experiences you value most in your life. The applicant whose greatest attainment is the software application he helped test sends a very different signal than the one whose crowning moment was chairing her community organization's fund-raising drive.

Similarly, *how* you describe your accomplishment also tells the admissions committee a great deal. If you give the impression that you rammed an achievement through with no regard for collaborating with teammates, schools may well question your team skills. The same interpersonal doubts may be triggered if your essay focuses on the procedural or technical aspects of your achievement rather than on the interpersonal dynamics. Finally, the committee will learn much from the reasons you give for valuing this accomplishment. If you say only that you're proud of this achievement because it led to an early promotion, they'll wonder why it didn't teach you deeper lessons.

The accomplishment essay, then, is considerably more than a résumé bullet point writ large. So put that sigh of relief on hold for now. Before discussing strategies for ensuring that your accomplishment essay gives adcoms the personal insights they seek, let's look at how schools ask the accomplishment question.

What Schools Ask

Many schools word the accomplishment question broadly to give you maximum leeway:

- "Tell us about your most significant accomplishment." (Berkeley Haas)

- "What achievement are you most proud of (studies, sports, professional life, etc.)?" (Hautes Etudes Commerciales [HEC])

- "What is the greatest achievement in your life?" (Western Ontario)

Because these questions give you so much freedom, you need to evaluate the accomplishment stories you choose with extra caution. Consider carefully before saying that your accomplishment was "getting into IIT" or scoring the winning touchdown in your high school championship game. Unless you execute these well-worn topics extremely well (and even when you do), you may give the impression that you have a narrowly competitive or superficial definition of achievement or that you're living in the past, with no significant accomplishments since the onset of adulthood.

Many schools deliberately narrow the potential scope of the accomplishment essay to force your answer in the direction they prefer:

- "Describe a significant professional accomplishment that demonstrates your potential for a successful management career." (Consortium for Graduate Study in Management)

- "What nonprofessional accomplishment are you most proud of and why?" (Yale)

These topics not only compel you to confine your definition of accomplishment to specific areas of your life, but they also signal what the school values. Since business schools are in the business of training managers, many obviously want to know about your work-life successes. Others, like Yale and Haas, value applicants' social impact vision and thus want to hear about your "not-for-profit" experiences.

Accomplishment questions also vary by the quantity of achievements they expect you to discuss. Harvard's "What are your three most substantial accomplishments?" is the classic formulation of the multiple-accomplishment essay. Here, the conundrum "Should I use a professional or personal achievement" solves itself. To avoid sounding like a work-obsessed drone or an unaccomplished underachiever, you may want to answer such multiple-accomplishment essays with one professional, one community, and one noncommunity personal accomplishment. Ideally, you also want each of your accomplishments to show you making an impact in different ways. For example, your professional success could show you having an impact through analytical skill and team leadership, your community achievement through teamwork and consensus-building, and your personal triumph through creativity and risk-taking.

Note that some schools use words like *impact, contribution,* or *creative solution* rather than *accomplishment* and *achievement* to invite you to talk about an accomplishment.

In the Schools' Words—

We are looking for very accomplished candidates in general, but particularly ones that can show a track record of leadership accomplishments in some organization, work or otherwise, where they have made something big happen that would not have occurred if they were not there. We are looking for big impact people who are able to size up situations, seize opportunities, mobilize people to act and get results. We want to see evidence of this.

—DICK SHAFER, CORNELL UNIVERSITY (JOHNSON)

A final accomplishment category grows out of business schools' frustration with the résumé-in-prose responses that accomplishment questions often inspire:

■ "What is the most significant change or improvement you have made to an organization with which you have recently been affiliated? Describe the process you went through to identify the need for change and manage the process of implementing change. What were the results?" (Indiana)

■ "We believe the key to effective leadership is the ability to transform theoretical concepts and ideas into action that can change the world. Given this perspective, please describe your most significant professional leadership accomplishment. In doing so, please describe how you transformed an idea into action, the challenges you faced, and the impact your leadership had on your team or the organization." (Michigan)

These questions virtually beg you to leap past simple descriptions and provide fully reflective analysis. So do so.

Choosing Your Story

What exactly is an accomplishment? Former admissions officer James Strachan usefully defines it as "an event or situation in which you successfully exerted a high degree of influence resulting in a sense of personal satisfaction that allowed you to learn something about yourself." That's a pretty broad definition, but it accurately reflects the scope schools are willing to give you.

In choosing which of your stories to wrap around this definition, start by asking yourself three questions:

1. What am I—off the record and in all candor—truly proudest of?

2. When have I had the greatest tangible impact on an organization (or individual)?

3. When has a positive experience in which I played a key role *changed* me or *taught* me the most? (See Writing Prompt Exercise 1 for other questions that may help you dig deeper in finding the right accomplishment.)

Define *accomplishment* as loosely as possible, and sift through your memory, scrutinize your résumé, interrogate your friends or colleagues. Chances are you'll find a story in which the depth of your impact was substantial and concretely, externally visible, one whose lessons you're still applying today, and one you still look back on with a quiet sense of pride. If you do, you have the makings of a killer accomplishment essay. If this brainstorm exercise generates too many candidates, revisit the self-marketing themes you created in Chapter 1. Which of your successes best supports your application's themes?

Determining exactly which one of your stories has the potential to make admissions officers sit up and actually feel enthusiasm is sometimes hard for you to gauge on your own. Becoming general manager at 25, producing your own award-winning independent film, winning a Fulbright scholarship, toiling in the White House, leading a $40 million IPO at 26, earning a spot on an Olympic team—the standout accomplishment can take a surprisingly wide variety of forms. Usually, however, such "wow factor" accomplishments combine distinctiveness in the actual attainment itself with a special zest, depth, or personality in the telling and analysis. Try to give admissions committees both.

Wow factor or not, the strengths that your accomplishment illustrates should corroborate the strengths you emphasize throughout your application. If your post-MBA goals, recommendation letters, and other essays market you as a global person, you may want your greatest achievement to have an international dimension.

Also be sure to calibrate the accomplishment you choose with the school's marketing position. A story that subtly communicates that you've devoted every waking moment to feathering your own nest may be poorly received at a school that prides itself on its social impact programs. And regardless of school, try to avoid professional successes that don't involve a team component. Save your solitary accomplishments for other essays.

Finally, as discussed in Chapter 1, consider your accomplishment story in light of the school's other essays. The same school that invites you to discuss either a professional or personal achievement may also give you a separate essay for discussing community involvement or your personal background. Consider focusing your accomplishment essay on a professional success—you may have no other chance to do so.

Structure

Merely describing an achievement is only a partial response to an accomplishment essay question. In fact, the "what" is only one of four components common to most effective accomplishment essays, namely: the accomplishment's surrounding context (including the challenge it posed to you), the description of the achievement itself, the outcome or results of your success, and the lessons you learned from it.

The Context and Challenge

The first one-quarter or so of a good accomplishment essay draws the reader into the essay in an engaging, vivid way. It sets the scene by providing a rough time frame for the action and just enough context so that the reader understands the enormity of the challenge you faced. In Renae P.'s sample achievement essay (accomplishment essay 1), she executes this initial context section in the first five sentences. Her first line grabs the reader's attention with three powerful but unattached nouns, "Stagnation, cynicism, disillusionment." Intrigued, the admissions officer reads ahead to see what these words apply to. The essay's first full sentence explains the suggestive opening and provides the fuller context. In the next two sentences Renae then magnifies the challenge with details. By the essay's fifth full sentence, she has begun describing the second component of the accomplishment essay: the achievement itself. This is the sort of efficiency you want to aim for.

The Achievement

Most applicants devote prodigious swaths of their essays to meticulous accounts of their achievement experience: "I did X . . . , then I did Y . . ." The true payoff of the accomplishment essay comes at its end, however, so it's essential that you keep your treatment of the achievement to the key events, with special emphasis on the variety of ways in which you tackled the challenge. In Renae P.'s essay, for example, she addresses her company's leadership problem by demonstrating several types of leadership. Each sentence hugs tightly to the particulars of the essay's opening scene, avoiding jargon and generalities. Though Renae's description of her achievement is logical and ordered, it's never dull. It has momentum and a touch of the dramatic ("How could we save the company?").

An accomplishment essay is after all a story, and if you can give it the drama of a good story, you'll lift it above the crowd. The use of plot twists or complications, unexpected detours, and moments of self-doubt or uncertainty add texture and interest to your essay, transforming the tedious exposition of a career data point into the kind of human-interest story admissions officers will remember. So, if you experienced some initial missteps before you enjoyed success, don't be afraid to describe them. They'll give your accomplishment true grit by showing you have the maturity to own up to errors and overcome multiple obstacles.

The Outcome

A clear statement of the ultimate result of your achievement gives your story closure and provides the hard evidence to back up your claim of success. As we discussed in Chapter 1, expressing that outcome in quantitative terms will lend concreteness and objectivity to your story. In the last line of Renae P.'s essay, for example, one sentence provides a multipart quantitative outcome. This kind of depth magnifies your accomplishment's impact.

In the Schools' Words—

Essays that clearly allow us to get behind the "accomplishments and achievements" and allow us to see what you learned from the experiences and how you made decisions are generally well received. They should also get a little "personal."

—ALEX BROWN,
UNIVERSITY OF PENNSYLVANIA (WHARTON)

The Significance

Business schools value the subjective lessons you draw from your accomplishments as well as their objective, bottom-line impact. But not just any subjective evaluation will do. The specific significance you place on your accomplishment tells schools how thoughtful or self-reflective you are, what you value (e.g., personal benefits versus team benefits), and how deeply you learn through new experiences.

Fortunately for many applicants, the emphasis that schools place on your subjective evaluation of your accomplishment gives you the opportunity to turn unimpressive bottom-line attainments into fabulous tales of personal growth and inner challenge. Deeply insightful analysis of your achievement's value may pull you "equal" to a star achiever who merely phones in the takeaways. Note, for example, how Naomi K. (accomplishment essay 2) develops a volunteer interaction with a single individual into an effective significant accomplishment by (1) humanizing her relationship with Lonnie through detail, (2) optimizing the accomplishment's impact through a sustained and well-executed "lessons learned" section (paragraph 3), and (3) using this lone triumph as the starting point for a second, wider-impact accomplishment.

Avoid any lesson learned that smacks of superficiality: "It was my most significant achievement because it led directly to my promotion four months later." Mention of external personal benefits, like raises and promotions, is the business of your outcome statement (the essay's third section). The significance statement should aim for deeper payoffs. Also avoid talking about lessons that sound like the kind of thing you think schools want to hear: "This experience was profoundly valuable to me because it offered me the humbling privilege of giving back to my deserving community in a meaningful way." This reeks of insincerity, whether the writer meant it or not. (Avoid extreme adjectives as a general rule. If you've

> While your specific accomplishments, even if truly exceptional, may not set you apart, what you learned and how you perceive their importance can distinguish you. In other words, show yourself to be an unusually perceptive, reflective, insightful person. Make your thought process, your unique perspective, set you apart.
>
> —*Linda Abraham, Accepted.com*

successfully communicated your accomplishment's significance, then such thesaurus words aren't necessary; if you haven't, then they won't help.)

Your accomplishment's significance, the life lessons it has taught you, must be genuine and personal to you. Unfortunately, the only way to make them so is to be honestly introspective and really explore the impact of the experience on you. Then describe that as directly and unselfconsciously as you can. Writing Prompt Exercise 2 at the end of this chapter offers some questions that will enable you to dig deeper to locate the lesson that fits. Remember, even if the school does not ask you to discuss the significance of an accomplishment, you should always do so.

Accomplishment Essays: What *Not to Do*

When you're writing your accomplishment essay, don't

1. Write about an accomplishment that isn't your own, either because it's really a *team* accomplishment in which your role was not distinct or because it's actually someone *else's* achievement (because you misunderstood the question).

2. Fail to be strategic about the accomplishment you write about. If your other essays focus on your professional life, you may want to devote your accomplishment essay to a community or personal story, even if it means you must relegate one of your greatest work-related achievements to a recommendation letter, your résumé, or the application data sheet.

3. Write about ancient accomplishments. Focus on something within the past two or three years (sometimes the school's question requires you to do so).

4. Select accomplishments involving your family, marriage, or romantic relationships. Unless your story is truly distinctive and you can write vividly about it, avoid these.

5. Describe the accomplishment but fail to explain why you value it or what you learned from it.

In the Schools' Words—

Achievements belong in employment history. Recognitions belong in "awards and recognitions," under Professional. Essays will briefly recite the facts of these but will focus more on the insights gained because of the achievements.

—MAXX DUFFY, FORMER ADMISSIONS OFFICER,
HARVARD BUSINESS SCHOOL

WHO ARE YOU?: THE SELF-REVELATION ESSAY

In one form or another every B-school essay question is trying to get you to open up and reveal yourself to the admissions committee. Are you the sort of person whom this most exclusive of exclusive clubs, the top-drawer business school, really wants as a member? What will you be like chatting it up after study group, floating opinions in class, officially representing the school as an alum? More directly than any other topic, the essays in this group try to answer these pivotal "fit" questions. With them, self-revelation is not optional.

Self-revelation essays should have a distinctly different tone than other essays, where opportunistically marketing yourself is the rule. Here, your goal is not to *sell* the admissions committee or make a polemical case but simply to *be* yourself—provided, that is, you're an amiable, balanced, mature, and interesting person. These are the worst possible essays in which to tell schools what you think they want to hear. No matter how facile a writer you may be, admissions officers have spent their entire careers reading between the lines, sifting the real from the bogus. If you try to fake them out, you will not win. Be yourself.

What Schools Ask

The self-revelation essay can take a great variety of forms: essays about values, activities, key events, strengths and weaknesses, biographical details—in short, anything that opens a glimpse into the real you. For the purposes of this section we've boiled all these possible topics down to five basic clusters:

1. Pure "who are you?" essays

2. Passion and hobby/extracurricular essays

3. Self-evaluation essays

4. Defining moment or learning experience essays

5. People, places, or things essays

Pure "Who Are You?" Essays

The "who are you?" essay questions comprise the straight-ahead "tell us about yourself" topics:

- "Please provide us with a summary of your personal and family background. Include information about your parents and siblings, where you grew up, and perhaps a highlight or special memory of your youth." (UCLA)

- "Write your life story in one page or less." (Virginia)

- "Creatively describe yourself to your MBA classmates. You may use any method to convey your message." (NYU Stern)

The trap these topics pose is the sheer breadth of the potential subject matter. Some applicants respond with a listless catalog of their life's chronology, often launched with an unpromising "I was born in . . ." An essay that offers too much will lack the detailed stories that really communicate your unique life experiences. Instead of shoehorning your entire existence into the essay, zero in on a theme or two (for example, a personal quality of yours or an unusual characteristic of your family) and then identify several separate anecdotes from different parts of your life that illustrate that theme. This strategy will give your essay coherence and enable you to go into enough detail to convey what's distinctive about you.

Since the goal of the pure self-revelation question is not to pry into your family secrets but to discover whether you're likable and interesting, your tone is crucial. Be engaging as Claudia G. clearly is in her sample essay (self-revelation essay 3). Avoid a flat, impersonal voice at all costs. If your own life seems boring to you, imagine how it will sound to an admissions committee!

Schools like Stern put an extra spin on the pure "who are you?" question by inviting you to describe yourself creatively—allowing you to abandon prose completely if there's a better way to express who you are. That three-quarters of all Stern applicants wind up submitting a written essay suggests how hard it is to come up with a nonwritten idea that really flies. If you do decide to eschew words, be sure your idea—whether it's a Web site, photograph, or product—truly captures who you are. Trying to seem creative for creativity's sake usually comes off as gimmicky. Should you decide to write an essay, don't despair if you can't dream up a clever format. If your description of yourself sparkles with personality and *joie de vivre* and the stories you focus on show you've led an interesting life, the admissions committee will forgive you for not writing it in crayon or iambic pentameter. Note, for example, how unflamboyant but effective Ashish S.'s essay is (self-revelation essay 1). By interspersing the unfolding narrative of a defining moment with flashbacks to other significant events in his life, he creates a memorable and creative personal portrait.

In the Schools' Words—

We have many creative folks out there, so we want them to show who they are through this essay. You can write an essay, write a poem/song, or even bake a pie. It is really up to the applicants to show who they are and what they are passionate about. Stern wants to get to know you.

—Julia Min, New York University (Stern)

Passion and Hobby/Extracurricular Questions

Passion and hobby/extracurricular questions try to get you to reveal yourself by finding out what your passions are. They are often framed specifically to learn about your hobbies and extracurricular interests:

- "What activities do you enjoy outside the office and/or classroom and why?" (Yale)

- "Outside of work, I . . ." (Kellogg)

- "What do you do for fun?" (Notre Dame)

How you spend your free time says more about you than what you do in the workplace, where your choices are often made by someone else. People who sustain deep personal involvements outside their work lives—particularly unusual ones—are more interesting than those who spend their off hours vegetating. Moreover, the history of your involvements tells schools something about your commitment and focus. Whether you enjoy volunteering as a dance instructor, collecting antiques, weight training, or working as a math tutor, your hobbies show that you are not all work—you know how to have fun.

Since many hobbies involve other people, learning about your extracurricular passions tells schools how you will respond in the many formal and informal group activities that define the business school experience. And since many B-school applicants are too young to have gained significant leadership experience at work, schools also look to these extracurricular essays to find evidence of leadership. If your nonwork commitments involve helping your community, especially in a leadership role, you'll be demonstrating the selflessness that admissions officers like to see in students and alumni. In his sample essay (self-revelation essay 2), for example, Rohit V. overcomes his professional status as a nonmanagerial technology type by telling an impressive story of pure leadership as a community group's marketing director.

Many applicants seem to assume that their response to this essay topic is being graded in bulk terms: the more varied activities they mention, the more impressed the school will be. The truth is that essays that focus on your lifelong interest in one or two activities (no matter how many other activities you're also passionate about) will almost always go over better. Rather than provide an exhaustive survey of your nonwork pursuits, steer the essay toward the activities that matter most to you and consume most of your free time.

Demonstrating an intensive enthusiast's knowledge of an obscure subject and/or dramatizing your passion through a specific memorable experience can produce essays with grit, credibility, and distinctiveness. Claudia G.'s knowledge of architecture in her essay (self-revelation essay 3), for example, is clearly no dilettante's passing enthusiasm. Consider focusing on the hobbies that may offset the negative stereotypes every profession drags behind it. If you're a computer programmer, writing about your love of math puzzles may feed social-skills concerns, but an essay about your leadership of a deep-sea archaeology team will surprise the admissions committee in the best possible way.

As always, it's not enough to simply describe your passion(s). You must account for your enjoyment, perhaps by explaining how you first became involved in your interests or by describing your emotional state while you're pursuing them. Has your long pursuit of this passion changed you or taught you anything about yourself or life? Better yet, if pursuing your passion has somehow enabled you to benefit others or improve an organization, say so and provide any hard evidence that substantiates this.

Admissions essays that lack passion can be damaging; "passion" essays that lack passion can be disastrous. You must make the readers experience your genuine enthusiasm for your personal involvements, and you must make them understand why you feel the way you do.

This second group of self-revelation essays also includes topics that frame the "passions" question much more broadly. Their focus is not only on your personal involvements and hobbies but more generally on what you care most deeply about:

- "What matters most to you and why?" (Stanford)

- "Please tell us what you feel most passionate about in life." (Columbia)

- "Describe something you feel passionate about." (Berkeley Haas)

Of course, you're free to respond to these questions as you would an extracurricular question, with stories about your personal involvements, but the wording invites you to discuss a wider and deeper range of topics. Because Stanford's notorious "what matters most" essay offers you seven or more pages in which to explore your topics and provides no other essay topics for non-work-related material, most applicants define *passion* broadly to include values and autobiographical stories in addition to extracurricular activities. That this is a wise move is suggested by the introspective and all-inclusive language in which Stanford once framed this essay: "Each of us has been influenced by the people, events, and situations in our lives. How have these influences shaped who you are today?"

The danger in such broad wording (what does "people, events, and situations" *exclude*?) is that you'll try to show what matters most to you in so many different directions that your essay will become a grab bag of events, significant others, and personal and community experiences loosely strapped together with a blanket theme (like the ever-popular "balance in life"). Honing in on a limited number of personalized themes and luminous, vividly etched moments is your salvation.

Self-Evaluation Questions

This group of self-revelation questions gets at who you are by asking you to evaluate yourself and your strengths and weaknesses, or to discuss how others do so:

- "Provide a candid assessment of your strengths and weaknesses." (Harvard)

- "Give a candid description of yourself, stressing the personal characteristics you feel to be your strengths and weaknesses and the main factors which have influenced your personal development, including giving examples when necessary." (INSEAD)

- "If a friend or family member were to describe your most defining quality, what would it be and why?" (Texas)

- "You have been selected as a member of the Kellogg Admissions Committee. Please provide a brief evaluative assessment of your file." (Kellogg)

- "Please identify and explain what you would consider the weakest area of your application." (Wharton)

These essays give you another slot in which to insert stories that flesh out the committee's picture of you while committee members run a reality check on your self-awareness. Do you have a mature, balanced understanding of yourself? Do you see the same strengths and weaknesses the adcoms have started to notice? Or do you live in perpetual denial? These essays also offer you a chance to gain credibility by simply being honest. If you come clean in these essays, admissions officers will be more willing to lend credence to your positive claims about yourself.

The strengths you discuss in this essay must complement (if not entirely overlap) the strengths your recommenders cite and your application as a whole communicates. Naturally, all business schools value skills like leadership, team skills, integrity, analytical ability, communication skills, and cultural adaptability, but each school broadcasts its own peculiar mix of valued traits, which you should be well aware of before mapping this essay. Don't just grab the three most likely "Darden strengths" and bend your stories to illustrate them. Ideally, your essay will blend "obligatory" business school strengths, such as leadership, with strengths that are really personal to you, like artistic ability or adventurousness.

Moreover, since *leadership, team skills,* and the like are broad terms that encompass many distinct traits, try to give your essay individuality by finding the particular traits that best capture you. Avoid strengths like persistence and dedication. They're not only vague and clichéd but will paint you as a worker bee rather than a dynamic leader.

The laziest and most common structure for self-evaluation essays is to take up each strength or weakness in turn, illustrate it with an example, and then awkwardly transition on to the next: "My second biggest strength is my . . ." To avoid this, find some common element or quality that your strengths share and weave your essay around that, or better yet, find a single story (a work project, for example) or activity (your bowling team) that will illustrate all your strengths and weaknesses in one fell swoop. It's awfully hard to be original when discussing traits you likely share with most of humanity, so remember that in this essay the creativity and uniqueness will derive from the special combination of strengths you cite and—most of all—from the stories you tell to illustrate them. If you can, draw explicit connections between your strengths and the specific B-school forum (class, study group, etc.) in which you plan to leverage it.

For most applicants, the minefield in the self-evaluation essay is the weakness section. This is not because most applicants have an embarrassing number of weaknesses—the vast majority don't—but because they refuse to admit they have any. Thus, admissions officers must trudge through a purgatory of "good weaknesses": perfectionism, workaholism, impatience with people with low standards, and so on. Such "strengths in disguise" may actually have worked 30 years ago when adcoms first encountered them, but trotting them out today only shows unimaginativeness, immaturity, and dishonesty—not especially becoming traits. True weaknesses, the kind schools want to hear about, are personal characteristics that most of us have and that can be reversed with sufficient awareness and effort: poor time management, procrastination, indecisiveness, and so on. Better yet, if the school's question does not require you to discuss personal or character weaknesses, consider discussing functional or professional weaknesses that an MBA can help you address, such as an overspecialized skills set, no finance training, lack of large-team leadership experience, no P&L exposure, and so on. In her essay (self-revelation essay 4), Mikiko U. maturely owns up to two negatives (undergraduate GPA and weakened recent community involvement), though for each she provides some mitigating context.

In the Schools' Words—

Adcoms are very good about spotting your weaknesses anyway, so you might as well show you at least have some self-awareness.

—ALEX BROWN,
UNIVERSITY OF PENNSYLVANIA (WHARTON)

Do more than merely "cite" your weakness. Give a brief example or explanation of how it has affected you, what specifically you are doing now to rectify it (classes, mentoring, etc.), and—if relevant—which specific B-school resources can help you purge this Achilles' heel for good. You don't want the self-evaluation essay to read like a static report card but as a snapshot of confident self-transformation—a savvy, evolving person working on his or her flaws, deepening his or her assets.

Defining Moment or Learning Experience Essays

Defining moment or learning experience essays enable the schools to discover who you are through the magnifying prism of a single defining, revealing, or testing event:

- "We all experience 'defining moments,' significant events that can have a major impact on our lives. Briefly describe such an event and how it affected you." (Harvard)

- "Describe a situation or learning experience that significantly changed your current goals or outlook on life. When describing the situation, include the actions you took and the results of those actions and describe how they led to changing your goals or outlook on your career choices." (Pepperdine)

- "'The unexamined life is not worth living.'—Socrates, *The Apology* by Plato. In light of the above quotation, please discuss a decision you have made that, in retrospect, has had a profound influence on your present circumstances. In hindsight, would you have made a different decision? Please explain." (Berkeley Haas)

These questions resemble other self-revelation essay topics in that they seek a glimpse of the real you through an event in your life. The special challenge in these essays is that they drastically limit the range of experiences you can draw from. No colorful assortment of diverse, heart-warming experiences will work here. You need a single razor-sharp moment in time that fundamentally changed you. For many applicants, that's a tall order.

Half the battle is identifying the event. It does not need to be some traumatic, movie-of-the-week moment (though those don't hurt), but it has to have left you a different person. To avoid suspicions of shallowness, you may want to steer clear of examples from your work life, though even these are fine if they had an unusual and far-reaching impact on you personally and professionally. You should also resist the temptation to discuss romantic relationships. However defining they may have been, they often aren't unusual or relevant enough to merit an essay.

Defining moment essays should usually have three sections: the description of the event itself (roughly half the essay's length), a section describing your feelings about the event and how it changed you emotionally or "inwardly," and a section detailing how you translated that internal change into action. Don't expect the power of the moment to speak for itself, even if it's traumatic enough to seem obvious. Admissions committees want you to walk them through the lessons and subsequent life changes. And whether the defining moment itself was positive or not, you want the takeaways to be uplifting—at least to the extent that they made you a better, wiser person. As much as possible, let the reader inside. Candidly describe your emotions in response to the event and your thought processes while coming to grips with it and moving on from it. But describe them calmly and maturely. You want the schools to admire you, not pity you.

People, Places, or Things Essays

A final tack some schools take is to "trick" you into revealing who you are by asking you to discuss other people, places, or things and their influence on you:

- "If you could step into any celebrity's shoes for a day, who would it be and why?" (Chicago)

- "Where is the most exciting place you have ever been and what did you learn from being there?" (Yale)

- "What is your most valued tangible possession? What is your most valued intangible possession?" (Berkeley Haas)

- "If you were given a free day and could spend it anywhere, in any way you choose, what would you do?" (Columbia)

- "Identify someone you regard as a hero, a leader or role model whom you admire. Describe how this person has influenced your development." (Harvard)

Thinking that these are "gimme" questions designed to lighten the admissions reader's load, unsuspecting applicants relax their guard long enough to write an indirectly and unintentionally revealing essay that strengthens their applications (or, much less likely, permanently scuttles them). Never forget that in the end all essays are about you.

"Most valuable possession" essays, for example, try to get a fix on who you are by what you value. One mistake applicants make here is to choose objects, like a Porsche Carrera or an M16 semiautomatic, that send unsavory signals to the schools. Focus instead on possessions that can serve as metaphors for your values, accomplishments, or skills, perhaps using one each to represent your professional, community, and personal lives.

Essays that ask you to discuss a particular place usually take the form of "ideal vacation" essays, which often inspire applicants to submit insipid travelogues about swaying palm trees in Cancún. Again, be strategic. Which of your key passions, values, or experiences have you not yet described in an essay for this school? Can any of them be expressed in terms of a place? Alternatively, consider focusing on a place that you associate with a revealing family or personal memory.

The most common version of the "people, places, or things" question is the hero, role model, or celebrity essay. "You can judge people by the company they keep" is the premise behind this topic. Without knowing anything else about someone, we know a lot by learning that one person's hero is Nelson Mandela, another's is Britney Spears, and a third's is his church's youth counselor. What each applicant does with those choices can, of course, be sublime or ridiculous, but the self-revelation is inescapable.

Aside from learning whom you esteem (and thus what you value in others, in yourself, and in life), these "other people" essays also enable schools to gauge how you establish and sustain productive relationships (that is, when you write about living role models). Schools can also use them to evaluate whether you are, in fact, the kind of person who is flexible enough to respond to another's influence and leadership.

Given these objectives, it's usually self-defeating to write about a distant historical figure whose influence on your life is not likely to be deep. Bill Gates, Lance Armstrong, Mahatma Gandhi, Oprah Winfrey, etc.—the list of over-used heroes is not especially long. So if you must go this route (and some schools do ask for *historical* figures), dig deep enough to find someone who can really help you stand out. Most effective are heroes or role models unknown to the admissions committee, such as your boss or mentor—people whose leadership you've actually witnessed as opposed to read about.

Whomever you choose, the focus of the essay should remain you. Discuss the two or three qualities you admire most in this person, with just enough historical context to orient the reader and show you know your subject. But avoid the most obvious traits like leadership and determination. Dig deeper! Then, as soon as possible, shift the focus from Joe Role Model to you. What is your personal history with this person? What aspects of his or her personality have you emulated? Which have you rejected and why? What lessons has this person's life offered you? Build your essay around answers to these questions.

The heart of this essay, then, is not a hagiography of your role model. It is the examples from your own life that illustrate you applying the lessons you gained from him or her. If these personal lessons and examples are strong enough, they can even overcome a clichéd (Mahatma Gandhi) or a dubious (Richard M. Nixon) choice. In his "three guests" sample essay (self-revelation essay 5), Fernando M. takes the risky step of choosing two ancient figures as his subjects (Socrates and the Egyptian king Khufu). He pulls it off, however, by choosing Sam Zell (not a household name) as his third subject, avoiding clichéd reflection, connecting each figure to his own life, and crafting a clever conclusion.

"Who Are You?" Essays: What Not to Do

When you're writing a "who are you?" essay, don't

1. Forget that the focus should be you. However outlandishly phrased, self-revelation essays are about getting you to spill the beans about your values, interests, and life experiences. Make sure your essay provides information unavailable elsewhere in your application and insights about you that corroborate the themes of your application as a whole. Don't waste unnecessary space on information that is not ultimately connected to who you are.

2. Choose inappropriate material. Not everything revealing about you is essay fodder. Some, such as relationships, is too personal. Others—religion, politics—are rife with danger because of their inherent controversy. If such risky topics are essential to who you are, frame your essay so as to defang them of their offensive potential. For example, focus on what your faith or political career have enabled you to do for others, not on doctrinal issues.

3. Fail to admit weaknesses. Failing to acknowledge that you have negatives when a question invites you to discuss them or palming off a disguised strength as a weakness damages your credibility with the admissions committee.

4. Write "passion" essays that lack passion. Because self-revelation essays always come down to you—someone you presumably are vitally interested in—your essay will have failed if it portrays you as a person not enthusiastically

engaged in your own life. An essay about you that's basically a bore leads schools to the logical conclusion . . .

5. Bite off more than you can chew. Since many self-revelation essays leave the scope of your answer up to you, your urge to communicate all your strengths may tempt you to spawn a kitchen-sink essay packed with three-sentence generalities about scattered shards of your life but bereft of examples and a unifying theme. Resist temptation.

VIVE LA DIFFÉRENCE: THE DIVERSITY ESSAY

What do a concert violinist, mortician, golf pro, and Web entrepreneur have in common? Probably nothing—except that they may all once have been classmates at a top-tier business school. When it comes to shaping MBA classes, adcoms' marching orders are "variety is the spice of life." In terms of occupations alone, typical top-tier programs have boasted everything from art dealers and zookeepers to plastic surgeons and helicopter ski guides. And the variety only deepens when geographic origins, cultural backgrounds, and personal pursuits are tossed in the pot.

Such rich diversity is the consciously crafted product of schools' judgment that we learn more from those we differ from than from pale reflections of ourselves. Because the word *diversity* still carries an affirmative action tinge, however, many applicants assume they're out of luck in the diversity department unless their grandmother was Mohican. Though it's true that schools show special favor to applicants from U.S. underrepresented minority groups—namely, African Americans, Hispanic Americans, and Native Americans—admissions statistics prove that schools define *diversity* much more widely than in strictly ethnic terms.

In the diversity essay, admissions committees are inviting you to help them sculpt a class of maximum variety. The pressure is on you to demonstrate your diversity, to convince the schools that you can enhance your classmates' experience more profoundly than can the next applicant. But how you accomplish that is left mostly up to you. What do *you* think makes you unique, the diversity question asks; what do *you* think your distinct contribution to your class will be?

What Schools Ask

Diversity essays reveal themselves through the key words *diversity* or *contribution*. However phrased, their common intent is to coax you to explicitly highlight the aspects of your profile that will add the most flavor to your class and benefit to your classmates. Some schools steer you toward defining diversity in terms of your life experiences, by asking you to discuss "aspects of your past or current life" or "your work and extracurricular background." Others shift the focus to your personality or abilities by inviting you to expand on your "personal characteristics," "outstanding qualities or characteristics," or "attributes or skills." But most schools give you maximum leeway by asking you, for example, to enlarge upon your "skills, knowledge, and life experiences" or "background, values, academics, activities, and/or leadership skills."

One variant of the diversity essay tries to determine your potential contribution by narrowing your focus to international or cross-cultural experiences:

- "Please describe any meaningful cross-cultural experiences you have had that highlight your understanding and appreciation of interacting with people from diverse backgrounds." (Vanderbilt)

- "Describe your international and cross-cultural experiences and how they will uniquely affect the classroom environment." (Fordham)

- "Have you ever experienced culture shock? What did it mean to you?" (INSEAD)

Because the range of stories that diversity essays allow you to tell is potentially so wide (and the space you're given, so small), deciding what to write about is the first stumbling block in crafting a standout essay.

In the Schools' Words—

Candidates who have traditional business experience worry that they need to be more unique, but at the same time nontraditional applicants worry that they don't fit the mold, and neither is the case.

—Julia Min,
New York University (Stern)

How can you know which aspects of your profile are really "diverse" or can actually constitute a "unique contribution" to future classmates? One way is by simply inventorying your life, as discussed in Chapter 1. Start with the narrow, conventional definitions of diversity—gender and ethnic background. If you are a woman or an underrepresented minority, then consider discussing that fact to whatever depth captures its importance in your life. Next, look at socioeconomic, cultural, and geographic types of diversity. If you overcame an economically disadvantaged childhood, identify strongly with your family's cultural roots, or come from a foreign country or a U.S. region underrepresented at your target school, these are diversity factors you will want to expand on in your essay.

Consider your hobbies and community activities. If they play central roles in your life or are atypical, they may also deserve a prominent place in your essay.

> There is no formula for distinguishing yourself. Rather, you must do so first by the specific anecdotes/experiences you describe and then, most importantly, by the *quality* of your insight from those experiences. In other words, don't look outward to distinguish yourself, look inward.
>
> —Linda Abraham, Accepted.com

Your specific profession and industry choice can also enhance your diversity if they are outside the MBA mainstream (or if you can show why your niche in a traditional MBA profession, such as consulting, is actually distinctive). Your education may have been unusual (e.g., your school's location or affiliation, your major or scholarships), your religious or spiritual life may be significant and unusual, your post-MBA goals may set you apart, even your sexuality or specific family dynamics (if handled properly) may convince the schools that your contribution could be distinctive. Skills or areas of expertise, unusual or challenging life experiences, even personal qualities or traits such as the gift of humor are all valid, potentially fruitful diversity topics. Thomas S.'s diversity essay (diversity essay 1), for example, offers a rich stew of "uniqueness factors," from extended experience in Japan and Germany as an "Army brat" to mature leadership in the navy and service on the diversity council of a federal intelligence agency—all narrated in an unusually witty and engaging style.

If after drawing up your personal diversity inventory you still think you're too unexceptional, don't fret. A diverse class doesn't mean a class filled with demographic outliers; it also means one that includes a goodly number of strong applicants with traditional, middle-of-the-road profiles. If you feel that's you, then tell your "normality" tale as engagingly and vividly as you can. Your charm and winning presentation can in themselves create the sense of potential contribution that schools look for. Personality, in other words, can be a "diversity factor." Many qualified applicants who believed schools eliminated them for diversity reasons actually eliminated themselves at the start by assuming they had nothing in the way of diversity to offer. Your diversity elements may not be terribly unusual taken individually, but together they may well make you memorably distinct.

In the Schools' Words—

I think a purposeful sincerity is your best strategy. Don't try to be unique, or tell us what you think we want to hear (I guarantee you we'll figure that out). Talk about the experiences that shaped you and what you've accomplished. Your individual talents and skills will come out.

—Jon McLaughlin, MIT (Sloan)

Aside from the content you choose, what can you do to ensure that your diversity essay really convinces admissions officers that you can make a significant contribution? First, you must provide vivid details and concrete examples that automatically individuate you because they're specific to your life. Since the words or themes you will use to label your uniqueness have probably been used before, it's your examples that will give your diversity essay its real singularity. Make sure they have color and bite. Second, it's not enough to simply name your diversity factors and drop in a few examples. You must also address the diversity essay's contribution component (sometimes stated in the question's wording, sometimes not, but always implied). That is, explicitly state how your diversity or uniqueness factors have benefited or educated you, what they've added to your life, and how they will benefit classmates. For example, what life lessons or insights did you gain from growing up in Mozambique or abandoning your budding career as a rock musician or chasing your passion for Tang Dynasty antiques to Nepal? And in what ways will you share these lessons or insights with your future classmates—by joining the African Students' Club? By playing for classmates during orientation week? By explaining antique auction bidding theory in class? In other words, show schools you've already begun envisioning how to share your special traits and interests within their program.

In the Schools' Words—

[International experience] can mean a lot of things. We look at the quality of this experience. Some people work in an international firm and talk several languages every day, and some travel a lot and live in other countries and never interact with people from other countries!

—JOHANNA HELLBORG, INSEAD

International and Cross-Cultural Diversity

The increase in international representation at American business schools is perhaps the most obvious way in which schools have diversified the MBA experience in recent years. None of the top-10 U.S. MBA programs today has fewer than 28 percent non-U.S. students, and the top European schools all boast international populations of 72 percent and higher. Schools value international exposure not only because new perspectives deepen the classroom learning experience, but because global experiences often go hand in hand with personal growth, tolerance, and enhanced professional value. As a result, the international or cross-culturally focused essay is an increasingly common variant of the diversity essay.

Of course, being international no longer automatically confers diversity points, as many applicants from India have discovered to their chagrin. Applicants from little-represented countries have a certain advantage in claiming diversity, it's true. But those from well-represented countries or who have modest international profiles can offset this with vivid, detailed, compelling descriptions of their own international stories and through the depth of insight and reflection they bring to their analysis of them. What did your international experience teach you about people, your own country, human difference (or basic sameness), or yourself? Note how in his essay (diversity essay 2), for example, Sandeep J. lifts the unexceptional fact of being an Indian serving an internship with a U.S. company to a whole new level by dramatizing his confrontations with and reflections on racism.

The Diversity Essay: What Not *to Do*

When you're writing your diversity essay, don't

1. Assume that *diversity* is defined only in terms of gender and certain under-represented ethnic groups or that the word *uniqueness* is limited to tales of being raised by cannibals or overcoming obscure medical conditions. Schools define both terms loosely.

2. Use "unique contribution" stories that really aren't all that singular—being a mother, being Canadian, making your high school's varsity basketball team. Dig deeper.

3. Focus on questionable, inappropriate, or negative uniqueness factors, such as your psychic gifts or your weekend recruiting work for underground terrorist cells. Stay positive and within bounds.

4. Try to cram too many uniqueness factors into your essay, producing a bland, all-inclusive porridge unsubstantiated by examples. Focus on three or four diversity themes.

5. Waste space informing schools how great diversity is. They know this; that's why they're asking the question. Talk about how great your own diversity is instead.

> **In the Schools' Words—**
>
> *Diversity is with a capital D—not just race and gender, but truly outlook, background, cultural, political, religion, full-time work experience, etc. It takes all forms and adds to the learning in the classroom.*
>
> —Kris Nebel,
> University of Michigan (Ross)

LEADING AND FOLLOWING: THE LEADERSHIP AND TEAMWORK ESSAY

"Five or six years after you receive your MBA," notes Kellogg's dean, Dipak Jain, "80 percent of your responsibility is managing people." Graduate management schools are about leadership, and one way they find it is by directly asking applicants for their best leadership stories. At the same time, schools also know that for many 26-year-olds, leadership is as much a work in progress as it is an accomplished fact. The leadership essay lets them extrapolate future managerial prowess from the hints and foreshadowings of lowercase leadership moments.

Teamwork is another matter. According to the *Wall Street Journal,* corporate recruiters rate the "ability to work well within a team" as the second-most important attribute of business school graduates—"leadership potential" ranking only sixth. For recruiters and business schools alike, there's no such thing as "teamwork potential." If you don't already have it, business schools may not want to give you the chance to pick it up between your finance and statistics classes. The teamwork essay lets schools judge that as an effective teammate you're already there, capable of synergizing with classmates from day one.

In the Schools' Words—

Since we are a management program, we do seek individuals who have potential for senior management or leadership positions in various types of organizations. Individuals who have already had management experience of some type may have an advantage, but leadership can also be demonstrated in extracurricular activities and in ways other than being the formal "manager" of a unit. If management experience has taken place working across cultures, that might add a twist that would be interesting.

—PETE JOHNSON,
UNIVERSITY OF CALIFORNIA BERKELEY (HAAS)

What Schools Ask

"Pure" leadership and teamwork essays unambiguously invite you to write about specific experiences or skills:

- "Discuss a situation, preferably work-related, where you have taken a significant leadership role. How does this event demonstrate your managerial potential?" (UCLA)

- "What have been your most significant leadership roles to date? What was the most valuable lesson learned?" (Kellogg)

To elicit more revealing answers, other schools phrase the question more unconventionally:

- "Evaluate yourself as a leader. Where have you demonstrated excellence?" (Minnesota)

- "Who is someone that you consider to be an inspirational leader? Why?" (Berkeley Haas)

- "Imagine you'll be taking a 72-hour car ride with two other individuals. If you could choose your travel companions for this journey, whom would you choose and why?" (Maryland)

Finally, some schools *combine* the leadership and teamwork essays into one:

- "Describe a situation in which your leadership and/or teamwork had a significant impact." (Yale)

- "'Team Fuqua' is a frequently used term when discussing the Duke MBA program. Great teams have great leaders with great ideas and great team play. Thus, 'Team Fuqua' means much more than teamwork. In fact, it builds directly from the core values of Fuqua, which are collaboration, innovation, and leadership. Please describe what you would bring to build on these core values and make Team Fuqua great." (Duke)

This last hybrid group underscores a crucial fact: leadership and teamwork experiences are often two sides of the same coin. Indeed, you can often find both leadership and teamwork experiences in the same accomplishment. As we'll see in the next section, it's often just a matter of emphasis.

Choosing Your Story

Choosing the best leadership or teamwork story starts, naturally enough, with knowing what leadership and teamwork are. Note that schools usually let *you* define the terms, since part of their purpose is to see what these words mean to you. So don't assume that *leadership* can only mean "telling people what to do" or that the word *teamwork* implies some corny rah-rah sports scenario. The upside of the interpretive freedom these essays give you is that you don't have to occupy positions of great formal authority or work in huge and diverse groups to impress schools with your leadership and team play. The downside is that you must show the schools through the way you execute these essays that you have given serious thought to what leadership and teamwork really mean and have found multidimensional ways to demonstrate them.

Leadership

Leadership can, of course, mean holding a traditional command-and-control position involving direct reports, sharply delineated hierarchy, and budget and P&L authority. But on the broadest level, leadership simply means assuming personal ownership of something in a group situation in order to create a positive result that would not have occurred without you. "In a group" is essential; on some level your leadership example must show you influencing the actions of others. At a minimum, then, leadership implies initiative, doing "more" than others, inspiring, being proactive, not reactive.

What do leaders do? Everything from motivating by setting a personal example, establishing and uniting people behind a vision, and training and mentoring to balancing short- and long-term goals, leading in crisis, and knowing when to let people go. What values do leaders demonstrate? Everything from charisma, initiative, decisiveness, and discipline to empathy, supportiveness, and selflessness. The longer you look, the more encompassing you'll find the idea of leadership to be. So even if you have no formal supervisory role, within leadership's wide definition you will surely find examples that you can develop into a leadership essay.

Starting with college, put the microscope to all your group experiences—work, academic, extracurricular, community, personal—and ask questions like these:

- Can you think of a time when you were specifically praised for your leadership skills?

- Have you ever been elected by a group of people for a position of responsibility?

- What methods do you use to motivate people?

- Do you have a philosophy of leadership? Has it changed over time?

- Have people ever followed your lead?

- Have you persuaded others to pursue a certain course of action?

Follow these questions (Writing Prompt Exercise 3 provides others) wherever they lead. Unless the school's question limits you, don't shackle yourself by searching for only work-related leadership stories. Because most applicants are still relatively low on the professional totem pole, their best leadership examples may well come from community or personal activities. Indeed, community leadership can often be more impressive because you're leading volunteers who don't have to follow you (or even be there), and you're frequently interacting with people at a more senior level than you would at work.

Teamwork

At the risk of sounding glib, the difference between leadership and teamwork experiences is often a matter of a pronoun. The very same accomplishment will often work well as a leadership or a teamwork essay by shifting the focus from "I" to "we." The project you described yourself as leading effectively through mentoring, delegation, or goal-setting skills was by definition also a team experience whose dynamic you can capture by focusing on diversity, cross-functionality, personality issues, and the like. Moreover, the traits that make a great team player—empathy, integrity, selflessness, adaptability, communication, etc.—are often the same as those that make a great leader.

Teamwork can take as many varied forms as leadership, from playing the peacemaker, the go-to assistant, or the jack-of-all-trades to being the cheerleader, the diligent worker bee, or the savvy politico. Likewise, you can find valid teamwork experiences in the workplace or classroom, in your church or community center, in sororities and fraternities or athletic fields, even in the family. Which story you choose will depend on which one shows you understanding and empowering teams best, but as with every essay you must choose topics strategically so all your strongest stories find their way into each school's essay set.

Structure

Leadership and teamwork are inherently people-centered topics, yet many applicants overload their essays with project-specific and procedural details instead of zeroing in on the human relationships. The four-part structure recommended below avoids this trap by encouraging you to devote as much space to the lessons learned as to the essay's "plot."

The Challenge

In this first section, provide just enough context—the time frame, the story's cast of characters, and your role—to orient the reader to the scene you're about to bring alive. Begin spelling out the leadership or teamwork challenge as soon as possible, as well as the specific obstacles you or your team faced in overcoming that challenge. In his essay (leadership and teamwork essay 2), for example, Hysam B. states his leadership challenge loudly and clearly ("supervise two first-year associates . . .") in only his fourth sentence.

It's fine to explain that your challenge was that a $5 million project was now three months over deadline and $1 million over budget, but the essay's *leadership-* or *teamwork*-specific obstacles should stem from people issues. Perhaps you were new to the project, two of your teammates were feuding, a new hire's learning curve was steeper than expected, or the client manager seemed to have walked right out of a *Dilbert* comic strip. Emphasize the differences and issues between people, not just the functional loggerheads and technical hurdles. Turn it into a human-interest story from the start.

Your Response

Your response is where you show how you addressed each of the challenges or obstacles spelled out in the first section by deploying several of your leadership or team-working skills. Think in terms of both traits and tactics. What three leadership/teamwork traits or qualities did you demonstrate in helping the group rise to the challenge? What were the tactical steps you took to overcome people issues? They don't have to be epochal. Taking the time to listen to a teammate or changing your personal style to steer around differences (cultural, functional, gender, age, racial, etc.) with another teammate is worth mentioning. Always describe the small human-level things you did to assuage egos, show gratitude, move people forward. These are the details that (together with the lessons learned) make leadership and teamwork essays work. If it's a leadership essay, show the school through miniexamples *how* you lead—inclusively? intuitively? analytically? If it's a teamwork essay, show the admissions committee how readily you can cede power or visibility when doing so helps the group.

If you have a leadership or teamwork philosophy, consider stepping back from the story for a moment to show schools that you can be reflective about leadership and team play, as Tim S. does in his essay (leadership and teamwork essay 1): "In a team environment, I normally play a very flexible role, either following if someone else has a better knowledge of the subject matter or leading if I am an expert on the topic." If you're very concrete and very "real" in the way you present your leadership or teamwork examples, you can go a long way toward offsetting any disadvantage posed by applicants whose essays recount higher-impact accomplishments but whose treatment of the leadership or teamwork issues behind the accomplishment comes off as false, jargony, or vague.

In the Schools' Words—

Most people have had the chance in their work experience or even school background to demonstrate leadership. Even if you have not had direct reports, most people have led teams and projects. All leadership experiences are valuable.

—Isser Gallogly,
New York University (Stern)

The Outcome

Your presentation of the outcome of your leadership or teamwork experience may be as short as a sentence, but it should help "prove" that you had the positive impact you say you did. Quantitative facts do this very effectively, but, again because leadership and teamwork essays are people-focused, qualitative and human-level impacts are also valued: saving someone's career, turning a dysfunctional team into bosom buddies, and so on. Note, for example, that Hysam B.'s leadership essay (leadership and teamwork essay 2) provides two separate one-sentence outcome statements because he describes two instances of leadership.

Lessons Learned

As always, schools want to see you step back from the Sturm und Drang of experience and give evidence that you're the sort who learns from experience.

Many applicants will slot in a few deep-sounding sentences and call it a night. Unfortunately, adcoms know that any reasonably intelligent person can snatch the latest leadership/teamwork "learnings" off a school Web site. To overcome their skepticism, you need to show how such leadership and team lessons stem organically from the details of your story. Hysam B.'s lesson—"I learned that demonstrating patience and sharing one's own knowledge are powerful tools for motivating people"—seems a natural and an "earned" product of the two leadership stories he's just told. Such statements show you are reflective and self-aware about leadership and teamwork, that you have thought about what they mean and are conscious of how to practice them.

One way to make your lessons learned seem organic is to show how your essay's central experience changed your idea of leadership or teamwork. Your essay could begin, for example, by stating that you used to believe that leadership meant, say, managing resources efficiently. After narrating a story in which you learned that leadership is about inspiring others to excel, you would then close the essay by referring back to your now obsolescent idea of leadership.

Leadership and Teamwork Essays: What Not to Do

When you're writing your leadership and teamwork essay, don't

1. Write about a group accomplishment in which your leadership role was indirect or nonexistent. Likewise, trying to force a leadership example to work as a teamwork essay will misfire if you were clearly the person in charge or if you show yourself interacting with teammates authoritatively rather than collegially.

2. Focus on the team's accomplishment rather than your interaction with the group. Yes, you must establish context and results, but team dynamics and what you did to shape them are much more important than blow-by-blow procedural details.

3. Fail to be specific and credible about the leadership or teamwork skills you possess. Drill down into your story to find the specific tactical leadership or teamwork skills it illustrates, and only then worry about extrapolating a general principle or lesson.

4. Forget to analyze the leadership or teamwork accomplishment or draw a lesson from it. The bare facts of the story itself are worthless if you don't analyze them to point out the myriad types of leadership or teamwork you demonstrated and identify the appropriate lessons to be drawn from them.

5. Draw obvious or clichéd lessons from your example or state obvious or clichéd types of leadership lessons. Don't say you learned that leadership means "taking

initiative and showing vision." Dig deeper than such umbrella words to find a more personalized message.

In the Schools' Words—

We are looking for very accomplished candidates in general, but particularly ones that can show a track record of leadership accomplishments in some organization, work or otherwise, where they have made something big happen that would not have occurred if they were not there. We are looking for big impact people who are able to size up situations, seize opportunities, mobilize people to act and get results. We want to see evidence of this.

—Dick Shafer, Cornell (Johnson)

NOBODY'S PERFECT: THE FAILURE ESSAY

No one likes to fail—least of all achievers with the smarts and drive to aim for the best business schools. For you, the only thing worse than failing might be having to admit mistakes to complete strangers whose verdict can decide your entire professional future! No matter how counterintuitive it seems, getting the chance to earn an MBA begins, for many schools, with admitting to a real howler.

As with the ethics essay (discussed later in this chapter), the failure essay enables schools to understand how you analyze difficult situations. Your ability to admit and coolly dissect a personal blunder evinces maturity and humility, qualities post-Enron-era business schools value dearly. Conversely, pretending you can outfox the admissions committee by slipping them a success wrapped up as a failure immediately announces immaturity—by (1) trying to pretend you've never failed and (2) thinking you can hoodwink admissions officers who've seen it all.

Failures are classic obstacles, and how you overcome difficulty says a lot about your character, resilience, and willingness to change in response to the feedback reality gives you. Moreover, admissions officers are people too. They love to hear "come-from-behind" tales in which the hero (you) overcomes his tragic flaw to redeem himself in the closing minutes. *Failure → understanding → redemption* is a traditional pattern in all storytelling; use it in this essay to rouse the reader's interest and sympathy.

Failure also often says good things about those who strive for the brass ring but miss. Ambition, boldness, innovation—these and other positive traits usually cling to those who "dare mighty things." Finally, responding to the failure question honestly will pay dividends all across your application. Once the schools see that you've been above board about your failures, they'll be much more inclined to take you at your word about your successes.

What Schools Ask

The classic business school failure essay is no doubt Harvard's: "Recognizing that successful leaders are able to learn from failure, discuss a situation in which you failed and what you learned." Nothing in this wording even remotely invites you to slip a "setback" or "letdown" under the radar. Harvard is asking for an out-and-out failure. Many applicants nevertheless react to this unambiguous phrasing like cornered ferrets, defensively denying that they could be anything less than flawless candidates. They narrate failures that are really 80 percent successes, team failures in which they played a marginal role, or moments of adversity in which their only lapse was being victimized by fate.

Precisely to avoid these kinds of nonanswers, many schools phrase the failure essay more expansively: "Describe when you were part of a team where the group process and/or intended outcome failed. What was your role, how did you contribute to the process or outcome, and what did you learn?" (Wharton)

Here, the focus has been shifted from *your* failure to your team's failure—a much lighter hurdle to clear. Other schools help you by using wording that softens the sting of *failure*:

- "Please describe a failure or setback in your professional or academic life. How did you overcome this setback? What, if anything, would you do differently if confronted with this situation again?" (Carnegie Mellon)

- "Discuss a time when you were faced with a professional disappointment. How did you handle the disappointment, and what did you learn from the situation?" (Texas)

There's a yawning chasm of difference between a failure and a setback or disappointment. The former means you personally were to blame; the latter means only that things didn't turn out as you wished. All such diluted variations of the failure question allow you to dodge the failure bullet. Nevertheless, unless you can draw powerful, revealing insights from a setback or disappointment, you should consider describing a true personal failure. Always read carefully to determine whether the question allows you to draw from failures in any part of your life or only from your professional or academic life.

In the Schools' Words—

Too little background can make the learnings seem unattached to what you experienced (and thus potentially somewhat artificial?) or the context of the situation unclear, and too much background might not leave enough space to talk about the learnings.

—Andrew McAlister (aka "Fanatical Fan"),
Wharton graduate and former admissions officer

Choosing Your Story

When brainstorming for the "perfect" failure story, remember that an *ideal* example will meet four criteria:

1. It was clearly your fault because you, for example, let someone down, conspicuously and unexpectedly failed to achieve a reasonable target, or misread or misreacted to a situation.

2. It sheds light on an activity or experience not treated elsewhere in your application.

3. It is no more than five years old but is not so recent that you haven't yet applied the lessons it taught you.

4. It reflects some positive aspect of your personality, such as initiative.

These aren't conditions that all effective examples will meet, of course, but they are an ideal to shoot for. Popular topics for failure essays include failed start-ups, being laid off, academic reversals, athletic failures, and rookie mistakes at work. But the best failures are often doozies of misadventure for the very reason that exceptional individuals often attempt things that others avoid, or they rise to positions where their mistakes are magnified by the scope of their responsibility. If you have made a truly distinctive, outsized failure, this may be just what the adcom ordered. After all, if you must come clean about a real failure, there's something to be said for failing big. So don't give them some milquetoast peccadillo—choose a blunder that only a big risk taker swinging for the fences could manage.

Structure

Since schools ask you to "discuss a failure," many applicants mistakenly burn through three-quarters of the essay's prescribed length detailing the ins and outs of their fiasco. The failure itself, however, is perhaps the least important part of the essay. At least as critical are your analysis of the failure, the lessons it taught you, and the ways you applied those lessons later on.

Context and Failure Statement

This first section of the essay—ideally a third or less of the total length—should give just enough information to pique the reader's interest and clarify that your failure was a real one, was indeed your fault, and had specific consequences. Since being able to stand up and admit failure is a key reason why schools pose this topic, your statement of failure should be unambiguous. You blew it. In Tun-jen L.'s sample essay (failure essay 2), for example, he states categorically: "I had failed to meet strongly set personal objectives. I felt an emptiness I had never known before."

But the failure statement should also be short and sweet. Avoid trying to wring pity from the admissions officers, and stay away from orgies of self-recrimination. As we noted in Chapter 1, the tone of your entire application should be positive; so keep this part of the essay factual, mature, and above all brief.

Analysis

The analysis section of the failure essay exists only to demonstrate that you have the self-awareness and analytical skills to dissect the causes of your failure. Don't use this brief section to try to shift the blame to someone else, rationalize your failure away, or strain toward a happy ending. Focus objectively and succinctly on what you did wrong and why. The only place for emotional expression in this essay is in stating your deep regret for the negative impact of your failure on *others*. No whining or wheedling.

Lessons

If you've played your cards right, you'll have reached the essay's halfway point (or thereabouts) with the pungent details of your blunder safely behind you and plenty of room still remaining for the essay's positive payoff: what your failure taught you. Aim for multiple takeaways to show how conscientiously and exhaustively you examined this "educational episode" to identify where you went wrong and how. Generally, the greater the magnitude of your initial failure, the more lessons you should be able to glean from it. Avoid banal, generalized lessons like, "I learned that leadership means taking responsibility for your mistakes"—that should be implicit in the much more specific and personalized lessons you discuss.

Much better are lessons like failing to turn to others for help; failing to listen; mishandling stress, conflict, or team dynamics; delaying a decision until you had more data; or failing to correlate ideal objectives with hard realities. What steps have you taken to ensure that you will not have to learn these specific lessons again?

In her essay (failure essay 1), Connie K. draws a very basic lesson from her difficult ethical failure: "This experience taught me that you must stick to what you know is true." If the lesson you learned was that you lacked sufficient self-knowledge about your skills, strengths, or career goals, you can actually leverage your failure to advance your case for needing an MBA. Note, for example, how Tun-jen L. subtly transforms the lesson of his failure—"to seek another path where I could commit my leadership as passionately"—into a justification for applying to business school: ". . . I am on that path today."

Lessons Applied

If your failure has a happy ending, it should come in the essay's last section, where you show yourself redeeming your earlier lapse. This part of the essay answers the essay's implicit questions: What do you proactively do after you've realized you failed? What corrective actions do you take? Brainstorm for a specific subsequent occasion when you encountered circumstances similar to those of your failure but responded differently and effectively because of the lessons your failure taught you. At the end of her essay (failure essay 1), Connie K. jumps three years ahead to show that although her failure taught her an ethical lesson, it also proved that her "business sense" had been right all along.

Failure Essays: What Not to Do

When you're writing a failure essay, don't

1. Write about a failure that isn't one. To say you failed because USC dinged your application last fall or because you once reduced costs by 15 percent instead of the 25 percent you intended is to misunderstand what schools mean by *failure.*

2. Describe a trivial failure. Recounting the time your fraternity's barbecue imploded may shed light on your skills as an organizer, but it doesn't meet the significance level business schools expect here.

3. Reveal a failure that exposes inexcusable flaws in your character. Getting fired for sexual harassment, stealing from your employer, or committing a capital crime are all true failures, no doubt, but they're far too egregious for schools to overlook.

4. Write too much about the failure itself. If you overload your essay with every gory detail of your lapse, you won't have enough space for the section that can redeem you—the lessons learned and applied.

5. Choose a failure that's more than five years old or whose subject matter is otherwise inappropriate. Failing to make your high school's chess club may well have scarred you, but its antiquity may cause the schools to assume you're evading the question. Similarly, failed relationships are too personal and too common.

BLACK AND WHITE OR GRAY: THE ETHICS ESSAY

Though schools like Virginia (Darden), Notre Dame, and IESE have long included ethics as integral parts of their educational mission, the classic ethics essay first surfaced in MBA applications following the corporate scandals of the 1980s, only to fade in popularity in the 1990s. With the Enron, WorldCom, and other corporate integrity implosions of the early 2000s, however, the ethics essay has come roaring back.

Many applicants paranoiacally assume that the ethics essay is designed to put their morals to some stringent litmus test. They brainstorm for examples that show them proudly refusing bribes, pointedly excusing themselves from insider-trading deals, or sternly rejecting other blatantly illegal schemes. They misunderstand the ethics essay's purpose. Admissions committees use the ethics essay to see how you analyze and propose solutions to thorny problems that lack black-and-white answers. Managers who expect to lead organizations well must be comfortable with ambiguity and have the emotional intelligence to find their way to solutions that balance complexities. Essays in which you pat yourself on the back for resisting an obviously illegal scheme (which admission officers would expect you to reject outright) tell them nothing about your ability to balance ambiguous alternatives or conflicting values.

Ethics essays also tell schools a great deal about your personality. When faced with complex challenges, do you turn to colleagues for help or work things out on your own? Do you think only about your own neck or do you show real concern for the impact of ethical scenarios on others? Finally, how you respond to ethics essays may tell schools something about the emphasis you place on social impact issues because ethics has a *social* dimension that is reflected in corporate social responsibility issues, such as labor and environmental policies.

What Schools Ask

The standard formulation of the ethics question is Kellogg's, "Describe an ethical dilemma that you faced and how it was resolved." Note that an ethical *dilemma* means a situation in which you must choose between alternatives that each have morally negative consequences. Choosing to resist an insider-trading opportunity is definitely a choice involving ethical issues, but it is not a dilemma because rejecting an illegal scheme is the only real *ethical* choice. Similarly, weighing whether to include bells and whistles on a new product that may attract new customers but, by increasing the price, may repel others is definitely a dilemma, but it is not an ethical one.

For schools that ask for ethical dilemmas, you must find an example in which ethical imperatives collide. Because such examples can be scarce, some schools adopt more relaxed language: "Describe a situation where your values, ethics, or morals were challenged. How did you handle the situation?" (Wharton)

This formulation lets you write about a true ethical dilemma if you've got one or, if you don't, about a more general ethical "test" (e.g., a bribe rejected) or value challenged (e.g., your cultural tolerance tested by a prejudiced peer). Other schools, like Dartmouth, give you an elaborately fictitious case study in which you must demonstrate your ability to weigh all the complexities, map out all the options, and identify a defensible compromise solution.

In the Schools' Words—

As soon as we doubt their ethics, they're gone. It's just not worth the risk.

—Jett Pihakis,
University of California Berkeley (Haas)

Choosing Your Story

With the exception of the failure essay, no essay may be harder to write than the ethics essay. For most applicants, one challenge is simply identifying an appropriate story. To inventory your own experience for possible ethical stories, look under every rock, including your community, academic, and personal experiences. The questions in Writing Prompt Exercise 4 may remind you of examples you've forgotten. The key is to search where ethical issues usually arise: at the intersection of competing interests, such as public versus private, individual versus organization, shareholder versus employee, labor versus management. You're hunting for gray areas, moments where your loyalties and instincts feel conflicted or collide.

In every real "gray" scenario some alternatives are likely to be more ethically pure and some more ethically dubious than others. Your most effective ethical choice may often be the one that strikes a balance or creative compromise. If in your example the ethically good choice seems too obvious or the potential ethical lapse seems small or nonexistent, then you may need to consider another example.

Structure

There's no rigid formula for organizing ethics essays, any more than there's one for distinguishing a true ethical dilemma from an imposter. Still, the five components described in the following sections are usually found in some form in effective ethics essays.

Context

Here you present introductory background information to give the readers their bearings and hopefully pique their interest. When did your ethical challenge occur? Who were the people around whom the event unfolded? What was your role? In Robert Y.'s sample essay (ethics essay 1), for example, he starts the essay in the middle of the action, deftly introducing the key ethical figure (Sue) and the context (an offered answer sheet after a grueling college road trip), all in the first three sentences.

This first section of the essay should then conclude with a forthright statement of the ethical challenge. As briefly as possible, state the crux of the dilemma or difficulty. Draw the reader into the nagging ambiguity of your dilemma, as Robert Y. does in his second, third, and fourth paragraphs.

Analysis

The heart of the ethics essay is your analysis of the alternative decision paths open to you and their potential costs and benefits. Remember that schools don't pose ethics essays to poke around in your scruples but to see how you tease out a course of action when all your alternatives seem poor. You should explain clearly whom your decision will affect and dispassionately weigh the pluses and minuses of each "solution," without appearing to judge the various participants or predetermine the outcome.

Your tone is mature and thoughtful, your attitude one of fair-minded concern for each participant, balanced with healthy self-interest and a bottom-line regard for the long-term benefits to your organization. You are a savvy team player with integrity looking for a pragmatic middle ground between moral naïveté and unscrupulous instrumentalism. Admissions committees are unlikely to applaud applicants who rigidly and noisily stand up for their moral principles when a nuanced, behind-the-scenes approach could have achieved the same ethical outcome with fewer sparks and trauma.

Because, like all effective essays, this should be a good story, look for ways to heighten the tension, by, for example, emphasizing the personal pressure you were under, expressing your own doubt, or quoting others who are convinced that one option is demonstrably better than the other. Notice that in doing all three of these, Robert Y.'s essay brings alive his moment of temptation.

Decision

Your analysis of your ethical challenge must eventually produce a clearly stated decision, solution, or compromise. Robert Y.'s comes with the unambiguous, "I refused to tarnish the legacy of those who played before me" at the end of his penultimate paragraph.

Follow your decision with a brief defense, in which you explain how it allowed you to remain true to your ethics while still preserving key relationships and supporting your organization's long-term interests. Don't defend your decision by quoting the Golden Rule or Kant's *Critique of Pure Reason*; defend it in concrete, human terms.

Consequences

Like any good tale, you must round out your ethics essay by telling the reader how it all turned out. Perhaps your coparticipants immediately saw the Solomonic wisdom of your solution and signed off on it. Maybe you were fired. Perhaps you had to fight for your decision—build alliances, persuade colleagues, change the ways of your ethically challenged colleagues. You can bet that admissions committees will love a solution that tested your interpersonal skills and shows you wondering aloud how your actions will affect others. In any event, explain what happened to each of the main actors in your morality play (including yourself), as Robert Y. does in his last paragraph.

Lessons

You should always try to draw the "moral" from the story, the lessons you learned and have applied in similar situations since. This is where you abstract the particulars of your ethical challenge into a larger insight or principle. If the best you can do is, "Honesty is the best policy" or "Do unto others as you would have them do unto you," you need to keep digging. This is an excellent place to connect the dotted lines between your themes in this essay and your other essays. If space allows you to work in a brief closing anecdote that illustrates how your decision led to later benefits or growth opportunities, then by all means do so. If you are unsure that you made the right decision, don't be ashamed to admit it. You won't be showing irresolution so much as honesty, self-awareness, and sensitivity to life's complexities, which is what schools are looking for.

Ethics Essays: What Not to Do

When you're writing your ethics essay, don't

1. Describe a situation that was an ethical challenge (e.g., deciding whether to comply with the terms of a contract) as if it were an ethical dilemma (where each alternative must be equally unsavory ethically).

2. Sound sanctimonious. Portraying yourself as a saintly figure floating chastely above the corrupt masses will invite schools to question your ability to handle the gray-area realities of business life. If, for example, you publicly repudiate your boss's wishes to protect your ethics without first seeking some quiet compromise solution, you may actually come across as impolitic and disloyal.

3. Omit one of the five elements of the ethics essay: (1) context, (2) analysis, (3) decision, (4) consequences, (5) lessons.

4. Make the unethical choice or consider the illegal act. If your scenario is not a dilemma and an ethically "right choice" therefore does exist, you must never show yourself choosing the unethical path. Likewise, you must never suggest that you seriously weighed the pros and cons of an illegal act or entertained yielding to the temptation of an immoral or illegal act. When it's illegal, it's wrong; no reflection is required.

5. Choose a bad example, such as a story in which the right, ethical choice is obvious or the downside of one of the ethical alternatives is minor. Also avoid inappropriate ethical examples, such as whether to be unfaithful to a spouse.

TRICK OR TREAT: THE CREATIVE ESSAY

As we've seen, the intent behind some schools' essay questions can be unclear. But in essay questions like the following, the adcoms' purpose can seem downright invisible:

- "Chicago GSB is seeking a mascot to represent our new facility, The Hyde Park Center. What would your choice be and how will it represent the attributes of the GSB?" (Chicago)

- "If you could imagine a life entirely different from the one you now lead, what would it be?" (HEC)

- "What well-known historical event would you have liked to have been involved in and why?" (London)

- "Write a newspaper article you might read in the year 2020." (Chicago)

OK, maybe if it was *your* job to select and train tomorrow's global business leaders, these wouldn't be the first questions you'd ask your applicants. But before you question the wisdom of the adcoms who chose these gems, recall the overriding intent behind everything schools ask: to find out who you really are and to learn whether you really want to join their program. However unorthodox, all these topics help them get answers to these key questions. First, they're distinctive enough to prevent you from guessing what the schools are after, which may just trick you into dropping your defenses long enough to reveal something genuinely personal. Second, they also effectively prevent you from cutting and pasting in other schools' essays, thus weeding out the casual applicant making a last-minute roll of the dice. Finally, because these questions have such creative what-if premises, they enable schools to determine whether you can handle curve-ball questions with imagination and resourcefulness.

Precisely because these topics are so cunningly flaky, there are no all-embracing rules for answering them. As a result, many applicants respond to them off-handedly—mistakenly thinking the adcoms asked them just to lighten their essay-reading load—or overliterally, earnestly elaborating an answer that sheds no new light on the applicant. No matter how irrelevant or outlandish these creative topics seem, you must expend the same effort on them as any other essay, and you must shed new light on you.

In one sense, NYU Stern's topic, "creatively describe yourself to your classmates using any method you choose," is the mother of all creative essays since you aren't restricted to words. Because this essay is so obviously autobiographical in its focus, however, we discuss it separately with self-revelation essays earlier in this chapter. Likewise, creative essays that leave the topic entirely up to you are essentially the same as open-ended optional essays, which we consider in the next chapter.

To help you see what admissions committees hope to glean from creative essays and how you should respond, let's take a brief look at some of the very typical creative topics we list at the beginning of this section. Chicago's mascot question is simply a variation on the standard "why our school?" topic. In framing it in this way, the admissions committee is not only testing your ability to identify the attributes that make Chicago unique, but also your creativity (and patience) in finding the animal kingdom metaphor that best captures them. HEC's Walter Mitty-esque topic should be approached as cautiously as essays that ask what you would do with the extra time in a 28-hour day or which career you would pick if you could choose any one. You want to focus on scenarios that show the better angels of your nature rather than purely materialistic or self-indulgent fantasies. You also want to avoid sounding like you're dissatisfied with your current life or that your ideal life is just an idle pipe dream rather than something you might actually be able to at least partly realize someday.

Finally, London's historical what-if essay is really just a variant on the "people, places, or things" topic we discuss in the self-revelation essays section. That is, you should choose a historical period that shows the school another side of *you*, and you should keep the focus of the essay on you as much as possible. Perhaps you would discuss the Great Depression of the 1930s because it gave your ancestors the values of prudence and frugality on which your family's firm thrived, or China's accession to the World Trade Organization because it accelerated the economic growth on which your post-MBA plans are based.

Whatever you choose, never forget that essays are always ultimately about you.

WRITING PROMPT EXERCISES

The most common flaw of business school application essays is lack of concrete detail. If you really want to stand out from other applicants, you therefore need to dig deeper than they do when writing your essays. The pointed, specific questions in the following four exercises will help you do just that.

Exercise 1

Sometimes applicants overlook accomplishments because they're too close to their own careers to appreciate what's distinctive about them. If the three core questions given on page 69 didn't help you find enough accomplishment essay material, try digging a little deeper with these:

1. Has your organization allowed you to concentrate on an area of growth or potential innovation? Describe your contribution so far and what impact that contribution could potentially lead to in the future.

2. If your responsibilities are narrow, are they still vital to your organization's future? Delineate all the ways in which this is so.

3. What's the most creative or imaginative thing you've ever done, either inside or outside your career? It doesn't have to be "artsy-craftsy" creative, just unquestionably "outside the box."

4. Think of the time when your voluntary intervention had the greatest impact on someone else. What did you do, how did it help him or her, and how did your intervention affect or change *you*?

5. Have you ever been formally recognized for something, such as receiving an official award for your contribution to an organization or being the subject of an article in a newspaper? Describe the circumstances of your achievement and how it made you feel.

6. Have you ever taken a major risk in or outside your career that succeeded? What motivated you? What was the result?

Exercise 2

The following questions can help you uncover the reasons why a particular accomplishment is or should be important to you:

1. Did the accomplishment help you learn a skill you didn't have before? Which one?

2. In what ways did accomplishing this achievement require you to take initiative, step out of your defined role, or perform above your accepted expectations?

3. Did the accomplishment give you firsthand exposure to the values that matter most to business schools, such as leadership, team play, communication skills, strategic vision? How so?

4. Did you view yourself or did others view you differently after the accomplishment? Describe that change.

5. Did you perceive any change in your role in the organization following the accomplishment? Did it lead to opportunities or responsibilities that you didn't have before?

6. Was the accomplishment something that earlier in your life you didn't imagine yourself capable of? Did you do anything in accomplishing what you did that looking back now actually surprises you?

7. In what ways did this accomplishment require you to think creatively or be innovative? What did you do that wasn't "by the book"?

8. Did this accomplishment teach you anything that made other, later accomplishments possible?

Exercise 3

The following questions can help you flesh out your leadership or teamwork stories:

1. Were the objectives your team pursued clearly established from the outset or left partly undefined? How did you go about solidifying them? How did you communicate them to your team?

2. What specific methods did you use to ensure that the project was proceeding apace? What steps did you take when it fell behind the expected pace?

3. Do you recall moments when you deliberately modified your leadership style to deal more effectively with specific obstacles? How did you determine which tactic to try, and were you successful?

4. Did the project ever require you to "manage up"—that is, get superiors to sign on to your methods or goals? How did you obtain their buy-in? Why do you think your techniques worked?

5. Which types of interpersonal interaction proved most effective for you? One-on-one meetings or group meetings? What specific tactics did you use to motivate people, and did you apply them on an individual basis or on the team as a whole?

6. What is the one aspect of your leadership during this project that you would change if you could? Why do you think you got it "wrong"?

7. Think about the teammates with whom you work most effectively. Name the three personality traits that make them so easy to work with. Now consider the teammates you work least effectively with—which of their personality traits pose the biggest obstacle in these relationships?

Exercise 4

Use the following questions to search for situations you may be able to use in ethics-related essays:

1. Have you ever been asked to do anything at work that you hesitated over for moral reasons or that somehow didn't feel right? If you had refused to do it, what consequences would you have faced?

2. Has anyone ever taken credit for your work or ideas, or have you ever observed this being done to someone else?

3. Have you ever witnessed a coworkers' misconduct and debated whether you should report it?

4. Have you ever been asked to withhold information from clients that might have benefited them had they known about it? Have you ever been asked to tell a client something that you knew to be untrue?

5. Have you ever been in a situation where adhering to the policies of your organization posed harmful consequences not intended by that policy?

6. Has a coworker ever shared information in confidence with you that could have potentially benefited or damaged your organization?

7. Have you ever been tempted to disclose information about your organization or its products that would have caused a potential customer to choose differently?

8. Have you ever been asked to modify a recommendation to clients so as to ensure their continued business?

SAMPLE ESSAYS

Accomplishment Essay 1: Renae P. (Admitted to Cornell)

Essay Prompt. Describe your greatest professional achievement and how you were able to add value to your organization. (400 words)

Stagnation, cynicism, disillusionment. Those adjectives fairly capture the spirit of High Concept Studios when my manager and I were recruited by a High Concept board member to turn the company around in 2001. As VP of New Film Projects, my new role was to direct our expansion into animation and comedy and retain our relationships with the three key directors in High Concept's $550 million stable. Though I believed in High Concept's potential because of its track record with drama and action films, when I first arrived it was immediately clear that its 250+ employees' morale had been dealt a severe blow by executive management's lackadaisical leadership. Though individually brilliant, the executives were not working cohesively, resulting in poor product positioning in the marketplace and a spirit of disorganization among employees, creative staff, and film distributors. *[Nicely demonstrates consensus-building skills.→]* Calling a meeting of the 6 full-time and 3 contract new projects employees who reported to me, I enjoined them to leverage their personal network among High Concept's other teams to find out what was wrong. Through them and my own contacts I also conferred with each of High Concept's five functional groups. *[←Shows that she works through others to find solutions.]* How could we save the company? What I discovered was that each group in the studio worked on a highly ad hoc basis, with little consistent integration of effort. The International Distribution group, for example, had initiated a new relationship with a Shanghai Film Distribution (SFD) unaware that the Domestic Distribution Group's deal with RKM Theaters explicitly precluded us from working with SFD. *[←Just enough detail to give story believability.]* This lack of communication and planning contributed to unacceptable overhead, and High Concept's near-sighted focus on short-term earnings meant sound, long-term thinking was unlikely. My solution, sanctioned by the CEO and general management, was to make the key processes of new project development and film promotion part of a single corporate-wide collaboration. Each film production team would be staffed with representatives from each stakeholder group, and as a company we would focus on no more than 10 to 12 film projects and key promotional campaigns at a time. By working with every group to determine the best tradeoffs between short- and long-term gains, I won companywide support that successfully focused our message so employees, creative staff, and distributors could respond. *[←Reinforces impression of strong team- and consensus-oriented leadership style.]* Within twelve months, our films were receiving increased coverage from industry publications and we had increased our profitable film ventures by 300%, setting the stage for our acquisition by industry leader RKO Studios in 2002.

Accomplishment Essay 2: Naomi K. (Admitted to Wharton)

Essay Prompt. Describe a personal achievement that has had a significant impact on your life. In addition to recounting this achievement, please analyze how the event has changed your understanding of yourself and how you perceive the world around you. (3 pages, 1,000 words)

Since 1997, I have been volunteering as a Big Brother for a twelve-year-old boy named Lonnie through the Alameda County United Way's Big Brother/Big Sister program. *[←Naomi's story is strong enough that she can get away with a direct, "uncreative" lead sentence.]* When I joined the organization, it was clear that Lonnie needed someone to boost his self-esteem. At the end of his school term, Lonnie's mother told me that he did not do very well in math so I also started to help him with his homework. We spent last summer doing extra math work, and I tried to spark his interest in math by explaining things to him using examples from his favorite activity: sports. Once he understood that math had practical value for things in his own life, he was able to catch up to other students. In the fall term Lonnie improved his grade from a C to a B. Hearing this news was one of the proudest moments of my life.

Later in the spring term, however, Lonnie experienced behavioral problems emanating from his inability to control his anger at his school, and the school authorities moved him to a special school. [←*Effective use of a "plot reversal": apparent happy ending leads to deeper challenge.*] He told me he missed his old school a lot and was willing to do anything for a chance to go back. He also admitted that he knew he might get his chance if he could control his anger. Seeing that Lonnie needed somebody to help him control his emotions, I worked to give him a sense of security and urged him to reason out the implications of the actions his anger drove him to. I also encouraged him to get a summer job to develop a sense of responsibility. He listened to and practiced my advice, and by the end of summer the authorities allowed him to return to his old school.

My friendship with Lonnie over the past two years is one of my proudest achievements because I have seen the tangible effect my help is having on his confidence and his life. The feeling that I can improve someone else's life by giving of myself is deeply satisfying. Before Lonnie let me help him, I used to divide the world into two parts: good and bad. The Good were the law-abiding citizens like you and me, and the Bad were the criminals we often see on TV being arrested. I firmly believed that all criminals had to be incarcerated and held responsible for their deeds. But by helping Lonnie through his behavioral problem, I realized that had all those "bad" people gotten help in their formative years, they might not have chosen the path they did. [←*Strong lesson learned: life is more complicated than she used to believe.*] Because of my experience with Lonnie, my whole outlook toward society and the world has changed. I no longer believe that incarcerating young people who break the law is the only solution. Though incarceration might help in the short term, the longer-term solution is to take care of the problem proactively. If we all were to devote some time and effort and influence to the lives of the less fortunate, the world would definitely be a better place to live in.

Motivated by the positive impact I had on Lonnie's life and the change it had on my outlook, I began participating in other community activities where I can make the world a better place. [←*Effectively uses impact of one personal accomplishment to tell a second personal accomplishment.*] While reading about the recent skirmishes between the Bosnian and Serbian armies, for example, I was moved by the sacrifices made by the Bosnian armed forces to protect their country from internal or external invasion. My research showed me that although the Bosnian Army provides sufficient financial support to families of soldiers killed during war, it does not provide the same level of support to the families of soldiers killed in internal counterinsurgency operations.

The amount of money the average American spends eating one restaurant meal could pay for an entire month's education and living expenses for one child of a slain soldier in Bosnia. I therefore decided to found an organization that would establish a scholarship fund for these children. [←*Shows impressive ability to translate her social concern into concrete action.*] My friends greeted my idea enthusiastically, and I soon had five volunteers who were willing to support the cause by paying a nominal amount every month for the education of these fatherless children. However, I encountered bureaucratic red tape when I presented Bosnia's Veterans Wives Welfare Association with my plan. To cut through it, I contacted the adjutant general of Bosnian Army, Lieutenant General S. L. Nemosevic, and detailed my plan directly to him. [←*Shows she can go straight to the top when necessary.*] Impressed by the idea, he promptly offered all the help he could give.

Leveraging my experience as a volunteer for Big Brothers/Big Sisters, I then formed an organization, *[organization name]* (Slavic for "helper of brave warrior") whose sole aim is to bring together host families and beneficiary families. The Adjutant General's Office provides us with the contact information and estimated financial needs of the families of the slain soldiers, and we match them with a host family living abroad who donates up to $30 a month. The beneficiary family is required to write the host family every month about the child's academic performance and furnish them and *[organization name]* with grade reports. [←*Paragraph is full of specific details that make achievement credible.*]

While talking to some Bosnians living in the United States about my plan to set up the fund, I learned that they were uncomfortable with the lack of transparency in the way funds would be disbursed. To address their fears and ensure the appropriate disbursal of the donated funds, I am now contacting Bosnia-based banks to help us facilitate a one-to-one transfer of funds between the host and beneficiary families. I am also setting up a web site (http://www.organizationname.com) to promote the cause amongst Bosnians living abroad. I plan to recruit more volunteers and meet a target of ten host families by year's end by starting low-cost campaigns like chain e-mails and by setting up information booths at Yugoslavian functions. [←*Magnifies impact of her achievement by showing she plans to expand it.*]

The change in my outlook that Lonnie effected opened my eyes to the responsibility each of us has to serve our local community, whether it's down the street or on the other side of the globe. Because Lonnie let me help him in his community, I was able to establish *[organization name]* to serve my own community by rehabilitating the families of soldiers who sacrificed their lives for Bosnia's security.

Self-Revelation Essay 1: Ashish S. (Admitted to NYU Stern)

Essay Prompt. Creatively describe yourself to your MBA classmates. You may use any method to convey your message: words, illustrations, etc. (2 pages)

Like any other test day, I was extremely nervous on August 3, 2003, and had slept poorly the night before. [←*Uses intriguing lead-in to pique reader's interest.*] The horror stories I had heard about Master Chang's black belt tests had been gnawing at me since I began my training, thirty-three months earlier. Knowing that this test was going to be even more grueling than that for my red belt, I was amazed at my courage in even showing up.

As I entered the gym, I remembered the beginning, the day I had asked the owner of the fitness equipment store next door what he thought of Master Chang. He said simply, "He offers real martial arts instruction. Most places don't." More than two years of continuous training and countless competitions against other schools' students had convinced me that the storeowner was right. I was part of a training program that had no equal. As my training progressed, I became fascinated by the philosophical underpinnings of our style of martial art, traditional Tae Kwon Do. I learned everything I could about the principles of sustaining determination and focus, maintaining an unassuming demeanor, and constantly remaining attentive to my surroundings so as to better respond to any situation. [←*Shows his dedication to this hobby has a deeper, "philosophical" side.*] The milestones of my journey to my black belt were still vivid: my first sparring match, my first successful spinning heel kick, the first time one of the high-ranking students told me my technique looked good. With each new achievement my resolve to complete the journey grew stronger.

So, despite our anxieties, here we were, the seven students who had risen through the ranks together, steeling ourselves for the most arduous exhibition we had ever experienced: the black belt test. But as I listened to Master Chang count us through our 1,500-crunch warm-up a feeling of calm fell over me. I was experiencing a pivotal moment in my life, but I had been through such moments before. I recalled the day in June 1997 when I decided to leave Indian Institute of Technology Roorkee to gain a Western business education at University of Michigan. [*Use of flashback here shows Ashish's response to Stern's invitation to be creative.→*] I had enjoyed my year at IIT, from the academic awards in my first semester and the invitation to join a prominent student club to making several lifelong friends. University of Michigan's fit with my goals was inescapable, however: an entrepreneurial atmosphere in the American business environment coupled with a substantive natural resources & environment program that would enable me to build my own environmental consulting company after graduating. When Michigan offered me an expedited spot in the semester beginning in January, I knew what I had to do.

At 600 crunches, I ignored the pain in my abdominal muscles and remembered the summer vacations in Ann Arbor I had spent working at Musgrave Enviro Systems. [←*Effectively uses the stages of the 1,500-crunch warm-up exercise to work in self-revealing examples from different parts of his life.*] I decided to work for Musgrave, a local environmental consultancy, because it would give me a working knowledge of environmental consulting. At Musgrave I learned how to do work in an analytical laboratory and gained an understanding of wastewater treatment and solid waste management as well as familiarity with local environmental regulations. Moreover, I was able to interact with environmental consultants, engineers, concerned citizens, corporate executives, and government officials—the dramatis personae of the industry. Dealing personally with all of these individuals showed me what they were like, what their jobs demanded, and how they responded to inevitable changes and problems. This six-month apprenticeship became not only a foundation but also a prerequisite for my career with my startup, New Earth Services, a colloquium on the art and science of environmental consulting.

At 1,200 crunches the pain and fatigue were harder to ignore, but I focused on the day two years before when I had stood glowing triumphantly in a reclaimed greenfield site outside Flint, Michigan. As I waited for Bundy Motors' attorneys to arrive for the final handover ceremony I reflected on the deal about to crystallize, my most significant to date. The Environmental Protection Agency's ruling against Bundy had vindicated New Earth Services' study of the hazards posed by the old Bundy facility and opened the door for a public buy-out of the site for remediation as a public park. My in-depth analysis concluded that there was sufficient equity in the deal to turn a profit and cash out investors. The deal made headlines in the local press and doubled New Earth Services' business. Standing there scanning the early spring grass, I felt a surge of pride at my accomplishment.

At 1,500 crunches, it was time to leave my life's pivotal moments behind and face my latest one: Master Chang. In a grueling four-hour marathon we were required to perform every strike, block, form, and board break we had learned before finally sparring with multiple attackers. Both our physical and mental stamina were tested as we threw unremitting combinations of kicks and punches with little time to stop and regain equilibrium. When fatigue brought me to the verge of full collapse during a flurry of push-ups, I fixed my mind on the number "10"—the percentage of students who ultimately earned their black belts from Master Chang—and rode through the exhaustion.

Three weeks later Master Chang presented me with a black belt before the entire advanced class. My martial arts career has taught me the same lesson as my entrepreneurial environmental consulting career: with dedication and determination anything is attainable. Humble perseverance is superior to impulsive audacity. Cumulative action speaks louder than words. [←*Effectively draws distinctive and well-earned lessons from his moment of truth and triumph.*]

Self-Revelation Essay 2: Rohit V. (Admitted to Kellogg)

Essay Prompt. Outside of work I . . . (2–3 paragraphs)

Outside of work I began working as a volunteer for the non-profit Network of Indian Professionals two years ago (NetIP; www.netip.org). NetIP is dedicated to community service, philanthropy, professional and cultural development, and the overall advancement of South Asian-Americans and their communities. All money raised is donated to charitable organizations. After eight months, I was elected to the NetIP board in the capacity of Marketing Director. *[←Impressive level of responsibility deepens reader's interest.]* When I took on the position, the organization was struggling. Increasing competition from numerous smaller organizations led to a steady decline in our membership, and a few of our past events had gone over budget, leaving us with little money. As Marketing Director I had to devise an aggressive but inexpensive strategy to increase our membership. The statistics revealed that over the last two years almost 200 members had not renewed their membership; membership retention, it was clear, was a greater problem than member acquisition. With twenty people on the NetIP board of directors, I proposed that each board member personally call ten members and receive feedback about what was lacking in the organization. *[←Needs only two sentences to demonstrate strong analytical, team-leading, and problem-solving skills.]* The members felt that the organization's value additions did not justify the $40 dues.

I came up with a two-pronged plan to address our members' concerns. First, I identified the various value additions that would interest NetIP members, such as savings with local business and services, the expansion of professional and networking forums, and the enhancement of cultural and social events. Our members had a diverse array of professional backgrounds, ranging from surgeons to small business owners. I saw an opportunity for our organization to create symbiotic relationships: members would receive discounts for services and products offered by other members who, in turn, benefited from the increased awareness of their presence. I negotiated perks for our members with local businesses catering to the Indian community, and initiated a program offering reduced membership dues to members who provided discounts on their services. Seventy members agreed to offer discounts. I also partnered with two professional organizations in the Kansas City Area that conducted excellent seminars on diverse topics of interest to the community. This strategic alliance allowed us to increase the potential scale of participation, which in turn made possible the organization of bigger events that reduced the member cost per event. *[←Effectively exploits an essay question that most applicants devote to a hobby to show his high-impact community leadership.]* Increasing our membership base through improved value additions was only half the battle. Another major hurdle was the lack of active participation in the NetIP activities; after all, a networking dinner fails if only a handful of people show up. To spark event-participation, I came up with another aggressive marketing scheme. Understanding the importance of advertising with local newspapers and radio stations, I decided we should have a media budget, and delegated the responsibilities to another board member. On my suggestion we sent our members a monthly newsletter publicizing the success of our events and promoting forthcoming ones. I also invited members from our partner organizations to attend our events at a discount, targeting areas with which we had no previous contact, such as the Bay Area schools with a substantial South Asian presence. Within six months of assuming my post as Marketing Director, participation for NetIP events improved by 30% and membership retention increased by 25%. [←*Results provide icing on cake for an impressive series of innovative solutions.*]

Working for a non-profit organization gave me an opportunity to come up with creative ideas to benefit the organization and unify the community. It also helped me strengthen my leadership skills and realize the full potential of my talents and abilities. I am now more devoted to innovative and assertive strategies even when it means taking risks; pre-empting potential problems and solving old ones, I have learned, is possible only with proactive, not reactive, solutions.

Self-Revelation Essay 3: Claudia G. (Admitted to Columbia)

Essay Prompt. Please tell us about what you feel most passionate. (250-word limit)

Not a single day goes by without me pausing for five minutes in front of the Renzo Piano Building Workshop (www.rpwf.org) in Paris to stare in fascination at the wooden models of Piano's projects. [←*Choice of unusual topic immediately sets essay apart and intrigues reader.*] My passion for this Italian genius's architecture is so strong I even arrange my holidays so I can visit his latest realizations, like the Hermès headquarters in Tokyo with its earthquake-resistant glass-brick façade and the legendary Potsdamer Platz in Berlin.

I am fascinated by architecture because I was raised on a construction site. [←*Somewhat jarring image deepens reader's interest while showing Claudia's sense of humor.*] That is, my parents designed our home's plans themselves, so I spent most of my time navigating around the legs of construction workers, masons, and architects—and "helping" them when I could. It was from these early memories that I developed my taste for the art of architecture, my faith in and respect for human work, and my vision of becoming a "business architect," a builder of businesses, in my own right.

My first visit in 1999 to the steel temple of architecture that is New York City was like discovering the fourth dimension! [←*Use of vivid metaphor for New York, colorful word choice, and exclamation point create effective tone for this "passion" essay.*] I have a literal passion for the Chrysler and Woolworth buildings, which, like such modern structures as Portzampac's LVMH headquarters, are masterpieces that were also at architecture's leading edge in their day.

Studying in New York I will witness the unveiling of countless exciting projects, including the new World Trade Center (though I wish they had chosen the Gaudi plan) and, above all, the New York Times headquarters by Renzo Piano. And to think that Columbia Business School is only 100 blocks from Times Square! *[Nice use of humor to close essay.]*

Self-Revelation Essay 4: Mikiko U. (Admitted to Kellogg)

Essay Prompt. You have been selected as a member of the Kellogg Admissions Committee. Please provide a brief evaluative assessment of your file. (1–2 pages)

Based on Kellogg's general criteria for evaluating candidates, the following is an evaluation of my file (in the third person). Grades are assigned to each criterion of the evaluation.

a) Mikiko's academic record (Overall Grade: A). *[←Use of grades and lettered sections with bullets helps essay stand out.]*
   - Mikiko had a terrific academic record in high school. Not only did she rank twenty-ninth nationally in Japan's high school exam, her performance on a college entrance exam (top 1 percent) also qualified her for one of the country's top six schools (Waseda University).
   - Mikiko's undergraduate academic record reflects her reduced focus on scholastics as a result of her extracurricular obligations. In various years, she was college champion, team captain, and university runner-up in field hockey and represented her class teams in five other sports. Although Mikiko makes no excuses for her decision to focus her energies on extracurriculars, I think we can agree her undergraduate academic performance does not reflect what she would be capable of at Kellogg. *[←Effective damage control.]*
   - As a graduate business student, Mikiko had an excellent academic record (3.62 GPA), which reflects her ability to handle academically rigorous courses in subjects similar to Kellogg's offerings.

b) Performance on the Graduate Management Admissions Test and the quantitative aspects of the applicant's work experience (Overall Grade: A).
   - Mikiko took the GMAT in October 2002 and scored 690. Given that she had limited time to prepare for the GMAT because she was working two jobs (Nikkei Financial and NihonCredit.com) while raising a family, her performance is comparable to her outstanding 720 score when she last took the GMAT, in October 1999.
   - Mikiko not only has B.S. in finance; she has enjoyed success in very quantitatively oriented jobs throughout her career. Combined with her academic performance in high school, college, business school, and on the GMATs, this points to an unusually strong quantitative orientation.

c) Career Progress (Overall Grade: A)

- Mikiko's solid experience in the investment space—both in an established multibillion-dollar corporation and in an Internet startup—have given her a perspective that will prove extremely valuable to Kellogg's primarily marketing- and consulting-focused student body.

- At Nikkei Financial, Mikiko has assumed many roles—associate, consultant, consulting manager, and investment manager. They have enabled her to see the international finance industry from within one of the fiercest and most fleet-footed competitors in the industry. In her last five years at arguably Japan's fastest-growing bank, Mikiko has learned lessons not only in investment and financial services consulting but also about the importance of having a solid strategy, sound vision, a willingness to lead change, and the ability to move extremely rapidly in the finance space.

- Mikiko's experience with NihonCredit.com gave her valuable insights into the high-profile world of Internet startups. Researching for and writing the business plan gave her the opportunity to view and plan the business as a general manager as well as a finance expert. The process of approaching investors and presenting the business plan and prototype taught her critical lessons in the importance of compressed new product development and time-to-market cycles, having an expert and "branded" management team, and the unparalleled power that a high-quality professional network can offer a startup. [←*Substantive overview of lessons her career has taught her avoids vagueness of many self-evaluation essays.*]

d) Extracurricular activities and community involvement (Overall Grade: A).

- Mikiko excelled in field hockey, golf, and basketball at various levels in Japan, and she was also a member of the university field hockey team while at Portland State University. Finally, she led a cinema club while attending Waseda University (1999-2001). These involvements demonstrate that Mikiko is a team-oriented person who believes in being fully engaged in every aspect of her life.

- Similarly, Mikiko's community spiritedness is indicated by her volunteering to teach origami classes to kids at the local recreational club while she was at Eribasu Bank in 2001-2002. And in 2001 she volunteered to balance the books for a national golf tournament at the same club. In 2000 Mikiko joined Japanese Women Professionals in its founding stages (see my essay 2).

- Mikiko's community involvement seems to have waned after 2002, but this may be related to her job at Nikkei Financial, which literally required her to travel every week between 2001 and 2003; the birth of her daughter in 2002; and her involvement in her start-up NihonCredit.com in 2002. Still, since 2003 Mikiko has been continuing to do what she can by helping to lift about 85 orphans out of illiteracy through monthly contributions in her Japanese hometown. Mikiko's track record here is very creditable.

In summary, I believe Mikiko has the ambition, ability, perspective, and drive to perform exceptionally well at Kellogg. With the training and professional network Mikiko can gain here, her career will surely reach the heights she envisions. Admit. *[Uses meaty examples rather than hard-sell rhetoric to make compelling case for admission.]*

Self-Revelation Essay 5: Fernando M. (Admitted to Chicago)

Essay Prompt. If you could pick three guests for a formal dinner, who would they be and why would you choose them? (300 words)

I believe that Socrates, Khufu, and Sam Zell would make the most engaging dinner companions. *[←Finds a combination of dinner companions that he can be sure no other applicant has used.]*

Socrates, the father of philosophy, believed that through our relationships with others and dialectic conversation we reach higher levels of truth and innovation. Though philosophers such as Sartre and Descartes were inward-looking, mankind has clearly progressed through social relationships. I would converse with Socrates about the meaning of life and the virtues of friendship and integrity that we both believe are the drivers of happiness.

Khufu, the builder of the Great Pyramid, worked with over 2.3 million stone blocks weighing 2½ tons each but still came within seven inches of achieving a perfect square at the pyramid's base. As a builder myself, I would ask him about the processes he used to engineer, plan, and execute the world's second-largest man-made structure without computers, machinery, or electricity. His knowledge may help me execute my projects with some of the same genius evident in his work nearly 5,000 years ago.

Sam Zell, the pioneer of the modern real estate industry and founder and chairman of the world's two largest publicly traded REITs, had the foresight and initiative to bridge the gap between the old real estate methodologies and a unified global model of a more perfect market. Since 1991, 15 percent of all commercial real estate has been placed on the public markets. I want to accelerate the spread of this metamorphosis by developing and securitizing properties internationally. I would ask Mr. Zell what compelled him to visualize the future of the market, how he formed the world's largest REIT, and what he envisions as the next great trend. *[←Chooses figures whom he can connect to different aspects of his life.]*

These innovators' exchanges with each other would be even more stimulating than our individual conversations. Would Socrates question Sam Zell's prediction that a near-perfect real estate market is possible? What would Khufu think of the world today? How would Zell advise Khufu on his use of materials and capital? This would be a dinner to remember! *[←Excellent conclusion goes extra step by actually imagining how dinner mates might "mix it up."]*

Diversity Essay 1: Thomas S. *(Admitted to MIT Sloan)*

Essay Prompt. Sloan is a very diverse place with over 60 countries represented. What will you bring to this diverse community? What do you expect to gain from the environment? (500 words)

Eating a hard-boiled egg at the summit of Mount Fuji requires a daring palate and the good sense to pinch your nose ever so lightly, to avoid being overwhelmed by the sulfuric odor from the area's indigenous hot springs. *[Highly vivid and unusual lead-in captures reader's attention.]* This odoriferous treat was my parent's idea of rewarding their 10-year-old for not complaining during a seven-hour ascent to the revered volcano's crater. I was of course most interested in my father's walking stick, branded with a dozen different Kanji inscriptions announcing the waypoints along our route. The walking stick remains a metaphor for my continuing journey to embrace international cultures and new experiences. This journey will accelerate as I forge relationships with Sloan classmates from diverse cultures and professions, sharing my passion to understand the viewpoints of others.

My open-minded approach to new ideas is in large part due to my international upbringing as a US Army brat, and my parents' efforts to expose my brother and me to the cuisine, customs, and philosophies of other cultures. While many Camp Zama residents succumbed early to "island fever," my parents were busy seeking exotic groceries and Indian spices, all the while looking for new students for their evening English school. Several nights a week, their students took over our living room, while my brother and I grew closer to their children, learning about Manga, Anime, and Tamiya auto and robot model kits. *[Continual use of vivid details makes essay come alive and projects Thomas's personality.]*

As a pre-teen in Heidelberg, Germany, I looked beyond our family's monthly Volksmarch to immerse myself in European culture. At a Boy Scout Jamboree in France in 1985 I first experienced linguistic helplessness as the guest of a Parisian family. Armed with a two-way dictionary, I tried in vain to explain that my faith prevented me from eating beef, resorting to charades involving cow sounds. This experience prompted me to enroll in my first French class, determined to achieve perfect pronunciation and accent. Now I can speak more languages than I can program, and in most cases, can appreciate their subtle emotions and humor. *[Engaging use of humor allows Thomas to "show off" his impressive multicultural profile without seeming boastful.]*

Later, my multicultural upbringing helped me to meet the challenges I faced as a naval officer. When one of my deputies was mistakenly accused of harassing a sailor in our division, my investigation revealed that he was in fact attempting to motivate and prepare a promising fellow Philippine-American for an accelerated promotion. In my role as a mediator, I tactfully guided him towards a gentler and subtler mentorship approach.

My success in promoting cross-functional teams earned me membership on the NSA's Cultural Diversity Council. With unprecedented access to the NSA Director, I led efforts to overhaul an unpopular personnel assignment process that affected nearly 5000 fellow military service members. My cultural sensitivity has also helped me in my consulting work in an increasingly global and competitive business environment.

Sloan's multinational and multicultural focus will allow me to apply my cultural diversity towards achieving my career goals. Product management requires a measured and careful balance of many equally important inputs and perspectives. At Sloan and beyond, this learned ability will help me to remain open-minded and embrace ideas from cultures and professions with which I have less experience. Just as the marks on my father's walking stick represented distinct segments of our journey up Mount Fuji, my classes at Sloan and the many connections I will forge with my classmates and professors are clearly defined steps along the route to reaching my goals. *[Nice conflation of opening walking-stick metaphor with closing school-specific takeaway statement.]*

Diversity Essay 2: Sandeep J. (Admitted to Columbia)

Essay Prompt. "What does it mean to you to live in a global community?" (350 words)

In 2003, when I began a three-month internship for Wipro Chemicals in Porter, Alabama, my assumption was that the racial discrimination I had seen in movies like *Mississippi Burning* was a thing of the past.

My job consisted in testing fine-powder chemical distillates used in house and car paint manufacture. My three teammates, three amazing black women in their 40s named Belle, Janice, and Katie, immediately adopted me, bathing me in their Southern hospitality. They always generously offered to share their lunches with me, and once Janice even invited me to her Baptist church. I was stunned at how simple it was to fit in and how naturally these warm people came to each other.

One day, as our "black team," so-named because as we worked our faces were always covered by black selenium powder, was having lunch, a white employee came up to me and said with a smile: "Do not feel obliged to lunch with 'em niggers." There was evil there, and I had not seen it. Stunned and disgusted, all I could do was utter a clumsy "I will think over it" and remain seated, sharing my food with my friends in silence. In that moment, I felt that there is nothing as important as brotherhood and community, even if that community must be formed through adversity. The next day, Janice and I visited Porter College and paused in front of the statue of its founder, who was also a famous segregationist. My hands-on education had begun. *[Effectively conveys powerful details through deft story-telling and vivid revelations of his feelings.]*

What threatens our global community most is intolerance, and we must never stop fighting it. In my country, fifty years after independence from British colonial rule, religious intolerance between Hindus and Muslims still hinders good relationships with our Pakistani neighbors. Visiting Russia with an Indian friend in 1999 I was struck by the way the average Russian person looked at us with curiosity but no warmth (except for Moscow students who wanted to tell us about the fall of the Soviet Union). Back in India, I learned that despite the close ties between the USSR and India from the 50s through the 80s, Russian people consider Indians to be indistinguishable from Afghanistanis and Chechens, two recent enemies. Although it was a relief to discover that India and South Asia did not have a monopoly on racism, I also saw how challenging it will be for all of us to finally achieve our global community. *[Skillfully broadens focus of essay's first story to encompass other stories that reinforce his tolerant, global outlook.]*

Leadership and Teamwork Essay 1: Tim S. (Admitted to Wharton)

Essay Prompt. At Wharton, the Learning Team, which consists of approximately five first year students, is often assigned group projects and class presentations. Imagine that, one year from now, your Learning Team has a marketing class assignment due at 9:00 a.m. Monday morning. It is 10:00 p.m. on Sunday night; time is short, tension builds and your team has reached an impasse. What role would you take in such a situation? How would you enable the team to meet your deadline? (Note: The specific nature of the assignment is not as important here as the team dynamic.) Feel free to draw on previous experience, if applicable, to illustrate your approach. (3 pages, 1,000 words)

I have shared rooms with people from many cultures and countries, from China to Germany and the United States, and worked with people from Italy, Venezuela, Australia, Sierra Leone, India, and Canada. Through them, I have gained a nuanced understanding of the dynamics of multicultural groups like Wharton's Learning Teams. In a team environment, I normally play a very flexible role, either following if someone else has a better knowledge of the subject matter or leading if I am an expert on the topic. If the topic is new to me, I am not afraid to ask questions to bring myself up to speed, and if I am an expert, I offer my expertise to my teammates and bring them up to speed. When we reach an impasse, I tend to step up and take the role of mediator and facilitator.

To help my Learning Team achieve its goal, my top priority will be to ensure that team members stay focused and do not vent their frustrations by "slinging mud." *[Works in personal examples to back up his teamwork claims.→]* At Capital Consulting, we routinely face extreme time pressures for meeting deadlines for client deliverables. More often than not, the strategy team and the implementation team will disagree about the customer's engagement requirements.

During one such situation, our strategy lead started blaming the implementation manager for not allocating enough resources to meet the next engagement phase on time. As the implementation lead, I quickly responded by asking her not to point fingers and to focus instead on the issue at hand. The immediate question was "What can we achieve with the consultants we have available?" not "Why don't we have more consultants?" or "Who is responsible for misallocating staff resources?" Everybody in the meeting agreed with me, and the discussion was immediately brought back on track.

I would also help my Learning Team by preparing a list of the topics that are absolutely essential for the assignment and then make sure that our discussions stay within the scope of those topics. This would enable us to avoid spending time on issues that are not really relevant and can be deferred. This approach has been successful for me in the past. While setting up a square-dancing club, Two-Steppers, for example, one of my partners insisted during one of our meetings that we needed to rent a larger hall in case our membership spiked. *[←Effectively pulls examples from different parts of his life.]* I pointed out that our current hall was adequate for our current needs and that I could not envision any scenario in which our membership would leap so quickly that we wouldn't have time to find a new hall. As the discussion dragged on, I realized that our time could be better utilized by discussing other important topics—like letting everyone know about the next dance. I proposed that we defer the decision since we didn't need a new hall to plan for next month's dance. All my partners quickly accepted the proposal, and we moved on to other important matters affecting the club.

Since the success of multicultural teams such as Wharton's Learning Teams depends on the active participation of all their members, I will make sure that all my team members participate in the discussion and express their opinions fully. One member of our team at Capital Consulting, Juan Encarnacion, is extremely bright but is not a native English speaker. I noticed that he was awfully quiet in meetings but in private would offer great ideas for solving problems and implementing added client requirements. To make sure he shared those ideas with everyone, during meetings I began asking him questions about topics I knew he had strong opinions about. As soon as he realized that everyone valued his insights Juan lost his inhibitions and is now an active participant in our meetings.

I would also ensure that my Learning Team's discussions remain enjoyable and that team members do not lose their sense of humor. By offering a mild wisecrack here and there, I make sure the meetings I am involved in at Capital Consulting remain lively yet focused. At the same time, I also understand the importance of not overdoing it and know how to quickly bring everybody's attention back to the main topic when humor ceases to serve the purposes of the team.

Finally, my Learning Team will face the challenge of keeping personality conflicts out of the discussion so each idea can be evaluated purely on its merits.

My experience at Capital Consulting is relevant here as well. For example, while attending client requirements meetings for Capital Consulting's largest client, I noticed that our two engagement managers always tried to shoot down each other's ideas for synchronizing the two phases of the engagement. To address this personality conflict I initiated the practice of gathering together all the team members' ideas at the beginning of the meeting, and then listing the pros and cons of each. I also urged each participant to support his or her idea by identifying the priority that our client gave to each phase and how our client would be affected if phase 1 completed before phase 2 and vice versa. This structured approach kept the discussion focused on the merits and demerits of the phases and their implications for the client—not on personalities.

[*Note that Tim only focuses on presenting a solution to the essay's hypothetical premise after he has introduced several personal examples.*] To enable my Learning Team to meet the deadline, I will draw up a list of the main issues and invite everybody to provide their input on simply identifying what the team's main objective should be. I will gently emphasize how important it is that we restrict all the discussions to the scope of the objective we have defined and make sure that everybody is on the same page. I will then proceed to ask for everybody's input on generating a step-by-step solution and work to build consensus after each step. I understand that at times consensus is hard to find. When that's the case, I will seek out some common ground and provide a solution based on that shared understanding. In short, I will use my personality as a consensus-seeking team player who has years of experience working with—and leading—multicultural teams to make sure my Learning Team achieves its goals and finishes the assignment with the active and focused participation of all its members.

Leadership and Teamwork Essay 2: Hysam B. (Admitted to NYU Stern)

Essay Prompt. "The ultimate measure of a man is not where he stands in moments of comfort and convenience, but where he stands at times of challenge and controversy."—MLK Jr. In your professional experience, describe a situation where you demonstrated leadership, relating it to the quote above. (2 pages)

As I passed Cliff in the hall he smiled and asked me whether I was excited to be the in-charge on the revenue tax checklists and the pricing testing for Deenen Lowe Funds, our largest Houston mutual fund client. We both knew the answer: Very. Throughout 1999 Cliff had been my in-charge for this client, but my performance over the past year had earned me his confidence as well as Amit's, the senior manager. My new role was to supervise two first-year associates, Shantel and Serge, in the price testing and the tax checklist for 12 mutual funds, representing billions of dollars in assets, while I completed the other audit work for two of those funds. It was the kind of challenge of my leadership skills that

Martin Luther King Jr. knew so well. [←*Refers back to MLK quote to signal that his response will answer Stern's question.*]

Auditing is a profession that you learn by doing, and Shantel needed to learn how to price and obtain descriptive data on equities, bonds, futures, and foreign currencies through hands-on work. I had enjoyed price testing, but Shantel was more interested in our technology clients, and she admitted to me and Cliff that she was anxious about taking a high-profile role on a client and industry she didn't know. So my first challenge was convincing her that she could come to me and I would help her find the price on any security she had trouble with. To motivate her, I also told her that even if she had little interest in mutual funds, she would draw on what she was learning here for the rest of her life. [←*Keeps focus on human dynamics.*]

A misstated price for any of the funds' many securities represents one of the biggest risks in an audit because investors might not buy or sell shares at a fund's true value. Although Master Funds had proprietary software that sped up the process of re-pricing securities, the work of following up on exceptions rested with Shantel and me. After teaching Shantel how to use Bloomberg, she had the technical knowledge necessary to re-price most of the funds' securities. However, for certain securities, particularly bonds, Shantel had to do intensive research, cope with informational dead ends, and use a drastically less technical, more interpersonal method for obtaining prices: the telephone. [←*Humor helps.*] At first Shantel was reluctant to call third-party traders because many of them were less than enthusiastic about helping someone who was not a client. I specifically reassured Shantel that if she kept trying the traders would eventually help. [←*Walks reader through actual manner in which he leads rather than just asserting it.*]

Between my new role supervising Shantel and performing the other audit work I was responsible for, I was feeling the pressure mount as Monica and Cliff sought daily updates and our deadline steadily approached. With only a few days to go, I remained calm, however, because Shantel had responded well to my encouragement and was becoming comfortable in her knowledge of the client and the industry. A day or so before the deadline I walked into the audit room and saw Shantel proudly wave the last outstanding confirmation at me. We not only finished ahead of schedule, but as the deadlines for the other parts of the engagement neared, people sought out Shantel's newfound Bloomberg skills for answers and information.

Much like Shantel, Serge had to learn the intricacies of mutual fund tax laws through hands-on work, with managers waiting and unyielding deadlines approaching. At first, Serge seemed the ideal pupil. He was extremely inquisitive, and though he was inexperienced with mutual fund clients, he shared my enthusiasm not only for mutual funds but also for the securities and the derivatives they invested in. Given that interest and the fact that the tax checklists were more straightforward than Shantel's work, I was surprised to discover that with the deadline for submitting the first checklists only a week away, Serge had fallen behind. I asked Serge what he thought was causing the delay, and he explained that the client's tax department was struggling with their new accounting system. With many of the supporting tax schedules missing, Serge worried that we might miss our first deadline. A process that I thought was going smoothly had thrown me another challenge. I had a feeling of déjà vu because a year earlier I had been in the same boat when my first deadline approached. From that experience I knew that completing the first set of tax checklists involved a steep learning curve, but subsequent checklists would go much faster. I reassured Serge and sat down to give him a thorough explanation of mutual fund tax law so he would have the knowledge to hit the ground running when we did receive the delayed schedules. By staying late to mentor Serge and shorten his learning curve, I ensured that we met our deadline. *[Blow-by-blow narrative style doesn't grow old because Hysam stays focused on the interpersonal not the impersonal.]*

As the engagement wound down, I caught my breath and smiled to myself over the events of the past five weeks. I was not so much relieved that I had dodged a bullet as gratified at how much I had learned in managing two crucial responsibilities at the same time. I had been placed in a situation in which the expectations of the partner, the senior manager, and Cliff were quite high. It would have been convenient for me to use my experience from the year before to complete the tax checklists or handle the price testing myself, but I wanted to be challenged and grow professionally. More important, I wanted to challenge Shantel and Serge so they would grow professionally. In doing so, I learned that demonstrating patience and sharing one's own knowledge are powerful tools for motivating people. I believe they are lessons Dr. King would have appreciated. *[←Nice understated conclusion to personable essay doesn't overstate MLK parallel.]*

Failure Essay 1: Connie K. (Admitted to Columbia)

Essay Prompt. If you could change one decision you have made, what would it be and why? (500 words)

"I need a million clients, Connie. Under one million clients, and I will be ridiculous in front of my shareholders." *[←Use of quotation puts reader in the middle of action with the story already under way.]* Only six months after joining Inforte Consulting, I was given the strategic assignment of determining whether a major telecom operator should use local loop unbundling (LLU) to enter the broadband market. My task would be to make the assumptions, gather the market data, and prepare a business case supporting the client's decision to invest in the roll-out of an LLU product.

Tough government regulations combined with LLU's immaturity as a technology made the business plan equation very tricky. It was also complex: the client was proposing to enter three separate markets (residential, small-and-medium enterprises, and corporate accounts) with three different telecom offerings (numeric voice, fast Internet, and video-on-demand). To manage this complexity, I developed a scenario-based approach that simulated the impact of various possible client decisions on market share, profitability, and return on investment.

The business plan was the most terrifying Excel model I have ever built! [←*Candid disclosure of emotions always effective.*] In the best-case scenario, our client could not reach profitability before 2006 with only 400,000 subscribers. Considering the level of risk, Inforte recommended based on my findings that the client wait before entering the LLU market.

Within hours the client's broadband program manager was on the offensive. He was convinced that his company could attract at least 200,000 more subscribers and achieve profitability one year before my rosiest analysis. My assumptions were "too conservative," he said; his shareholders needed "more attractive" numbers. Although I was a mere first-year strategy consultant, I stood my ground. The best-case scenario could not be "improved" unless we artificially increased LLU's rate of penetration in the short-term.

I tried to document all my assumptions but, because of the client's approaching meeting with its shareholders, my partners said it was too late. Still, I stuck to my findings, but my partners declared that my six months of business experience did not give me the knowledge to intervene in a strategic assignment involving a multi-million-euro investment. After two days and two restless nights, I finally surrendered. I would submit the plan the client wanted provided I could get out of the assignment. My partners accepted. For days I felt like someone with a bad hangover. [*Vividly captures emotional pressure of difficult moment, keeping reader's interest.*]

Two months later, the client's board decided not to launch the LLU product because the assumptions the broadband manager had insisted on were too optimistic! My "hangover" returned with a vengeance. Returning to my original report, I gave them the figures I had believed in all along.

This experience taught me that you must stick to what you know is true. Though I was ashamed at my decision to boost the figures, ultimately both the client and the marketplace vindicated my business sense. It took three years for the regulatory conditions to improve and the LLU technology to mature. When it did, the same client called me back to implement the LLU project. Today, I am the engagement manager on this project, which launches this January.

Failure Essay 2: Tun-jen L. (Admitted to INSEAD)

Essay Prompt. Describe a situation taken from school, business, civil or military life, where you did not meet your personal objectives, and discuss briefly the effect. (20 lines, 300 to 350 words)

The moment remains so vivid: the crutches, the colonel's office, the train ride home, and the weeks of soul searching that followed. [←*Use of specific images pulls reader into essay.*] The day I lost my military aspirations I had to face the fact that I had failed to meet strongly set personal objectives. I felt an emptiness I had never known before.

All Taiwanese males have to fulfil their military obligations, but only volunteers can seek to join the elite Special Forces Corps. During its gruelling three-week selection process, 30 percent of recruits are either rejected or willingly leave. There I was fresh out of college, surrounded by 40 highly motivated young recruits hailing from every part of Taiwan, and stationed in a remote Yu Shan (Mount Jade) barracks. The only one with a college education, I often thought I wouldn't make it. But I did make it, and from that proud moment on I never looked back. I went on to finish boot camp and became one of only 5 out of 40 recruits selected for Non-Commissioned Officer College. Once again I volunteered to go.

I rose to corporal and became an instructor for 12 recruits. I learned the meaning of responsibility, the value of team spirit, and the challenge of maintaining high morale in the toughest environment. But most importantly, I learned what leadership really was. I truly enjoyed the disciplined military environment and I gave it my all, pushing hard to rise to lieutenant. My efforts were rewarded when I became the only one of the 40 original initial recruits to attend Officer Candidate School. It was what I had been waiting for. [*Tun-jen's extended narrative of success builds tension because reader knows disappointment is coming.*]

I was proud to wear the uniform of an aspiring officer and to be close to fulfilling the objectives I had set myself. Then in an instant it all ended. During a seemingly innocuous T'ai chi ch'uan match I fractured my left foot, tearing the ligaments in my ankle. My military career and hopes of becoming an officer were ended. I have matured a great deal in the two years since then. The experience taught me to accept and learn from my failures, but also to seek another path where I could commit my leadership as passionately. I am on that path today. [←*Makes sure not to end essay on negative note.*]

Ethics Essay 1: Robert Y. (Admitted to Wharton)

Essay Prompt. Describe a situation where your values, ethics or morals were challenged. How did you handle the situation? (500 words)

Sue smiled as she offered me the completed structural reactions answer set. "I aced the same course last quarter," she beamed. An ardent Tennessee Volunteers' fan as well as my dorm's RA, Sue had responded to my complaint about my unfinished problem set, due the next day, by suddenly vanishing from the room. As I reflected on the exhausting NCAA finals tournament trip that was now forcing me to contemplate an all-nighter, Sue reappeared, holding a guaranteed "A." [*Opening paragraph sets up ethical challenge, then Robert breaks away to fill in the background story.→*]

I had heard stories about unfair academic advantages given to college athletes, but until that moment I had remained naïve about them. Because Tennessee is on the Honor System, the responsibility for maintaining the integrity of one's academic work lies entirely with the student. I never worried about ethical violations because I knew I could never ask someone to help me cheat on a test or assignment. "Stand up for what is right," my dad has always said, "even if you're standing alone." Then he would smile and say, "It's lonely at the top!"

Adjusting to the academic rigors of a top-tier university was a challenge, but when I earned a spot as a walk-on basketball player my freshman year, "challenge" took on a whole new meaning. The grueling three-hour practices, countless hours of game-film study, and long road trips all seemed a small price to pay, however, when we earned a top seed in the 1999 NCAA Division I Men's Basketball Tournament. We were good, and made it all the way to the Final Four in Denver. It was an incredible experience, from the police escorts and media events to the thousands of fans. Despite our yearlong dedication, we lost the semifinal game in overtime. Devastation does not begin to describe the mood on our flight back to Tennessee. [*After dramatically describing setback, Robert deftly returns to opening scene.→*]

It was that devastation and exhaustion that Sue heard in my voice as she stopped by to ask how I was doing. I mentioned my problem set in passing, and 10 minutes later she was offering me my first taste of the ethical temptations even the most scrupulous college athletes will face. My first thoughts were "no one would know" and "she approached me, right?" Clearly, my usual sound judgment was still clouded by the vivid memory of that scoreboard back in Denver: Tennessee 82, Oregon 83. But I also felt an overwhelming annoyance that Sue felt I should be treated like a "dumb jock". [*←Effective pivot from considering temptation to rejecting it.*] As a walk-on, I had earned my Tennessee acceptance letter just as much as she had! Besides, I wasn't the only person whose honor was at stake. I represented not only the Tennessee men's basketball team but all collegiate athletes. I refused to tarnish the legacy of those who played before me.

In a perfect world my story would end with an all-nighter in the library and a brilliant score on my problem set. Well, my world was far from perfect that day, and I went straight to bed. I woke up at 6 am and barely managed to complete the problem in time. It's the only "C-" I've ever been proud of.

4

The Required Optional Essay

When is a good time to write an optional essay? Always. Everybody has an interesting story. I love to see what people choose.

—Dawna Clarke,
University of Virginia (Darden)

For most applicants the optional essay is either an afterthought glibly tossed off or a dreaded challenge to defend the indefensible. The deceptive little word *optional* accounts for the first misperception, and the second stems from the optional essay's traditional role as the place where you explain your F in freshman-year calculus, those six glaring months between jobs, or the reasons why your supervisor won't write a recommendation letter even though he's your biggest fan.

Admissions officials are all over the map when it comes to the advisability of submitting the optional essay. Some love them; others speak of them with thinly veiled impatience. Ultimately, it's you who must decide whether adding yet one more essay to the adcom's heap will put you over the top or transform sympathy into exasperation.

WHAT THE SCHOOLS ASK

Almost every business school today allows applicants to submit an optional essay or at least "additional information" of some kind. In fact, a great many

129

business schools provide the same instructions, a variation on, "Is there any further information that you wish to provide to the Admissions Committee?" Since such open-ended wording invites abuse, schools like Cornell (Johnson) pointedly add "This essay is for clarification purposes only."

In the Schools' Words—

I would caution you to limit it to stuff that truly adds to your application. Too much additional information might not be viewed in a positive light, as we really do read all of the applications! I would use the optional essay if needed, but try to avoid too much information that is not requested.

—Pete Johnson,
University California Berkeley (Haas)

Some schools narrow the focus by hinting darkly that you should address "aberrations," "areas of concern," "extenuating circumstances," or "aspects that need explanation." A smaller subset steers you toward specific topics that they want to hear about if they're relevant to you. For example, NYU Stern invites you to explain why you haven't submitted a letter of recommendation from a current supervisor, George Washington asks you to "explain any academic inconsistencies," and Wharton helpfully offers a grab bag of possible topics: "unexplained gaps in work experience, choice of recommenders, inconsistent academic performance, significant weaknesses in your application."

But the typical business school's optional essay remains an extremely open-ended invitation to talk about exactly what you want to:

■ "Additional information that will highlight unique aspects of your candidacy . . ."

■ "Background information you would like the admissions committee to take into consideration . . ."

■ "Anything else you would like the Admissions Committee to know . . ."

Because business schools range from discouraging optional essays to positively welcoming them, your decision whether to submit one will need to be highly school-specific.

TO WRITE OR NOT TO WRITE?

The bottom-line question is: should you write an optional essay? Though 60 to 70 percent of all Michigan State applicants submit optional essays, at schools like Dartmouth (Tuck) and UC Berkeley (Haas) only about half do. And it's a good bet that of those who don't, the majority view optional essays as strictly for applicants with "excuses" to give—about grades, test scores, or missing recommendations. Blessedly free of these negatives and already thoroughly sick of essay writing, these applicants probably don't give the optional essay another thought. This argument has appeal. If applicants are tired of writing essays, imagine how admissions officers must feel about reading them. Why throw away the goodwill you've carefully built up over four required essays by exhausting their patience with a fifth?

That's the "don't write" argument. But as the title of this chapter suggests, there's another, more positive case to be made for writing the optional essay. First, banish the thought that optional essays are only for "extenuating circumstances." The number of schools that hold to that narrow definition is greatly outnumbered by those whose instructions welcome "any other information" you care to give. As for the argument that the optional essay will only turn an impatient and bleary-eyed reader against you, the truth is it might—but only if you write a rambling, off-the-cuff, valueless porridge of an essay. The tired-admissions-officer argument is not a reason to avoid submitting an optional essay, just an ineffective one. Committees may be overworked, but they're also professionals who like nothing more than discovering qualified and distinctive applicants who match their school's culture. It's by deepening their confidence in your possession of all three of these qualities—ability, uniqueness, and "fit"— that the optional essay can do you a world of good.

So, should you write one? The answer is—it depends on whether the school's required essays have allowed you to project all your themes and stories, on whether the school's optional essay is the restrictive "clarification only" type or the broad "any other information" type, and on whether you truly have one more insightful essay left in you to write. The optional essay invites you to look at your candidacy in the clear, bracing light of reality. You may in fact not have one more revealing and distinctive story, and that's OK. If you don't, admit it, and don't rub the committees the wrong way with something dull or unfocused.

In the Schools' Words—

Quite a few applicants do submit an optional essay either to explain something on their application or to strengthen their application by showing us a different side to them.

—Go Yoshida, University of Chicago

The more selective the school, the greater should be your presumption that you do indeed have more to tell. Taking these schools up on their offer to skip the optional essay may send the unprepossessing message that you have only a limited number of accomplishments or distinctive experiences to share. Submitting a (good) optional essay sends the opposite message: "There's more where this came from. I've done a lot!" If you're top-20 B-school material, you really ought to have new and important material to add. In risk/reward terms, the potential downside of writing an optional essay is greatly outweighed by the upside of submitting an essay that adds one more compelling new component to your profile.

Finally, just as visiting the campus a second time communicates your intense interest in a school, so too the optional essay signals that you are willing to expend extra effort to win admission. After plowing through dozens of applications that seem casually tossed off, or, worse, don't even bother to get the school's name right, your extra effort will help you stand out from the pack. View the optional essay then for what it is, the business schools' sincere effort to ensure that they've given you every opportunity to communicate your full story. It's an invitation to strengthen your application, not weaken it. So take it.

WHAT SHOULD YOU WRITE ABOUT?

As we've seen, there are two basic categories for optional essays—the bad and the good. The bad encompasses all the "clarification" and "extenuating circumstances" topics; the kinds of things you're likely to discuss only because failing to will raise admissions officers' suspicions. The good is everything else—the purely discretionary topics that you choose because they will tell the schools something new and important.

Whichever category you choose, remember that it's only human nature for the readers to approach your optional essay with slightly less gusto than they read your first, so be as direct and concise as possible. Since you are giving them an unrequired essay on an "invitation-only" basis, you should spend at least as much time on it as on a required essay. The added quality you give it can resuscitate the readers' waning attention and overcome their natural skepticism about an "extra" essay.

The Fine Art of Damage Control

Allaying admissions officers' concerns about curiosities or weaknesses in your application is the most common use of the optional essay. With the exception of failure essays, no other essay invites you to reflect so intently on your weaknesses. Since the obvious goal of a successful application is to project the positive, you should try to keep your excuse or explanation for a negative out of your optional essay and slip it instead into a data sheet in the application or in passing as a small part of another essay. Why? First, using the optional essay to explain a negative draws attention to it, so you want to use the optional essay only for occasions when the negative will automatically draw the reader's eye and when your explanation for it can't just be unobtrusively tucked somewhere else. Second, the optional essay is almost always the last essay, and you don't want the reader to leave your application chewing on an excuse or a negative.

If an explanation is necessary and you can't squeeze it in somewhere else, the optional essay is a legitimate place to air a negative. But even here, you want to conclude the essay with an example or two that show that you have overcome or are overcoming the negative, whether it's a low GPA, an employment gap, or, heaven forbid, a criminal conviction. In other words, it's not enough to explain negatives in optional essays. You must also show recovery.

The two most common ways of doing damage control are (1) making the case, with evidence, that what appears to be a weakness really isn't, and (2) acknowledging the weakness but building the case that you've grown past it. Personal hardship is perhaps the most effective single explanation for application weaknesses. If such factors legitimately explain your application's blemish, then you should devote an optional essay to them. Convincingly explaining such hardships may not only get you admitted; with some schools they may also earn you a scholarship.

Sample essays 2 and 4 at the end of this chapter effectively explain away application negatives by discussing extenuating circumstances with maturity and concision. As Mohamed E. and Peter J.'s essays show, the difference between a weak explanation and a compelling one is more than fancy wording. If your reason for botching the GMAT is flimsy, don't expect nimble-footed prose to gloss it over. Better to avoid the optional essay altogether. In contrast, if your reasons reflect complex factors or circumstances beyond your control, you should exploit the opportunity that the optional essay offers you.

For damage-control optional essays, brevity is most definitely the soul of wit. Short essays of one hundred to three hundred words will often discuss most application blemishes in all the detail that's likely to do you any good. Get in and get out fast.

GMAT Scores

There are really only two explanations for low GMAT scores that carry weight with admissions committees. The first is that some extraordinary circumstance occurred just before or during the test session itself that unfairly affected your performance. Such circumstances can range from the obvious—your spouse was hospitalized the night before, an auto accident on the way to the test center—to the borderline: you weren't feeling well during the exam, the testing environment was noisy or too hot or cold, or you weren't able to concentrate for some concrete reason. Since the marginal explanations can conceivably be made by anyone and are difficult to substantiate, you should think twice about mentioning them in your optional essay.

Other iffy explanations—for example, you were working too hard supporting your sick mother to afford a Kaplan GMAT prep course—can, if true, serve as optional essay topics, but don't expect the committee to give them much weight. In describing such extraordinary circumstances your tone should be direct and unemotional—avoid woe-is-me dramatics. And don't belabor them with excessive detail.

The second legitimate explanation for low GMAT scores is that there has always been a disconnect between your standardized tests scores and your academic performance. If true, this may indicate that you are a member of that small minority whose intellectual aptitude is simply not accurately measured by tests like the GMAT, GRE, or SAT. Note that this "outlier" defense will work only if you can point to a clear pattern of standardized test scores that seem to bear no relation to your high grades. For example, you scored a cumulative 900 on your SATs but were in the National Honor Society and class valedictorian.

Both these explanations apply to very few applicants, and if you aren't obviously one of them, you should not address your GMAT scores in your optional essay. Most important, just because you are disappointed with your GMAT score doesn't mean you should devote your optional essay to explaining it. If you got a 680 and the school's median is 700, don't bother.

Optional essays about GMAT scores should never consist only of your explanation for the score. They should include a positive and specific case that the disappointing scores are either unindicative of your real abilities or that you have already taken steps to offset the doubts they raise.

Poor Grades

Many applicants think they should use the optional essays to do "damage control" on the lone C they suffered in freshman-year basket weaving. The truth is that these minor lapses are too trivial to waste space on. If the cause of your GPA lapse was brief and the result of a specific situation (a strange grading policy, for example), then state this in one or two sentences in an addendum to the school's data sheet, and avoid the optional essay altogether. Grade-focused optional essays should be limited to scenarios like the following:

- A string of Fs and Ds during a bad semester or two or in core business courses.

- A lower GPA in your last two years than in your first.

- A bell-shaped GPA curve, in which your strongest grades came in your sophomore and junior years.

■ A lower GPA in graduate course work in comparison to your undergraduate years.

What explanations for poor grades carry weight? A weak but all-too-common one is the "lack of focus" argument. This only begs the question—why did you lack focus? It's one thing if you struggled because you're the first person in your family to go to college and simply needed time to adjust. It's quite another if you devoted your freshman year to becoming your fraternity's unofficial kegger king.

The best explanations emphasize concrete factors, preferably those outside your control. If you had unusual and unavoidable family obligations or had to work full time to self-fund your education (as Peter J. did in sample essay 4), admissions officers will surely cut you some slack. Even factors over which you had control can sometimes constitute persuasive explanations. The defense that you viewed college as an opportunity to grow and gain leadership experience through unusually deep extracurricular commitments can work if your extracurricular involvements were, in fact, substantial, sustained, and atypically broad. Use specific numbers to demonstrate your level of commitment.

Whatever your reasons may be, explain them succinctly, objectively, and maturely. In any event, take responsibility, and draw a lesson from the episode: "I learned that I must better balance my outside commitments and study." The first explanatory part of your essay should be equaled or exceeded in length by your positive statement about the things you've been doing since that make a repeat of this scenario unlikely. Give examples that show how you have developed better discipline and a responsible attitude toward work and school, such as the rising GPA and dual degrees that Peter J. earned as he learned how to juggle work and study (sample essay 4). If the problem was time management (as it was for Peter), consider discussing recent time management feats, such as juggling a full-time job and a master's program.

No Recommendation from Current Supervisor

Many schools recommend that you explain why you have chosen to omit a recommendation letter from your current supervisor. This is not an application weakness in the same sense as poor grades or test scores. The schools simply want assurance that it is not because your supervisor has a low opinion of you.

Most applicants omit a letter from a current supervisor because they don't want to jeopardize their chance for advancement if no business school admits them. Luckily, business schools fully appreciate the delicacy of this situation, and if you've been with your current employer for under a year, an enthusiastic letter from your previous supervisor is an acceptable alternative. In this case, you need not devote your optional essay to explaining. Just insert a two-sentence note in your application stating that you're submitting a recommendation from your previous manager instead. This frees you to devote the optional essay to more valuable and relevant information.

Another acceptable reason for omitting a letter from a current supervisor is that you are self-employed or work for a family business (letters from family members don't carry much weight). In these cases, inform the school that you are submitting letters from clients, colleagues, or vendors who can comment authoritatively on your candidacy. If you're unemployed, devote the lion's share of the essay to what you've been doing during your time between jobs.

What if the real reason you've omitted a letter from your current supervisor is that you're unsure he or she would be enthusiastic? Simply inform the school that the recommenders you are using are exceptionally well qualified to comment on your performance and potential and back this up with evidence—and leave it at that.

Employment Gaps and Weak Extracurriculars

Admittedly, it's hard to spin current unemployment in a positive way, but the circumstances behind your jobless situation can have a mitigating effect and should usually be explained. For most schools, joblessness of under, say, two months need not be given the full treatment of an optional essay. If you were terminated for cause, there's probably little you can say that will help you anyway. Don't devote an optional essay to the matter, but be ready to discuss it objectively, maturely, and nonnegatively if you interview with the school. Don't, however, deny your joblessness on your application data sheet, résumé, or anywhere else.

If you were terminated because of a companywide downsizing in a lousy market, you need not be defensive or apologetic. Many are in the same boat, and, while a negative, schools won't regard it as a deal breaker. Use the optional essay to provide ministories about the activities that have been occupying you since you got the pink slip, such as classes or community involvements.

Business schools have very high standards when it comes to extracurriculars and community involvement. If you're weak in these areas, don't use the optional essay to explain it away. Instead, write a sincere and detailed essay about an activity that highlights the compassionate and selfless qualities that community activities demonstrate, such as taking care of one's child as a single parent or providing an unusual amount of care for family members.

Other Extenuating Circumstances

The range of weaknesses that applicants may need to discuss in the optional essay is hardly limited to grades, scores, recommendation letters, gaps in employment, or lack of community involvement, of course. If you're a reapplicant, the optional essay may be the only opportunity you have to make your best case for all the ways you've improved since you first applied. The impact of visa restrictions on career plans, an abbreviated stay in medical or law school, a transcript showing more than three universities or a six-year undergraduate career, reasons for deferring admission a year ago or for needing a second MBA—all of these raise concerns that the optional essay can go a long way toward alleviating. In his essay (sample essay 2), for example, Mohamed E. makes a convincing case that his family emergency justified a round-two application, though as a reapplicant he was expected to apply in the first round.

Less typically, the optional essay can help you make the case that, for example, being wheelchair-bound is not an impediment, that the clinical depression you suffered in college is a thing of the past, or that you were among the many honorable employees at Enron or WorldCom. The bottom line is the same: schools offer optional essays not to smoke out negatives but to give you a chance to explain them honestly, succinctly, and positively.

Positive Optional Essays

Despite the popularity of the damage control essay, most schools are quite open to optional essays that don't "explain" anything at all—they just provide new insights into or information about your application. So what should you write about? One effective strategy is to return to the self-marketing handle we discuss in Chapter 1—the four- or five-theme message you've been trying to convey across your application. Have you illustrated all these themes sufficiently in the school's required essays? Perhaps you intended to discuss the weekly advice column you write for the *Quincy Herald*, but couldn't fit it into the available topics. Your optional essay could be the place to highlight this unusual, creative hobby. Perhaps you're trying to offset your "techie" background by emphasizing your interpersonal and communication skills. In that case, your optional essay could dramatize a work situation in which you worked subtly behind the scenes to build momentum for a key decision. Or it could focus on your rise through the ranks at your local Toastmasters club. The range of possible uses is enormous. Just don't repeat a story you mentioned elsewhere in the application.

Since the optional essay represents your last chance to market yourself to the admissions committee and you don't want to outstay your welcome, avoid writing about prosaic workplace accomplishments or "football hero" type essays. Look for that one remaining story that only you can tell and that will deepen the committee's sense that you are a distinctive person of many parts. Unusual hobbies that reveal another side of you, travel experiences that show you expanding your sense of self, the part-time business you started out of your garage, running for local political office, or serving in the military, even what you've learned about multiculturalism as a participant in a cross-cultural relationship—the more outside the box your story or insights are, the more benefit you may gain. And don't equate effective or unpredictable optional essay topics with exciting ones. An essay about your passion for cooking, the harpsichord, or stamp collecting could enhance your distinctiveness just as much as an essay about skydiving or mountain climbing (both of which the committee will certainly have encountered before).

As a general rule, avoid the glib, loosely structured "I-dashed-this-off-in-a-minute" exercise. Admissions officers like color and humor as much as the next person, but not as a substitute for having something substantive to add. If your point is that you'll make your future classmates' learning experience fun, then find a story with a beginning, middle, and end that illustrates this.

In the Schools' Words—

The optional essay is your opportunity to tell us anything that you haven't had the opportunity to cover in the other four essays or in your interview. Common responses have to do with explaining extenuating circumstances, hobbies, travel experiences. I definitely recommend completing it.

—Dawna Clarke,
University of Virginia (Darden)

Work-related stories can also work as optional essays; just be sure they really add value. If you work in an unusual industry and you haven't had a chance to communicate what makes it distinctive, enjoyable, or challenging in the required essays, then the optional essay is your chance. In his essay (sample essay 1), for example, Paul S. offsets Chicago's limited essay opportunities by using the optional essay to discuss an impressive leadership story.

Using the optional essay to expand on your goals only makes sense if your goals or future industry are unusual or unusually complex. If the post-MBA plan you outlined in essay 1 is to return to Bulgaria and modernize its wine-making industry using Western technology, it's quite possible you have more interesting things to say on the topic than the goals essay gave you room for.

As we saw in Chapter 3, business schools love "overcoming hardship" essays. They frankly admire the fortitude and character it takes to rise above difficult circumstances and tend to reward it with offers of admission. Ideally, you worked your "obstacles overcome" stories into your required essays—it's the kind of material you will want to highlight. If this was not possible, however, or if you have more than one such tale, the optional essay can help. Imagine an applicant who was so enthusiastic about her hobby that in pursuing it she developed a rare medical condition, one that, ironically, forced her to abandon her passion. Powerful story, right? Well, taking advantage of an optional essay, that applicant exponentialized the power of her story by recounting how she founded a national not-for-profit organization to support research into her rare illness. The story helped win her admission to a top-10 business school.

Another approach to the optional essay is to drive home your desire to attend your target school. Space limitations may have prevented you from doing more than quickly surveying the school's virtues in the required essays (some schools, like USC, lack a specific "why our school?" question). In the optional essay you could—making sure you don't repeat yourself—portray your "fit" in a more personal and focused way, by, say, narrating your recent campus visit, talking about the alumnus who is your role model, or spelling out your plan for starting a student club. Kristy S. does just this in her optional essay (sample essay 3), closing her meaty case for her potential Harvard contribution by referring to conversations with HBS alums.

Reusing leftover essays from other schools for another school's optional essay is a legitimate strategy but only if you do two things. First, recycle an essay that gives your essay set greater balance. If required essay topics forced you to devote three-quarters of your essays to professional topics, then use one of your leftover essays to discuss community or personal topics in the optional essay. Second, purge any wording that signals that in its former life this optional essay was Duke essay 3 or UCLA essay 1. You also need to add wording that informs the committees why you are submitting this extra essay. Because optional essays leave the topic up to you, the burden is on you to disclose the essay's topic to the committee. Don't assume or hope adcoms will figure it out.

OPTIONAL ESSAYS: WHAT *NOT* TO DO

In your optional essay, don't

1. Abuse the length limits or write more than two pages. Keep optional essays as short as possible. If a school does not state a limit, then hold yourself to the length limit of that school's typical required essay. The University of Chicago, for example, has one 750-word essay and two 300-word essays, so your optional essay should not exceed 300 words.

2. Go into agonizing detail about the cruel conspiracy or bad karma that led to your D in Object-Oriented Programming. Even if every word you say is true, the committee may wonder about your sense of proportion. Essays of explanation should never belabor the negative.

3. Lie. Don't even think about explaining your poor GMAT score by spinning out some fiction about your grandmother being kidnapped by a sect of militant environmentalists.

4. Whine or complain about an unhappy outcome. By all means explain the circumstances of your setback, but take personal responsibility for it. When

the admissions officer evaluates how much weight to assign to your weakness, your mature mea culpa will reflect well on you.

5. Repeat any substantial story, anecdote, or accomplishment from your other essays. If you devoted two paragraphs in a required essay to your passion for Civil War reenactments, don't elaborate on the story in your optional essay. You've already scored all the points your unusual hobby will bring you.

6. Tell stories that are so personal that they can have no relevance to graduate management study. These usually involve topics such as failed relationships or deeply personal events that would make the committee uncomfortable. Such stories might even backfire by causing the committee to wonder if you included the story just to win sympathy.

7. Enclose photos of your cocker spaniel, your 700-page treatise on Syncretism and the Epistemology of Being, or a video of your last bowling tournament. Admissions officials will usually welcome one short news-relevant article about (or by) you, but any other creative attempts to stand out will usually come across as manipulative or cheesy (or both).

8. Write epic summaries or cute throwaway stories that provide no substantial new insight or information. Avoid optional essays that consist of disjointed, relatively trivial leftover topics with no unifying theme.

9. Create your optional essay by carelessly cutting and pasting in another school's essay. If your essay starts with "My defining moment was the day . . . ," "I wish the admissions committee had asked me . . .," or "If I could be present at any event . . . ," the committee may wish you luck with Harvard, Kellogg, or Chicago (respectively) but view your application to its school less favorably. Remember that admissions officials are well aware of what other schools ask.

10. Use the optional essay to explain a negative episode but fail to conclude it with a positive example that shows you learning from or overcoming that negative.

WRITING PROMPT EXERCISES

Tackling an open-ended essay topic can be daunting. The following four exercises minimize the challenge by walking you step by step through the writing process for a typical optional essay.

Exercise 1

Play the admissions officer for a moment. Step back from your application—or better yet, give it to an objective friend—and ask yourself whether it all coheres. Is anything missing? Did your friend hand it back to you and say, "I still don't understand why you left Goldman Sachs for Ernie's Carpet Empire" or "Why exactly did you major in marketing if your goal was always entrepreneurship?" or "How come your résumé is the only place where you mention your world trophy in archery?" If you or your readers discover such anomalies, you have a potential topic to explore in the optional essay.

Exercise 2

Assume that the topic you decide to write about involves clarifying an ambiguous episode or explaining an extenuating circumstance. You must map out the most concise, objective, and mature explanation possible. If the episode is significant enough to warrant an essay, chances are it's a subject you're touchy or even emotional about. You need to eliminate your subjective, defensive take on the situation and describe it as analytically as possible. One way to do this is to banish for the moment the question of how the committee will judge the substance of the situation (a bad grade, poor test score, employment gap). Pretend instead that what they're really judging is how succinctly, soberly, and responsibly you can *describe* the situation. Or, alternatively, imagine that you're a CEO evaluating a wayward business unit. You wouldn't be interested in blame or guilt but in the realities of the situation and what you can do to fix it. Adopting this case-study mindset will enable you to describe your extenuating circumstance in precisely the kind of clear, compact, and responsible tone the admissions committee expects. And by doing so, you will have set yourself apart from the many applicants who hem and haw, cast blame, and generally sound mealy-mouthed.

Exercise 3

Edit your case analysis of your extenuating circumstance until it reads with the terseness of an executive abstract that Jack Welch might actually read all the way through. Count the words; if there are more than 300, begin editing again. You're done when you can't cut any more without changing the essay's meaning or accuracy. Now, insert one sentence that maturely accepts responsibility for the situation and another sentence that draws a specific, actionable lesson from the situation. If your lesson is, "I learned that I need to balance my work and academic commitments," rework the sentence until it sounds more personal, more "earned": "I learned that before obligating myself to two substantial commitments, I need to evaluate how dedicated I really am to each and work out a time-management plan that enables me to give my best to both."

Exercise 4

Now you've reached the heart of the essay: why your extenuating circumstance is hardly worth remembering because of the number of times you've vindicated yourself since it happened. Return to your lesson statement: "I learned that before obligating myself to two substantial commitments, I need to evaluate how dedicated I really am to each and work out a time-management plan that enables me to give my best to both." Now search your experiences subsequent to the extenuating circumstance for roughly analogous situations in which you proactively evaluated two substantial time commitments, weighed the benefits and sacrifices of each, determined how much time each needed and how interested you were in both, and then worked out a feasible schedule that maximized your energies for both activities. Also describe the other, less important activities you had to give up to fulfill these two obligations, and describe any habits or tactics you adopted to optimize your time. Finally, conclude with a factual, even quantitative, outcome that demonstrates that you successfully lived up to both outcomes: "By year's end I had earned my master's (with honors) while presiding over a 15 percent increase in my department's productivity." This same framework can help you whatever your extenuating circumstance may be.

SAMPLE ESSAYS

The following four sample optional essays suggest just how many different forms the optional essay can take: from pure explanation essay (samples 2 and 3) to accomplishment essay (sample 1) and contribution essay (sample 4).

Sample Essay 1: Paul S. (Admitted to the University of Chicago)

Essay Prompt. If there is further information that you believe would be helpful to the admissions committee, please feel free to provide it.

A recent but pivotal experience taught me how to become a leader and work effectively in a crisis. [←*Provides an explicit theme statement up front so committee knows why he's submitting this essay.*] The year 2001 was bad for the economy, and the building supply industry was no exception. As a part of a restructuring plan Builders World Supply announced that it would be relocating and downsizing its distribution center in Portland. About 250 people were going to be affected, and only a few would be offered the opportunity to relocate to our Denver operations. People began to panic, and morale plunged. [←*Nicely captures the human dimension of a business problem.*] It seemed impossible to summon the collective motivation to complete the ongoing shipments and at the same time close down the department. Colleagues I had known for years and befriended began leaving the company, and the situation worsened when my supervisor turned down Builders World's offer to relocate and left the company. In this moment of crisis, the company's management asked me if I could step in and make sure all the shipments were made, sell the equipment to raise $100,000, and relocate the office and remaining equipment in Denver. I promised them I would. [←*Effectively conveys both the esteem in which he was held and his sense of responsibility to others.*]

Since my business career has always been relationship oriented, I was very concerned about the needs of my Portland colleagues. On their behalf, I approached management and negotiated better severance and retirement packages. I also used weekly meetings to remind them of the department's 25-year-old reputation for quality, which they themselves had worked so hard to create. I personally asked them not to jeopardize that good name during the department's last weeks. My colleagues rallied around me to move ahead with the shutdown. I was touched by their positive, personal responses. One customer service rep even offered to sacrifice his two days of vacation to meet a ship date. [←*Concrete, telling example anchors paragraph.*] To thank everyone for their good work, I went to some lengths to get the funding to organize farewell parties.

For some of my colleagues' issues, I had to deal with the labor union. For example, on behalf of Builders World's management I successfully negotiated with the union to prevent junior colleagues who had critical skills from being "bumped" by senior colleagues who had seniority in the same job classification but could not be trained in these skills in the time left. This meant compensating these colleagues for the lost potential opportunity, which I was happy to see done. My leadership approach worked, and in five months I was able to wrap up the center's operations and raise $125,000 rather than the requested $100,000 through equipment sales. [←*Quantitative evidence of results always works.*] I learned I had the people, motivational, and administrative skills to lead well in a moment of organizational crisis. As a result of my leadership approach, I was also able to earn the very close friendship of some of my former colleagues. In fact, after my GSB interview my wife and I will be flying to Portland to attend a party given by my ex-colleagues. [←*Again, simple detail proves his theme that he is a people-oriented manager.*]

By way of conclusion, I would like to clarify to the committee that my disappointing verbal score on the GMAT does not mean my oral and written communication skills are inadequate. I regularly make group presentations to customers, submit written weekly project reports to my management, and have authored five papers on distribution management published in prominent professional journals. I am ready for the University of Chicago Graduate School of Business in every respect. [←*He could have slipped this into a separate addendum.*]

Sample Essay 2: Mohamed E. (Admitted to Wharton)

Essay Prompt. The Admissions Committee believes the required essays address issues that are important to your candidacy. If there are extenuating circumstances or concerns affecting your application that you feel the Admissions Committee should be aware of, please elaborate here (e.g., choice of recommenders, unexplained gaps in work experience).

I would like to take this opportunity to explain why I waited to apply in Round 2 of the admissions process. [←*Direct statement of purpose tells committee why he's submitting this extra essay.*] I understand that the admissions committee strongly encourages reapplicants to apply in Round 1, as there are fewer materials to submit, and because early application demonstrates interest in the program. While I attempted to complete my application in time for the Round 1 deadline, I knew starting off that it would be an uphill task because of the circumstances surrounding my brother's health, which required me to go to Qatar twice. In fact, I had recognized the time constraints I would face while discussing my reapplication with the Admissions staff after my first application was denied. I followed their advice to continue working on my application until I was fully satisfied with it. I believe I have completed the application to the best of my ability and just in time before I go home again to Qatar to help my family survive my brother's death. [←*Effectively shows that he can maturely and conscientiously balance two opposed obligations.*] I would like to assure the admissions committee that my decision to apply in Round 2 only demonstrates that my interest in the program is so strong that I committed myself to putting together the best application I could. [←*Keeps committee on his side by keeping essay length to absolute minimum.*]

Sample Essay 3: Kristy S. (Admitted to Harvard)

Essay Prompt. Is there any other information that you believe would be helpful to the Board in considering your application? Please be concise.

I would like to use this space to underscore in specific terms what I can contribute to Harvard Business School (HBS). [←*Direct, up-front statement of essay's raison d'être.*] Because of my combined education in medicine and insurance [←*Nicely highlights her unusual professional niche*] as well as my extensive work experience in both fields, a central focus of my consulting career has been to help physicians and insurers work more effectively together by enabling them to overcome the restrictions their particular career training and business approaches place on their ability to solve business problems. In this respect, the Harvard MBA program is ideal for me because its general management approach will give me the skills and broad perspective I need to further integrate the business/medicine "synthesis" that lies at the heart of my consulting experiences and entrepreneurial plans.

The uniqueness and frequency of my experiences in South America and El Salvador will also allow me to enrich case discussion at HBS. [←*Effectively draws on another of her application's distinguishing features: global exposure.]* Although I will gladly contribute my understanding of the unique cultural, political, and economic conditions in these countries, it will be from the perspective of someone who has tried to help these societies change from the familiar environment of crony capitalism to the unfamiliar but more rewarding model of the Western risk-driven market capitalism. This challenge of transition is faced not only by El Salvador and South America but by third-world companies and monopolies around the world. I am eager to bring my readiness to help lead change to HBS, which expects no less of its students. *[Shrewdly plays to Harvard's self-image as the place for world-changers.]*

Since 1999, I have had the chance to visit Harvard Business School on three occasions, most recently in late September of 2003. *[←Highlights unusual number of campus visits given she is international applicant.]* After participating in classes in Accounting & Control and Entrepreneurial Management taught by Mark Bradshaw and Laura Nash I came away more confident than ever that HBS offers a learning experience that I can both benefit from and contribute to a great deal. Long conversations with Ricardo Garcia, Antonio Marcial, and Bernardo Aluino—all HBS graduates at McKinsey's Mexico City office— have also reinforced my confidence that HBS is exactly the right choice for a "McKinseyite." *[←Effective use of individuals' names to show her networking and due diligence skills.]*

It is my strong ambition to contribute to and learn from the HBS experience and the Harvard community, and I hope you will give me the opportunity to prove it.

Sample Essay 4: Peter J. (Admitted to the University of Chicago)

Essay prompt. If there is further information that you believe would be helpful to the admissions committee, please feel free to provide it.

I would like the admissions committee to know that my undergraduate GPA is not an accurate measure of my academic abilities. Because my parents could not pay for college and I did not want to take on loans, I chose to work. *[←Leads with his strongest material: he had time commitments that other students did not face.]* My work experiences in college, both at JSM Real Estate and as a Resident Advisor, proved to be excellent and worthwhile experiences. As a real estate associate at JSM, I was able to see the lessons of my business classes applied in real situations. As a Resident Advisor, I was able to gain valuable leadership experience. *[Deftly turns a negative fact into a platform for showing off positive experiences.]*

When I developed the time management skills to balance work and study, my GPA rose and I was able to earn dual degrees, a Bachelor of Arts degree in

Russian and Eastern European Studies and a Bachelor of Sciences degree in Accountancy. [←*Provides the "happy ending" that mitigates his negative.*] My degree in Russian and Eastern European Studies was for avocational purposes. It enabled me to understand my heritage and learn how to read and write in Russian. My fluency in Russian has enabled me to contribute to the Russian community of Nashville by tutoring and mentoring new immigrants. My degree in Accountancy, which led to my licensure as a CPA, was for vocational purposes and has proved to be indispensable to understanding the way businesses function.

I ask the admissions committee to view my GPA in my last three years in college as well as my professional successes since college as the true indication of my ability to participate in Chicago's rigorous program. [←*Respectfully and humbly closes a damage control essay that's actually a highlight reel of his application's strengths.*]

CHAPTER 5

Credible Enthusiasm:
Letters of Recommendation

> *A balanced recommendation is a beautiful recommendation.*

—PAMELA BLACK-COLTON,
UNIVERSITY OF ROCHESTER (SIMON)

Sometimes the last item read in an applicant's file, sometimes treated as a pro forma rubber stamp, occasionally the element that saves or damns a candidate, the letter of recommendation occupies a unique place in the business school application. It is the only element in the admissions folder in which a third party is given the chance to weigh in on the applicant's qualifications. Because it is the element over which the applicant has the least control, the letter of recommendation is the application wildcard.

Called by some schools "letters of evaluation," "career progress surveys," or "confidential statements of qualification," recommendation letters by any name are critical to your chances of admission. A well-written, detailed recommendation can sound almost like an endorsement from your organization itself, lending your application an air of credibility that's hard to equal. A supportive recommender can enthuse about you in a way that you cannot, at least without sounding like a raving egotist. And as a more experienced professional with broader managerial exposure, your recommender will have observed aspects of your skills that you aren't likely to see yourself. Recommendation letters can do what no other parts of your application can; so make sure you execute them well.

This chapter differs from every other in that it concerns an application document that you should not write. Almost every business school insists that applicants not write their letters of recommendation themselves, even when their recommenders ask them to. Many of these same schools do encourage you, however, to proactively help your recommender craft letters that really strengthen your application. This chapter will help you and your recommender do just that.

First, we need to consider what business schools use letters of recommendation for, and what they seek in them.

WHAT DO RECOMMENDATION LETTERS DO ANYWAY?

You're probably thinking, "Why all this fuss over documents that are almost always dripping with praise? How can schools take letters of recommendation seriously?" There's no denying that the vast majority of letters of recommendation are positive endorsements. But consider that experts estimate that anywhere from 10 to 20 percent of the recommendation letters schools receive are actually negative—not lukewarm, negative. Add to this the sizable percentage of recommendation letters that, although apparently positive, contain one telltale deal-breaking hint, and you begin to see why schools scrutinize letters of recommendation as closely as they do.

The experienced adcom member knows how to read between the lines, to gauge when a negative remark is a legitimate weakness and when it's a ding trigger, to separate the fulsome praise from the hard accomplishment. The percentage of positive recommendations may be huge, but there's a much smaller universe of genuinely enthusiastic and knowledgeable recommendations.

Because schools seek different qualities in their applicants, a good letter of recommendation will mean different things to each school. In general, schools use letters of recommendation to determine whether you can handle their program academically and whether you have the kind of senior management potential to eventually make the school shine. On the broadest level, schools use recommendation letters to learn about your hard (technical, analytical) and soft skills (interpersonal, communication), but also about something more important than skills—your personality and character.

Letters of recommendation also serve a corroborative function. They tell the school whether the people who work directly with you view your contribution in the same way you do. Have you been overspinning your achievements in your essays? Are you really the fast-track star you portray yourself as? Recommendation letters provide the reality check. But such corroboration is more than merely factual. Schools are looking to see if your recommenders also confirm your themes, the self-marketing handle you've been pitching in your essays. A recommendation letter that confirms all the factual claims you make about your position and achievements but contradicts the spin you've put on them will hurt you. For example, to evade the "techie" pigeonhole, suppose you downplay your technical expertise in your essays and highlight your informal project leadership and mentorship roles. In his letter, your recommender confirms that you are an unusually skilled software developer who has played key roles in developing six of the company's flagship applications—just as you claimed. However, he fails to back up your leadership claims, instead enthusing rhapsodically about your brilliant software development and testing skills. Admissions officers, wondering if you really have senior management potential, slide your file into the wait-list box. Dissonance between recommender and applicant can be fatal.

On a more subtle level, schools can also use letters of recommendation to gauge whether you (1) know how to read people well enough to discern enthusiastic recommenders from the lukewarm and (2) have the negotiation skills to convince busy recommenders to do you a big favor.

Ask a roomful of admissions officials what they value most in a recommendation letter, and you'll invariably hear two words: candor and specifics. They want to know that the recommender is being honest with them and that praise is tempered with objective evaluation. In other words, they want concrete credibility. Does this really mean that schools will favor an applicant whose recommendations discuss "areas for improvement" over one whose recommendations deny any weakness? It does. No one is perfect, and a recommendation that offers no negative comment loses believability (though, of course, your credibility can also be communicated by specifics and examples). As you and your recommenders follow the advice contained in this chapter, remember that elite business schools don't admit applicants because they have no blemishes. They admit them because their positives are so consistently striking and substantial as to outweigh their faults.

LENGTH

Generally speaking, the higher your target school lies in the business school food chain, the more likely it will view a long recommendation letter favorably— provided it's meaty. The big exception to this is Harvard Business School, which now limits responses to each question on its recommendation form to 250 words. The simple reason for this is that longer letters show the recommender's enthusiasm. (The sample letter at the end of this chapter—which helped the applicant earn a spot at Columbia—is a case in point.)

Though long letters can certainly backfire if they lack examples, are written poorly, or are excessively long, they do tend to show that the recommender thought highly enough of you to take the time out of her busy day to write an extensive endorsement. Harvard notwithstanding, few business schools place length restrictions on recommendation letters. They want recommenders to feel encouraged to say as much as they want to. In fact, admissions officers have a dismissive nickname for short letters—"coffee-break recommendations."

When is a long recommendation too long? Two to three pages (single spaced) is fine if it's full of examples; four pages should be viewed as an outer limit.

SELECTING RECOMMENDERS

The question of whom to ask for your recommendations can get complicated, but some rules of thumb will help:

- Start by asking who knows you best, through direct interaction over a sustained period (ideally, six months or more).

- Then ask yourself who is likely to provide a truly enthusiastic endorsement.

- Finally, focus primarily on professional references.

These "screens" should give you a manageably short list of potential recommenders.

The complications arise when (1) you don't want to risk telling your current employer of your business school plans or (2) your screening process still leaves you with too many candidates, and you're not sure which mix of recommenders will make your best case. We address the first scenario in the next section, so let's focus on the question of ideal mix here.

The goal is to obtain letters of recommendation that capture the broadest range of your skills, experiences, and themes. This breadth will not only portray you as the kind of well-rounded applicant schools covet, but it will also enable you to minimize the overlap between the stories each recommender tells. One way to achieve this breadth is by choosing recommenders from different periods of your recent career: current employer and recent past employers (going back no more than three years). Another approach is to choose recommenders from your current or recent employment who have each seen different sides of you: your current direct manager, a current manager in another department whom you worked with in a different capacity, an external client or customer who glimpsed another side of you. A final approach to ensure breadth is to choose a mix of recommenders from your professional and nonprofessional activities (though, again, lean toward the professional). A manager from work will obviously have seen you in a very different context than your supervisor at Make-A-Wish.

How do you decide which of these approaches will generate the best blend of recommendations? By returning constantly to your initial enthusiasm and knowledge screens, by determining who knows you best, and by deciding who will write the strongest endorsement. If you keep these three criteria in mind—enthusiasm, direct knowledge of you, and breadth of insight—your chances of identifying the most effective mix of recommenders will be high. It's fine if two recommenders refer to one or two of the same achievements, but they should provide a different perspective on each. In fact, themes like leadership and teamwork are so broad that three recommenders should be able to provide original slants on your achievements without repetition.

If you're shrewd in your choice of recommenders—and they come through for you—you'll have taken a crucial step toward convincing the admissions committee that you deserve a spot. For most applicants, the first step is to secure a letter from a direct supervisor.

FIRST LETTER: DIRECT SUPERVISOR

Ideally, your first letter will be from your current boss. Yes, schools say they understand why you may not be able to ask your current manager, but you should try to give schools what they prefer, not just what they'll live with. Because schools recognize how risky it can be to ask your immediate manager for a letter, they look favorably on applicants who do. Don't conclude too quickly that approaching your boss is impossible or "dangerous."

The one exception to the direct-supervisor rule is if you are applying to business school within six months or so of starting a new job. Your new boss may not know you well enough to write an effective letter. Your schools may actually prefer a letter from your previous manager.

If you absolutely cannot get a letter from your current manager, then you must get a letter from another manager at your current employer who knows you well or from your immediate manager at your most recent employer.

In the Schools' Words—

Recommendations are an important part of your application. We would like one of your recommendations to come from your current supervisor. Your current supervisor is in the best place to provide insight to you as a business professional leader. . . . We are looking for people who can provide true insight into your character and potential. It is always a good idea to choose your recommenders carefully. Also, you should brief and prep them to help you tell your story. Provide them with your résumé, essay one, talk with them about your goals, and educate them on the school.

—ISSER GALLOGLY,
NEW YORK UNIVERSITY (STERN)

"GOD" LETTERS

It should go without saying that procuring a recommendation from a CEO type, celebrity leader, or higher—the so-called "God" letter—will hurt your application if the deity in question doesn't really know you. It should go without saying, but hundreds of business school applicants will do exactly that in the coming year. Don't be one of them. You may think that a VIP recommender's willingness is an exploitable ace in the hole, but such letters are a bad idea for two excellent reasons. First, the VIP recommender is unlikely to know you well enough to say anything that will interest the committee, and, second, your ace-in-the-hole strategy is actually surprisingly common. Schools are inundated by brief, unhelpful letters of reference from VIPs. Rather than being impressed, they wonder at your judgment.

SUBSEQUENT LETTERS

Admissions committees love letters from supervisors. These professionals have the seniority and leadership experience to judge employees, and evaluating people is frequently a key part of their managerial role. Their opinion comes with built-in credibility. Assuming that your immediate supervisor wrote your first letter, your second letter should come from your immediate supervisor in your last job or perhaps another manager at your current job who knows you well. Particularly if you're self-employed or work for a family-owned business (letters from Dad are out), clients, suppliers, or your accountant, lawyer, or venture capitalist can also make good business-related recommendations.

Though professional-related letters are always preferred, your second recommendation can also come from an extracurricular source. This could be your supervisor at a community organization, provided that your performance for that organization was unusually strong, you believe your community profile needs more bolstering than your professional side, or you're applying to a school that views "social impact" applicants favorably. Except for schools like Stanford that require them, letters from peers should be avoided unless you really have no stronger supervisory alternative. This is because peers will rarely have been in a formal evaluative role over you. Schools view their endorsement as skeptically as they might a letter from a friend.

Some schools allow current students to write brief "unsolicited" letters of support (called "green sheet" letters at Wharton) on the applicant's behalf that do not count against the applicant's total recommendation count. You should obviously take advantage of this opportunity to provide new information or broaden support for your application if you can.

Since schools insist that recommendation letters be recent and come (primarily) from business associates, avoid dusting off the academic recommendations you filed with your college's career placement an eon ago. With rare exceptions, schools discourage academic letters not only because, for most applicants, college was a long time ago, but because schools glean all the academic-related information they need from your undergraduate transcript and GMAT scores. Too often, academic letters sound half-hearted and distant, referring only to classroom grades rather than to extracurricular leadership or other activities that schools might actually be interested in learning about.

In the Schools' Words—

Answering our specific questions certainly helps. We understand when a busy person prefers to write one letter to a few schools, but the applicant should still ask the recommender to be aware of what we are asking and try to cover that, even if it's not in the format of our questions.

—GWYNETH SLOCUM BAILEY,
UNIVERSITY OF MICHIGAN (ROSS)

THE DELICATE ART OF APPROACHING RECOMMENDERS

Now that you know whom you'd like to ask for recommendations, don't just fire off a few e-mails and wait for the effusive praise to pour in. A careful, proactive strategy toward approaching and coaching your recommenders can make all the difference between a disastrous "recommendation" and a letter that will actually be helpful and appropriate.

The first step is gauging whether your prospective recommenders are willing. In fact, you want them to be more than willing; you want them to be downright enthusiastic. The best method is to forthrightly ask them if they think they can write a strongly supportive letter. If you encounter anything short of unhesitating consent, you may want to consider someone else. Recommenders sometimes agree to write positive letters but then, in the spirit of objectivity or worse, submit tepid or vague letters that harm more than they help. A recommender who is writing a letter only out of courtesy or duty will probably accept an opportunity to back out if you offer one. So phrase your request in language that invites unenthusiastic recommenders to recuse themselves.

The Drill

Let's face it, devoting the multiple hours required to write a detailed letter of recommendation is a big favor. Give your recommenders enough time (two to three months is ideal), and make your initial request in a face-to-face meeting (or two). Bring with you all the supporting documentation you think they need (or will read). Definitely give them

- Your résumé.

- Your schools' official recommendation letter form and stamped envelope, or instructions for filling out the online form.

- A cover memo or general statement explaining why you need an MBA, what your post-MBA goals are, what you think is unique and compelling about your candidacy (traits, not just skills), which examples (accomplishments) and themes you want this recommender to discuss, and which schools you're applying to, with a list of the qualities they seek in applicants.

Consider giving your recommenders

- Your essays, if you've written them (you did start early, didn't you?). (Note a risk here: the recommender may simply import material from your essay with no new insights or information.)

- Talking points for answering each of the questions on the recommendation letter form.

- Highlights and/or quotations from the recommenders' performance reviews of you.

- A sample letter of recommendation if you have one.

- Accepted.com's "10 Tips for Recommenders" (at www.accepted.com/mba/LettersRec.aspx)

Be sure to tell your recommenders when you need the letter and how much time you realistically expect the process to take. Provided you don't overdo it, all this information can ensure that your recommendations complement your essays while minimizing the chances of a backfiring letter. Make clear that the recommender must respond to each item in the school's form with at least one specific and detailed example. Far from scripting the recommender's response, your supporting documentation may actually jog his or her memory about accomplishments and skills that you overlooked. In any event, your impressive organization and thoroughness is also likely to put recommenders in a frame of mind highly conducive to praise.

Educating Your Recommender

You will be the best judge of whether your recommender really understands the recommendation process. Managers in management consulting and investment banking, the two traditional MBA feeder industries, are likely to be veterans (or beneficiaries) of the MBA recommendation letter game and so may require little guidance. If you work for a small company or a firm in an industry where MBAs are less common, you may have to do some hand-holding.

Your recommenders may be used to the brief reference letters, sometimes used as letters of introduction in the business world, and dash off your letter accordingly. Similarly, they may think they should approach your letter in the same spirit as your annual job reviews, where a tone of rigorously neutral objectivity rules. In either case, they may believe that an impersonal corporate tone confers weight and authority. Edify them: recommendation letters should start not from a position of neutrality but from energetic advocacy.

WRITING YOUR OWN?

More and more recommenders, weighed down by work and other responsibilities, are asking applicants to draft their letters of recommendation for them. Even if your recommender intends to use this draft only as a starting point, you should resist this request for one good reason: business schools don't like it. The whole point of asking a third party—your boss—to provide some outside perspective on your potential and qualifications is defeated if that outside perspective comes directly from you.

Given that typical admissions officers read thousands of recommendation letters over their careers, rest assured that they have a sixth sense about non-genuine letters. The personal idiosyncrasies of your writing and thinking style are difficult to hide, and after plowing through your essays, the admissions officers are now likely to be acutely sensitive to them. Even if you try to adopt your recommender's voice, the similarity between your essays and your letters of recommendation is likely to be all too clear.

But the likelihood of getting caught is not the only argument against writing your own letters. It's that writing your own recommendation will probably produce a mediocre letter. You are unlikely to be able to view yourself in the way that a more experienced manager will. Your recommender will probably highlight stories or personal traits that you wouldn't. Admissions officers will immediately sense that your ventriloquized recommendation letter isn't offering any insights or experiences not already found in your essays. Besides, even the most egotistical applicants will be hard put to describe themselves with the same delighted, spontaneous enthusiasm that truly supportive recommenders exude.

In the Schools' Words—

It shouldn't appear as if the applicant wrote the recommendation. [Writing it yourself] definitely will hurt your application. Coaching recommenders is one thing, but the letter they write should definitely be their own.

—Don Martin, University of Chicago

By writing your own letter, in other words, you'll be trading an opportunity to provide a fresh, deeper perspective on your candidacy for warmed-over versions of your essays. So do your best to convince your recommender to write the letter himself or herself. If you can't, try to find another recommender who will. Needless one hopes to say, writing *and* signing the letter for the recommender (also known as forgery) is illegal and unethical.

If you really feel you have no choice but to write the letter for the recommender's signature, consider an alternative that will keep you out of the process. Accepted.com can interview your recommenders for you and transcribe their comments into a formal recommendation letter for their revision and signature. This removes you from the process, as the schools want, and saves your recommenders from the hassle of slaving over nouns, predicates, and indirect objects. They may not have two hours to write your letter, but they are likely to have 30 minutes to convey their comments over the phone.

USING THE SCHOOL'S FORM—OR NOT

Lining up letters of recommendation is not what it used to be. In the good old days, you could ask your boss and a former professor to draft shortish, semi-detailed letters of endorsement; paperclip them to the school's "grid" recommendation form; and wait by the mailbox for the good news. Those days are gone. More and more schools are insisting that your recommendations come only from work-related sources and that recommenders respond to each specific question on the school's form. How to satisfy the schools' requirements without permanently alienating your recommender? One approach is to craft a letter that encompasses *all* the questions asked on each of your schools' recommendation forms.

Most schools say they are open to receiving whatever type of letter recommenders want to send provided it answers all the school's specific questions. This approach will mean that your schools receive longer letters and answers to questions they didn't ask. But since most schools are flexible about length, this is a minor downside. A more significant downside is that this "all-in-one" letter will make it difficult for you to slant your recommendation letter toward the particular strengths of individual schools. For example, you might want to emphasize achievements that underscore your marketing strengths in your Kellogg letter but your finance and entrepreneurial strengths in your MIT (Sloan) letter. You may well conclude that sacrificing such customization is a small price to pay for ensuring your recommender's goodwill.

Though all-in-one recommendation letters do not need to repeat each of the numbered narrative questions on the schools' recommendation form, the recommendation letter should be organized clearly enough so that the schools know exactly when the writer is shifting from one question ("strengths or talents") to another ("weakness or areas for improvement").

In the Schools' Words—

Make sure they fill out the form, and attach a letter answering the questions, but that letter can also address other schools' questions (at least for us). Don't not address one of our questions though!

—ALEX BROWN,
UNIVERSITY OF PENNSYLVANIA (WHARTON)

A second, far riskier approach is to have your recommender draft a school-specific letter for the school you most want to get into (or for schools, like Virginia, that insist you use their recommendation form), and then hope your other schools "won't mind" that some of their questions are left unanswered. A variation of this approach is to line up a different set of recommenders for your "safety" or less desirable schools. Their letters may not be as strong as your A team recommenders, but then again you may not need them to be. Your main recommenders will appreciate the lighter burden.

A final approach, of course, is to hope you have the kind of godsend recommenders who are willing to work with you on individual letters for all your schools. Even here, however, simple humanity compels you to limit the letters to some manageable number.

In the Schools' Words—

We would like the recommenders to fill out our form but realize these are very busy people. We do not look negatively on letters of recommendation that are in letter form but address our questions. We do not like to receive generic letters of recommendation attached to our form—there are reasons why we ask the questions we ask on our form and hope that the recommender will address them in some format.

—SALLY JAEGER, DARTMOUTH (TUCK)

STRATEGIES FOR RECOMMENDATION QUESTIONS

The content of most schools' recommendation letters is remarkably similar. Every school asks the recommender to describe the length and context of their interaction with you. Likewise, virtually every school requires recommenders to comment on your strengths and weaknesses, and the vast majority asks for comments on your career potential and analytical and team/interpersonal skills. Similarly, a smaller but still substantial number of schools ask for comments on your leadership ability, most significant improvement over time, communication skills, impact on your organization, integrity or ethics, and performance relative to peers.

Of course, there are also topics that only one or two schools ask about: your sense of humor (Wharton), your ability to thrive in a case-method environment (Harvard), your self-confidence (UCLA), response to constructive advice (Stanford), and so on. If you create the "all-in-one" recommendation letter we discuss in the previous section, it's important that you include these school-specific questions too. They reflect the school's self-image, and you want to acknowledge that.

Before discussing specific strategies for approaching the most common recommendation letter questions, let's consider a feature that should be common to all of them: examples.

The buzzword on recommendation letters among admissions committees today is *behavioral*. Schools are rewording and sometimes replacing their questions to make it harder for recommenders to answer in general, unrevealing ways. Behavioral questions push the recommenders to provide situational examples that prove you have the skills they have claimed for you by showing those skills in action. An example of a behavioral question is Stanford's, "Please provide the most constructive piece of feedback you have given the candidate. In doing so, please detail the circumstances that caused you to give the feedback, and describe the candidate's reaction both immediately and subsequently." It's impossible to answer this question effectively with vague language not tied to a specific event.

Bottom line: the days when schools trusted recommenders' flat assertions about applicants' skills are gone. They want credible evidence. Note, for example, how Subodh J.'s sample letter at the end of this chapter contains no fewer than 10 concrete examples.

As we've seen in earlier chapters, the most common and persuasive evidence is the example or anecdote, which can usually be structured as a three-part equation:

1. What was the problem or challenge that you the applicant or your organization faced?

2. How did you use your particular skill to resolve the problem or challenge? That is, what steps did you follow in applying this skill and overcoming the specific obstacles you faced?

3. What was the positive outcome (expressed quantitatively, if possible)?

As in essays and résumés, numbers give schools hard data they can hang their hats on, magically transforming the nebulous into the tangible. If your recommenders back up all their claims and examples about you with concrete numbers, your letters will gain the weight and credibility that give your application momentum. Another type of evidence that builds credibility is quotations, as from clients, other managers, or the recommender's own performance reviews of you.

Finally, it's not enough to provide stellar examples if you don't also provide the context for understanding them. In other words, your recommender shouldn't just state that you presented your market analysis to the CEO, she should explain that only one other associate has ever done that in the history of the firm.

STRUCTURE

Recommendation letter forms can vary a great deal from school to school, but the majority shares the same basic structure and seeks similar kinds of insights. In addition to introductory and concluding paragraphs, recommendation letters often include sections on these topics:

- Duration and context of recommender's relationship with you.
- Your strengths or talents.
- Your interpersonal and teamwork skills.
- Your weaknesses.
- Your career potential.

We discuss each in turn in the following sections.

Introduction

Although recommendation letters are increasingly Web-based documents, they have traditionally followed the format and conventions of a standard business letter, including the brief general introduction: "It's my distinct pleasure to write this letter of recommendation on behalf of . . ." or "I'm delighted to have this opportunity to wholeheartedly endorse Joe Blow for admission to . . ." Even a sentence or two of bright, positive language can establish a tone of enthusiasm that, ideally, will pervade the entire letter.

The recommender can then follow this with a sentence that summarizes the key qualities she'll be focusing on in the letter. It's difficult to avoid platitudes in these lead-in paragraphs, but admissions officers have an uncanny ability to sniff out the insincere. The recommender can give these general sentences concreteness by staying focused on what's distinctive about you: "Svetlana's unusually analytical mind, gift for building rapport, and natural sales skills make her one of the most promising young managers I have encountered in 20 years in the industry."

Your recommender may even consider opening the letter creatively with an anecdote about the first time you worked together, the first time you revealed the person behind your professional persona, or a moment when you exceeded the recommender's expectations. This approach will vividly demonstrate the recommender's special relationship with you and immediately distinguish the letter from the stuffy norm.

The introduction is also a good place for the recommender to provide a few sentences of background information on herself—where she earned her degree(s) and which organizations she has worked for and in what capacity, up to her present title. Such information enhances the recommender's credibility as someone whose opinion merits respect. Recommenders who have MBAs should obviously note this fact, especially if they are alumni of the school in question.

The opening paragraph can conclude with an explicit description of the pool of peers against which the recommender is comparing you, including the approximate number of people in that group: "all the marketing managers I've worked with in my career," "the 25 peers in Wue's consultant training cohort," "the 50 odd MBAs I've interacted with professionally," "the 30 analysts under me in the Equities Research division." The recommender than quantitatively ranks you among this group: "top two account representatives," "upper 5 percent." This ranking statement can also be inserted at the end of the letter or in response to a school's specific question for it. In Subodh's sample letter, for example, his recommender appropriately saves this "pool comparison" statement for Columbia's specific question "How does the applicant's performance compare with that of his or her peers?"

How Long and in What Context?

This is the de rigueur first question of every recommendation letter. Because it asks a straightforward factual question, there's very little "positioning" your recommender can do for you here: she either knows you well or she doesn't. If she does, she can make that knowledge crystal clear by very specifically noting the range and depth of interaction she's had with you. This is where many applicants falter by assuming that this is a "no-brainer" that can be answered in a single sentence: "I've known Caldwell since October 2002, when he began reporting to me as business development manager." Your recommender needs to go deeper than this.

The recommender must detail your professional relationship with her: How did your recommender first get to know you? Did she hire you? What qualities did she first notice in you? What were your job responsibilities when you first began working with the recommender? What, early on, was your hierarchical relationship with the recommender? Did you report directly to her? How often would you meet or talk with her? Continually (offices or cubicles side by side) or intermittently—twice a day, once a week? If only once a week, did you meet only formally in meetings, for example? If so, were these group or one-on-one meetings? How have your professional responsibilities and hierarchical reporting relationship changed over time? How frequently do you interact with the recommender now and in what sorts of circumstances—ongoing daily interaction, meetings, travel situations? If you no longer work together, when did you last work with your recommender and how often do you keep in touch? These are the sorts of detailed questions you need to address.

If this seems like overkill, remember that if your recommender can establish early on that she has extensive and sustained knowledge of you, she will have created a climate of credibility that will make all her upcoming assertions about you more believable. Conversely, if your relationship with the recommender is not as close or as longstanding, you may want to keep this paragraph short and sweet—or consider another recommender.

Having established this detailed context as succinctly as possible, the recommender can conclude this section by explicitly asserting her authority to recommend you: "For these reasons, I believe I'm in a particularly strong position to comment authoritatively on Caldwell's skills and potential."

Strengths or Talents

In many ways, this is the most important part of the recommendation letter—the recommender's opportunity to describe what really makes you special and to back it up with examples. Which strengths should you emphasize? Again, avoid "hard-working" or "diligent." These qualities are assumed and will hardly distinguish you from others as a potential senior manager. You want the strengths that your recommender discusses here to complement the three or four themes illustrated in your essays. The themes need not match identically, of course.

Some variance between essays and recommendation is good because one of the functions of a recommendation letter is to provide new information. So if your recommender details three strengths, two could be the same strengths you cited in your essays, for example. The same rough ratio might also govern the overlap between the stories described in your essays and those in your recommendations. That is, two could be unique to this recommendation, and one could be a story you also discussed in your essays.

The recommender should describe your strengths straightforwardly in a theme sentence or two: "One of Rajesh's special talents is decisive decision-making." The body of the paragraph (several sentences in length) should consist of evidence sentences that cite specific examples of your strength. These examples are the payload of the recommendation letter—the proof that your recommender isn't just blowing laudatory smoke rings. Without them, your letter is sunk.

If you are, for example, a finance professional or IT consultant, it goes without saying that you have strong technical or analytical skills. Encourage your recommender to focus on strengths that might not be assumed in your profession, such as leadership, creativity, interpersonal skills, or strategic vision.

Interpersonal and Teamwork Skills

So much of your time in business school will be spent in groups that for most applicants the recommender's response to questions about teamwork and interpersonal skills is more important than his comments on your analytical or quantitative skills (which in any case the admissions committee can assess through your transcript, GMAT score, and résumé). Moreover, because people skills are a broad and amorphous talent, they must be demonstrated in your recommendation letter through examples, examples, examples. Note that in Subodh's sample letter, for example, his recommender goes out of his way to provide sustained and specific evidence of Subodh's skill with superiors, peers, and subordinates.

One way of grasping how important people skills are to business schools is to consider the sheer variety of interpersonal terms that show up on schools' recommendation form grids:

Handling conflict

Building consensus

Motivating teams

Negotiating successfully

Mentoring subordinates

Demonstrating multicultural skills

Interacting with peers

Interacting with subordinates

Making presentations

Influencing others

Communicating well orally

Exhibiting a sense of community

Inspiring trust and confidence

Respecting others

Demonstrating integrity

Being personally accountable for one's behavior

The interpersonal ideal may well be the applicant with a friendly, even fun-loving demeanor who treats people with respect while inspiring them to do their best. But there are as many "right" ways to show interpersonal and team-work skills as there are terms for it. Be sure to provide your recommender with the details of your finest interpersonal moments. They need not be formal work examples. Sometimes the most effective examples are informal stories like going beyond the call of duty to help a colleague with a personal problem or lifting your group's morale through some personal gesture.

A recommendation that hints at the wrong kinds of interpersonal adjectives—*arrogant, harassing, prejudiced, antisocial, socially inept*—can have a decisively negative impact on your chances of admission.

Weaknesses

No section of the recommendation letter is more dreaded, important, or misunderstood than the "weaknesses" question (sometimes euphemized as "areas of improvement"). Most letters whistle past the graveyard when it comes to addressing weaknesses. They either ignore them ("If Ralph has any weaknesses, I am not aware of them.") or dress up virtues as vices ("perfectionist," "works too hard"). Both approaches fail because (1) they're frankly hard to believe, and (2) too many applicants use them. They fundamentally misunderstand the purpose of the question.

In reality, schools expect your recommenders to be quite supportive, so they do not include the weakness question expecting to learn of horrific faults like "abusive" or "unscrupulous." (A small fraction of recommenders do, of course, report such deal-breaking weaknesses.) Rather than flushing out the bad apples, the main purpose of the weakness question is simply to learn where otherwise outstanding applicants need further development. Many applicants' paranoia about this question's dark intent leads them to immediately think in terms of *personal* weaknesses, and, unsure which kind are acceptable, they offer weaknesses that are really strengths, like "perfectionism." Some schools, like Dartmouth, make it harder to wriggle out of the weakness question by asking the recommender for *three* areas needing improvement.

But unless the school's question insists on a personal weakness, a much safer approach is for the recommender to identify *professional* weaknesses. For example, your recommender may commend you on your superb financial analysis and corporate finance skills but advise you to gain formal training in portfolio analysis, venture capital, and international finance. These are hardly weaknesses schools will hold against you—indeed, they strengthen your case for needing an MBA! In other words, steer your recommender toward discussing weaknesses that (1) complement the reasons for needing an MBA given in your goals essay and that (2) no one would expect you to have overcome at this point in your career. The recommender must, however, be specific about these functional or professional weaknesses or the schools may suspect another attempt at evasion.

It may be that your weaknesses really aren't functional, of course. What personal skills weaknesses are acceptable? It's often a question of degree. A weakness—"poor communication skills"—that can expedite your file to the ding bin becomes tolerable if it's a mild and correctable form of the flaw: "Needs to polish her oral presentation skills." Such repairable weaknesses can include everything from a "tendency toward linear thinking," "too quick to compromise," and "still too risk-averse" to "immature about corporate politics" or "too deferential toward senior management," and the like. If your personal weakness is not an egregious vice, doesn't routinely impede your effectiveness, and can be rectified, then admitting it may not damage your chances of admission.

Usually, citing one weakness is sufficient (unless the school asks for more), but a two-sentence response won't cut it. The recommender should provide a brief example in which you demonstrate the flaw. He should then indicate what you have been doing to rectify it (if you have), followed by another more recent example of the new and improving you. (Since weakness questions ask for current flaws, the recommender should not imply that you've completely eliminated the weakness.)

Don't fear the weakness question. Even one frank, detailed admission that you aren't the first perfect human being will go a long way toward overcoming the skepticism that schools bring to each new glowing recommendation letter. By providing contrast, weaknesses can actually accentuate your positives.

Career Potential

If the last three recommendation topics have focused on your past and present, this last key topic is all about your future. Though worded differently from school to school, it essentially asks the recommender to assess your likelihood for future success. Since the recommender obviously can't know how things will turn out for you, it's tempting to fire off a short, general-sounding paragraph along the lines of, "Tony will succeed at whatever he sets his mind to." This won't score many points with the admissions committee, so it's best to approach this question in the following three concrete ways:

1. *Past record of atypical success.* The recommender can quickly cite the evidence that you have succeeded at an atypical pace thus far in your career: early promotions, special management training programs, "high-pot" status, unusual raises and bonuses—anything that shows you outperforming your peers. The recommender can then make the logical deduction for the admissions committee: your past history of atypical success strongly suggests that your unusual success will continue.

2. *Business school and goals.* First, the recommender can explain why she believes you want and need an MBA. The recommender with an MBA can draw from her own experience of the MBA's affect on her potential. The recommender without an MBA can simply mention the hard or soft skills that she believes you will gain in business school. Second, the recommender can provide the committee with as much detail as she has about your post-MBA goals. The greater the detail, the more thoughtful and forward-looking you will appear. This will increase the likelihood that the committee will believe you will actually realize your potential. In discussing goals, the recommender should always make clear why she thinks these goals are reasonable and achievable for you.

3. *Five or ten years ahead.* The recommender can sketch out a likely scenario (synchronized with your goals essay, of course) for you five or ten years down the road—including job title, industry and type of employer, or general responsibilities. This can graphically indicate how much potential she really thinks you have. That is, a recommender who states you will be roughly on a par with your peer MBAs ten years from now may not impress the committee. Conversely, a snapshot of you outperforming your peers would confirm the recommender's strong sense of your potential.

Conclusion

Like the introductory paragraph, the conclusion sums up the main themes that distinguish you and, with a ringing final endorsement, completes the sustained tone of enthusiasm that should characterize the letter. If the recommender has not ranked you against your peers, he or she can do so here. Unless you're using an "all-in-one" recommendation letter, the name of the target school can be repeated here to emphasize that the letter is tailored to the school. In his sample letter, for example, Subodh benefits from his recommender's own Columbia connection, which he shrewdly elaborates on in the letter's closing paragraphs.

It's usually also a good idea to have the recommender share his or her direct phone number with the committee: "Please don't hesitate to call at (123) 555-7890 if you have any questions whatsoever about Caldwell." This further demonstrates the recommender's enthusiasm by showing that he or she is willing to say even more. It also lends the letter a note of authenticity since no applicant forging a letter would invite the committee to uncover the deception.

LETTERS OF RECOMMENDATION: WHAT *NOT* TO DO

With respect to letters of recommendation, don't

1. Choose your recommenders poorly. Avoid VIP recommenders who know your first cousin's second wife and met you only once for 30 seconds. This mistake also includes family members and friends or former professors who gave you an A five years ago but never talked to you.

2. Write it for the recommender. Why? Because schools don't like it. Find a recommender who thinks enough of you to write it himself or herself. If all else fails, find a consulting service like Accepted.com that can interview the recommender for you, saving him or her time while keeping you out of the process.

3. Omit examples. This is recommendation letter sin number one. Letters that lack anecdotes or stories to flesh out the recommender's claims are almost worthless in the committee's eyes.

4. Use vague, generic language. "Bill is a top performer with a really sharp mind and a winning personality." This is an empty, uncompelling claim. Schools want substantiated facts and anecdotes that reveal personality and distinctiveness.

5. Adopt an impersonal, dry "corporate" tone thinking this lends gravitas and credibility. A recommender who continually refers to you as "the applicant" will sound like he regards you as a mere cog in the corporate wheel or, worse,

can't recall your name. Similarly, an entire letter of sentences like "Project deliverables were aligned with Ricardo's scope analysis, impacting our strategic benchmarks across all metrics" can ruin an otherwise enthusiastic letter.

6. Wander from the question. Too many recommendation letters suffer from attention deficit disorder. Eager to be enthusiastic but even more eager to avoid specifics, the recommender begins praising one of the applicant's strengths but then quickly moves on to four more without ever illustrating the first.

7. Pretend you have no weaknesses. Many applicants are so psyched out by their competition that they believe a letter that admits even the slightest weakness will scuttle their chances. The opposite is actually true: a letter that omits a weakness loses credibility and invites suspicions that some sinister personal failing is being covered up.

8. Attempt to evade the weaknesses question by using stale, overused, generic weaknesses like "perfectionism," "works too hard," or "too hard on himself." Better to mention the functional deficiencies that you're going to business school to fix.

9. Contradict your application's themes. Don't be a quant-savvy marketer in your essays, résumé, and interview but a quant-challenged marketer in your recommendation letters. Stay on message.

10. Focus only on factual achievements rather than portraying yourself as someone with a unique set of strengths. A letter that's chock full of impressively detailed accomplishments is light-years stronger than a vague letter devoid of examples. But the ideal letter will place such accomplishments in a broader context to show why your performance was atypical and will connect them to the themes ("innovative leadership," "international profile," etc.) that unite your whole application.

WRITING PROMPT EXERCISES

The following four exercises will help you apply the advice offered in this chapter by giving you step-by-step instructions for key stages of the recommendation-writing process.

Exercise 1

Assuming that you follow schools' preferences and don't draft your recommendations yourself, the only writing you'll do in this phase of your application is the cover memo you give your recommender to guide him through the process. Look at the items that we recommended you definitely give your recommender earlier in this chapter for the topics your cover letter should discuss. You should already have done your résumé. If you've approached your application process strategically, you'll have started or even finished your essays. If so, you'll notice that almost all the topics you should cover in your cover memo were addressed in your main goals essay: why you need an MBA, what your post-MBA goals are, and what you think is unique and compelling about your candidacy (traits, not just skills).

In drafting the memo for your recommender, briefly summarize the themes and stories of each of your essays in one or two sentences. If you haven't started your essays, preparing this note will serve as an excellent method for data-mining the themes and stories you want to tell. Don't worry about the length of the cover memo; just make sure it covers all the core stories and positioning themes that define your application. When the content is down on paper, begin whittling it so the memo runs no more than one or two pages.

Exercise 2

Now comes the crucial part. You have a cover memo that indicates what stories and themes you've told in your essays. But if you want a recommendation letter that truly complements your essays, you need to take this cover memo to the next level by proactively guiding the recommender toward discussing other examples, unused in your essays, that also illustrate your themes.

Suppose you discussed three or four work-related accomplishments in some detail in your essays. Assume that your recommender will need at least four or five examples to answer the school's recommendation questions. Also assume that it's OK for one or two of these examples to be the same accomplishments you discussed in your essays (though seen from a different angle). To identify the remaining three examples, scour your résumé, your performance reviews for the past two years, and your memory for untold gems that reinforce your themes and that your recommender personally witnessed. (Second-hand accomplishments— "As I later learned from Akira's project manager . . ."—are rarely effective.)

Now, align each of these accomplishments with the theme (leadership, team skills) it best exemplifies. Then flesh it out using the three-part equation we discussed earlier in this chapter: (1) problem or challenge, (2) how you resolved the problem or challenge, (3) tangible positive outcome of your solution. Finally, add to your cover memo any details that you'd like the recommender to include or aren't sure he'll remember, gratefully hand it to him, and let him do the rest.

Exercise 3

As we've seen, an effective recommendation letter is not only detailed and enthusiastic but strategic. Besides guiding your recommender toward discussing the accomplishments that reinforce your essays' themes, you can also ensure that he helps you combat the assumptions that admissions officers may bring to your application: the quantitatively challenged sales rep, the interpersonally unpolished techie, the individualistic entrepreneur who never saw a team he didn't try to run, the investment banker without a social conscience, and so on.

First, list the generalizations about skills or personality traditionally associated with your industry or profession. Pull out your résumé and essays, and, perhaps with a friend's help, check if any part of your application is unintentionally telegraphing these stereotypes to the admissions committee. Is your résumé stuffed with a bit too much technical jargon? Does your list of community involvements start looking patchy after the second activity? If you do find anything that subtly hints at your profession's stereotyped weakness, ask your recommender to help you offset it with stories that work against type, perhaps by giving him outlines of examples that refute them. An applicant who has no international experience could encourage her recommender to discuss the details of her success on a multinational team. The solo entrepreneur could ask his recommenders to describe the team-building exercises he implemented at his start-up.

Exercise 4

Ensuring that your recommenders write effective letters comes down to the granularity of their comments about you. Consider one of the most common recommendation letter topics: your impact on your organization. Broad claims like, "Lian's impact on our division's bottom line has been extraordinary" will die on the vine if they are not followed by an incisive and persuasive example. You can help your recommender dig out those examples by first asking yourself the right questions about your impact in the organization. Suppose you're a manager of a hospital. Ask yourself fine-grained questions like these:

1. How did you handle changes in demand for patient care?

2. What new technology did you introduce at your hospital?

3. How did you enhance your hospital's performance on regulatory surveys?

4. In what ways and by what percentage did you reduce costs without compromising quality of care?

5. How did your hospital improve in patient satisfaction metrics?

6. Did you implement any strategies for managed-care contracting in your hospital?

7. Did you negotiate contracts that benefited the hospital?

8. How did you handle noncompliance issues?

Bring out the full extent of your impact by asking the right questions. Then give this information to your recommender.

SAMPLE LETTER OF RECOMMENDATION

Here's an example of everything an effective recommendation letter should be: meaty, enthusiastic, and balanced.

Subodh J. (Admitted to Columbia Business School)

I am very happy to have the opportunity to recommend Subodh Jain for admission to the MBA program of Columbia Business School. Subodh has outstanding analytical skills and exceptional individual and interpersonal attributes that will make him a truly exceptional contributor at Columbia and a brilliant leader. [←*Brief introduction establishes tone of enthusiastic endorsement.*]

What is your relationship to, and how long have you known the applicant? Is this person still employed by your organization? (Yes/No) If "No," when did he/she depart?

I first met Subodh at the beginning of 2000 when he joined Satyan Partners, the strategy division of Satyan Consulting, as an intern. At that time I was a manager entering my sixth year with Satyan. Over the course of the following two years I had the privilege of supervising Subodh during several strategy engagements, representing fifteen full-time months, with leading Asian personal computer manufacturers. [←*Specific information on nature of recommender's relationship with Subodh builds credibility.*] In January 2002, following an engagement during which we developed the integrated desktop PC strategy for IndiaPC, Subodh decided to join Dell where he took on the operational responsibility of launching their new corporate laptop offerings in Japan. At the time, Dell Japan was the last PC maker to enter the market. Today, with more than 10% market share, Dell Japan is poised to become the fifth largest personal computer maker, just behind NEC.

Following Dell's successful launch in Japan, I heard Subodh was thinking of seeking out a new challenge. I immediately met with him to convince him to return to Satyan Partners, which, happily, he did in autumn 2003. Very soon after his return we had the opportunity to work together on a company-wide operational review for China Computer's entering president. It was our last engagement together. Subodh notably demonstrated his ability to deal with senior members of the Executive Committee, especially with Mr. Xie Lee, the current head of the Consumer Desktop Division. Subodh also showed his ability to put his technical expertise into practice.

Subodh is still working with Satyan Consulting and enjoying continued success. He recently sold his first engagement, which he is currently managing. As for me, in 2004 I left Satyan to return to my home city of Chennai where I work as a freelance consultant to senior executives at Wipro and Tata Group.

Provide a short list of adjectives, which describe the applicant's strengths.

To name only a few of the most relevant adjectives, Subodh is extremely bright, curious, versatile, efficient, autonomous, team-oriented, ethical and very mature. The following questions/answers will help to better substantiate why I think these characteristics accurately represent Subodh. [←*Rather than just list adjectives, recommender refers reader ahead to the rest of the essay where these adjectives are illustrated with examples.*]

How does the applicant's performance compare with that of his or her peers?

When working with Satyan, I considered myself privileged to work with a group of twenty-five highly talented and motivated individuals. As a Senior Manager I have had the opportunity to manage several consultants who "keep me on my toes". By that I mean that they do not hesitate to challenge my ideas and force me to better myself.

I can truly say that Subodh is the most talented person I've worked with in what is a very strong peer group of twenty-five people. [←*Bold statement of extreme praise makes letter stand out from less enthusiastically endorsed applicants. Will he back it up?*] I'm not the only one to think this. Our staffing meetings would oftentimes dissolve into heated discussions over who would have the privilege of adding Subodh to their team. He is what we refer to amongst ourselves as a "Fast-Tracker". Subodh received the "far exceeds requirements" notation on his last five evaluations. This is the highest possible ranking and is only awarded to the top 3% in an office. [←*Provides substantial detail to support "most talented" claim.*]

What makes him so effective?

Subodh learns extremely quickly, is very curious and has the versatility to succeed in any context. After only four and half years of work experience, he has proven his ability to adapt and succeed both in consulting and in industry. Moreover, his software background provides him with much stronger analytical and quantitative skills than most of his peers. During the IndiaPC assignment in 2001, Subodh built a marketing plan with multiple variables that enabled us to model customer acceptance scenarios and compare them. This greatly helped the client make his $175 million investment decision. Few senior consultants could have done this job. [←*Brief example effectively demonstrates analytical skills.*] Combined with his experience in corporate strategy and marketing, this analytical/quantitative skill makes Subodh an "all-terrain" consultant, able to go through complex Excel models and contribute to more qualitative and business-driven projects.

What further sets Subodh's performances apart from those of his peer group are his autonomy and initiative. Subodh will not wait for his project manager to tell him what to do; he will systematically suggest a course of action and propose an implementation plan. Once a plan is agreed upon, he will take full responsibility for delivery and will typically far exceed expectations. This was the case during the last engagement we worked on together for China Computer. The project identified several initiatives for driving efficiency and liberating upwards of $1.5 billion in free cash flow. Subodh contributed significantly to this project by assuming the full responsibility for a whole segment of the project—the consumer laptop division—representing one fourth of the total synergies. Normally, this type of project is awarded to a manager, but we felt Subodh had the required skills and maturity. As usual he proved us right. On the strength of this project in particular he won his ticket to be promoted to Manager in June 2004. [←*Second set of key strengths is also backed up by concrete example.*]

Another important characteristic of Subodh's is that he has excellent relational skills with clients and does not require the same level of guidance as most of his peers. He is not just a consultant but also a true counselor to his clients, which is demonstrated by the repeat business he generates. Once clients have worked with him, they ask for him specifically. Recently, for example, IndiaPC, who remembered his contribution in 2001, directly contacted Subodh. Subodh went on to sell this client an $800,000 project; a feat rarely achieved by first-year managers. [←*Third set of strengths backed up by concrete example.*]

How has the applicant grown during his/her employment with you? Please comment on the applicant's maturity.

Subodh has progressed at an exceptionally rapid pace in all dimensions expected of a consultant: analytical capability, aptitude to "storyboard", client impact, ability to take on growing responsibility within projects and manage cross-functional teams.

Furthermore and as previously discussed, Subodh has also been able to develop his marketing skills and recently sold an engagement to IndiaPC in difficult market conditions. I believe that this latest achievement is in good part related to his experience in industry. I can remember that our discussions were often punctuated by Subodh's concern for putting his consulting experience to the test of business reality. And indeed, I witnessed a positive difference in his abilities after his eighteen-month Dell experience. On top of his former assets, Subodh had developed a better knowledge of operational constraints and had more empathy for the client.

As far as maturity is concerned, one clear sign of it is that despite his growing reputation and influence Subodh has remained true to himself: easygoing, always helpful and extremely professional. In short, Subodh takes his work and clients very seriously but does not take himself too seriously which, in my mind, is a very strong sign of maturity.

Comment on the applicant's ability to work with others, including superiors, peers and subordinates. If the tables were reversed, would you enjoy working for the applicant?

Subodh is very easy to work with. All stakeholders in a project always appreciate him because he naturally creates good personal connections thanks to his smiling personality.

As previously stated, senior managers, partners and clients will specifically request Subodh for almost any type of project because of his autonomy, versatility and efficiency. Subodh clearly understands the roles, responsibilities as well as the strengths and weaknesses of these stakeholders. He knows when to involve the right players to maximize his work's potential for success. This was confirmed to me when I observed the way he worked with managers on several assignments. He was able to quickly understand each environment and efficiently adjust to different styles of management.

Subodh's peers respect his judgment and will often times turn to him as they would to a project manager for expert advice. More importantly he contributes to the success of all projects because he is a "true team player". I have personally and frequently seen Subodh help a colleague complete an assignment after he himself had already put in a sixteen-hour day. During a strategic project that we worked on for six months I saw another example of his commitment to the team. Because of some last-minute adjustments we had spent all night working on a business plan. Our presentation was at 8:00 am and by 6:00 am we had hardly finished. Subodh took it upon himself to finalize the deck and get everything ready so that I could take a shower and gather my thoughts prior to making the presentation to a twenty-person project committee. Trust me, had he not offered to do this, what turned out to be a successful presentation could have been a disaster. [←*Revealingly specific anecdote shows Subodh's human side.*]

Subodh's subordinates value the fact that he sets out a clear direction, takes the time to work closely with them, and "teaches" them the skills required to be a good consultant. First, in terms of knowledge transmission, Subodh has the ability to adapt to his audience and make tricky concepts sound simple. This greatly helped us integrate consultants into assignments that required strong technical backgrounds. Secondly, Subodh has an excellent capacity to translate technical insights into something meaningful for the client's business.

Finally, I would enjoy being managed by Subodh because he gains respect; he does not impose it. I know that he would provide me with strong direction as well as the room I need to develop my own views and opinions. Moreover, he would provide the input and support I would need to improve my deliverables and myself.

In what ways could the applicant improve professionally? How does he/she accept constructive criticism?

Subodh's attitude towards seeking out professional feedback is exemplary. In each of the five evaluations I conducted on him, he explicitly asked for weaknesses and made sure to work on them for the next evaluation. He is one of the rare consultants who is more interested in the feedback session than the discussion about pay and bonus, although this also mattered to him, of course.

As I said previously, Subodh is superbly talented, and as one of our very best consultants, he does not have many weaknesses. However, as his background is in engineering he would definitely benefit from the formal management training provided by the Columbia Business School MBA program. He will acquire new skills and knowledge such as financial analysis, entrepreneurial management, and organizational behavior that will complement his own technology expertise. Interacting with Columbia Business School's diverse student body will allow him to broaden his perspectives and overall boost his ability to anticipate and manage change. Subodh is a very talented person and clearly a future leader, so the MBA will round out his skills. [←*Recommender takes advantage of Columbia's request for a professional weakness by naming functional areas Subodh can address in business school.*]

How well has the applicant made use of available opportunities? Consider his or her initiative, curiosity and motivation.

Subodh is inherently curious. When most consultants are presented with a new project they will typically ask if it is a strategy engagement and if it is in their industry of choice. In contrast, Subodh seems to first ask himself what he can learn from working on the project. In terms of his initiative, as previously discussed, this is an area where he definitely sets himself apart from his peer group. For example, on a project in which his team lacked information about new technologies such as home-based networked computing, Subodh decided to organize a four-week benchmark in London, U.K. He first got a few agreements in principle to meet with some U.K. start-ups and then successfully sold the idea to our Managing Partner and the client. The benchmark proved very helpful to the client and became a reference used by Satyan practitioners throughout the European practice, involving five offices and representing more than five hundred consultants.

Another example of Subodh's motivation to make full use of opportunities is the work we did on integrated desktop PCs in 2001. [←*The recommender's repeated ability to cite supportive examples makes his enthusiasm for Subodh seem eminently logical.*] Early that year Subodh was asked to work on an initial assessment of the integrated desktop PC business plan for a competitive manufacturer. While he knew almost nothing about this technology he rapidly became a reference with the client at both the engineering and marketing levels, and delivered much more than was initially asked of him. As a result, he was instrumental in turning this small engagement into a fifteen-person project that lasted for nearly a year and a half. Three years later, when the client wants to further develop integrated desktop computing, he asks for Subodh.

Comment on your observations of the applicant's ethical behavior.

Subodh is a straight shooter. He calls it as he sees it and does not shy away from stating his opinions. On one occasion, a client had asked us to "stretch" the numbers for a business plan. We were considering following the client's request, because we were getting a lot of pressure from the client and internally. But Subodh vigorously reminded us that doing so might well serve our interests in the short term but it could ultimately come back to haunt us.

Given the amount of pressure on us, it really took a lot backbone for Subodh to speak his mind and defend his opinions. I honestly cannot think of any other consultant in Subodh's peer group who would have held their ground in the face of direct resistance from the Managing Partner. [←*Impressive claim.*] Furthermore, and more importantly, he was simply right.

What do you think motivates the candidate's application to the MBA program at Columbia Business School? Do you feel the applicant is realistic in his/her professional ambitions?

Subodh is a realistic person. Unlike many consultants I have encountered, he has always adopted a pragmatic and hands-on attitude in the way he sets his goals and makes decisions. In the years 2000-2001, like many technology consultants, Subodh had many opportunities to join start-ups working on very promising technologies such as wireless home computing or PC-based home theater technology. Notwithstanding those attractive possibilities, Subodh decided to work on the launch of integrated desktop PCs, a technology that is encountering important success in India today. In retrospect, this choice happened to be the right one at the time. While this could be viewed as chance, I know for a fact that Subodh considered all options available to him and chose the one he felt was the most realistic, had the best chance of success, and would best enable him to develop professionally. Because of the maturity of integrated desktop PCs as a technology and the conclusions Subodh had drawn from his four-week benchmark in the U.K., Subodh finally chose integrated desktop PCs versus wireless home computing and PC-based home theater, which were not yet mature technologies for the Indian market.

This exemplifies why I am convinced that Subodh has realistic professional ambitions and that his decision to apply to Columbia is well thought through. Personally, I think that Subodh's solid experience in industry and consulting is the key to understanding his wish to attend an MBA program now. This is truly the perfect time for him to complement his skills and experience with the richness, rigor and diversity of a Columbia MBA. I am convinced that Subodh has the required talent to achieve his goals and make the most of his past experience in developing new PC technology on a large scale.

As regards Subodh's choice of Columbia, I like to think I had a slight impact on his preference. I can remember how attentive he was when I would tell him about my personal experience working in New York as a consultant during my graduate studies in electrical engineering. I frequently used the services of Columbia's library and learned to appreciate the quality of your facilities. Subodh and I had these discussions quite early in our relationship but I recall that Subodh was already very interested in the prospect of studying at Columbia. [←*Personalizing Subodh's application to Columbia by mentioning recommender's own esteem for Columbia is a nice touch.*]

Obviously, Subodh's choice of your MBA program has much to do with its outstanding reputation. However, I would venture to say that the renowned diversity and hands-on approach of your program are likely the key drivers of his choice.

Are there any other matters, which you feel we should know about the applicant?

I sincerely believe that Subodh would prove a valuable addition to your esteemed MBA program. I believe that his experience, strong technical expertise and well-rounded personality will make him an asset to your program and his classmates. Moreover, he is simply a great person to be around. He possesses a contagiously positive outlook on things, is the personification of the term "team player", has a strong sense of ethics and is consistently driven to better himself and his environment.

There is absolutely no doubt in my mind that Subodh possesses the skills to successfully graduate from your program and hold up the Columbia tradition of excellence in the international business community.

Sincerely,

Parting Thoughts

If you've invested your valuable time and money in this book, it's probably because you know as well as anyone what an MBA can do for your career and your life. You know it can do more than give you world-beating management skills and an intense learning experience you'll never forget. It can also open doors, launch lifelong friendships, and change the way you understand yourself and the world.

Like anything offering that much value, there are no magic shortcuts into the Promised Land. After helping hundreds of applicants win admission to the world's best business programs, I can assure you that the essays that will get you in are not those with the best-executed "mantra," the cleverest angle, or even the most polished prose. The essays that succeed do it through honesty, self-knowledge, and effort. The odds of application success are directly proportional to the amount of candid personal insight and time you put into your essays.

Admissions officers recognize sincerity and hard work, and time after time they reward it. So be real, and give each essay the time it needs to really capture you. Good luck!

Bibliography

Abraham, Linda. *Best Practices for 2005 MBA Admissions* (Los Angeles: Accepted.com, 2004).

———. *Submit a Stellar Application: 42 Terrific Tips to Help You Get Accepted* (Los Angeles: Accepted.com, 2004).

Abraham, Linda, and Cindy Tokumitsu. *The Consultant's Guide to MBA Admissions* (Los Angeles: Accepted.com, 2004).

———. *The Finance Professional's Guide to MBA Admissions Success* (Los Angeles: Accepted.com, 2004).

Asher, Donald. *Graduate Admissions Essays* (Berkeley, CA: Ten Speed Press, 2000).

Bouknight, Omari, and Scott Shrum. *Your MBA Game Plan* (Franklin Lakes, NJ: Career Press, 2003).

BusinessWeek Guide to the Best Business Schools, 8th ed. (New York: McGraw-Hill, 2003).

Carpenter, Phil, and Carol Carpenter. *Marketing Yourself to the Top Business Schools* (New York: John Wiley & Sons, 1995).

Chesla, Elizabeth. *Write Better Essays in Just 20 Minutes a Day* (New York: Learning Express, 2000).

Crews, Frederick. *The Random House Handbook*, 6th ed. (New York: McGraw-Hill, 1991).

Curry, Boykin, and Brian Kasbar, eds. *Essays That Worked for Business Schools* (New York: Ballantine, 2003).

Danziger, Elizabeth. *Get to the Point* (New York: Three Rivers Press, 2001).

Frank-Pedersen, Robyn. *Get Your M.B.A. Part-Time* (New York: Simon & Schuster, 2002).

Gilbert, Nedda. *Business School Essays That Made a Difference* (New York: Random House, 2003).

Harbus editors. *Sixty-Five Successful Harvard Business School Application Essays* (New York: St. Martin's Griffin, 2004).

Housman, Jon, and MBA Jungle editors. *The MBA Jungle B-School Survival Guide* (Cambridge, MA: Perseus, 2001).

Kaufman, Dan, Chris Dowhan, and Adrienne Dowhan. *Essays That Will Get You into Business School* (Hauppauge, NY: Barron's, 2003).

Letteau, Lara, and Bryan Goss. *Applying to a Top MBA Program: From Decision to Admission* (self-published).

Mendonca, Alan, and Matt Symonds. *Getting the MBA Admissions Edge* (N.p.: The MBA Site Ltd., 2001).

Miller, Robert H., and Katherine F. Koegler. *Business School Confidential* (New York: Thomas Dunne Books, 2003).

Montauk, Richard. *How to Get into the Top MBA Programs*, 2d ed. (Paramus, NJ: Prentice-Hall, 2002).

Murphey, Alice, and Shari Holmer Lewis. *Business School Admissions Advisor* (New York: Simon & Schuster, 1999).

Royal, Brandon. *Eighty-Eight Great MBA Application Tips and Strategies to Get You into a Top Business School* (Singapore: Pearson Prentice Hall, 2004).

Stelzer, Richard J. *How to Write a Winning Personal Statement for Graduate & Professional School* (Lawrenceville, NJ: Thomson Peterson's, 2002).

Stewart, Mark Alan. *Perfect Personal Statements* (Lawrenceville, NJ: Thomson Peterson's, 2002).

Strachan, James L. *How to Get into the Right Business School*, 2d ed. (Lincolnwood, IL: VGM Career Horizons, 1999).

Tanabe, Gen S., and Kelly Y. Tanabe. *Accepted! 50 Successful Business School Admissions Essays* (Los Altos, CA: SuperCollege, 2004).

Vault editors. *The Business School Buzz Book* (New York: Vault Inc., 2004).

The Wall Street Journal's Guide to the Top Business Schools 2004 (New York: Simon & Schuster, 2003).

Whitcomb, Susan Britton. *Résumé Magic* (Indianapolis, IN: JIST Works, 1999).

ABOUT THE AUTHOR

Paul Bodine is the senior editor at Accepted.com, one of the oldest and most successful online admissions consulting services. He is a graduate of the University of Chicago and Johns Hopkins University. His clients have consistently earned admission to such elite business schools as Harvard, Stanford, the University of Pennsylvania (Wharton), MIT (Sloan), Northwestern (Kellogg), Columbia, and the University of Chicago. He lives in Southern California.